AMERICAN MIRROR

AMERICAN MIRROR

*Social, Ethical and Religious
Aspects of American Literature
1930–1940*

By
HALFORD E. LUCCOCK

NEW YORK
COOPER SQUARE PUBLISHERS, INC.
1971

Originally Published and Copyright © 1940 by
The Macmillan Company
Reprinted by Permission of the Halford E. Luccock Estate
Published 1971 by Cooper Square Publishers, Inc.
59 Fourth Avenue, New York, N. Y. 10003
International Standard Book No. 0-8154-0385-2
Library of Congress Catalog Card No. 75-156806

Printed in the United States of America

FOREWORD

"EVERYTHING NAILED DOWN is comin' loose."

This observation, made by the angel Gabriel to de Lawd in Marc Connelly's *Green Pastures,* produced in 1930, might well stand as a summary of a good deal of the history of the nineteen thirties, both in the United States and throughout the world. A great many things that seemed securely nailed down have been "comin' loose." The reflection of that experience of a collapsing world in American literature during this decade has been voluminous and varied. It furnishes an interpretation of permanent value for understanding the tumultuous years.

It is the purpose of the present volume to examine some characteristic portions of this literature with particular attention to its social and ethical and religious aspects. The spread of the experience of these ten years is too vast and confused to be interpreted by any neat formulas; the present time is far too early to allow any valid judgment on reactions to this experience as reflected in the significant writing of the time. Yet it is hoped that by consideration of parts, at least, of the creative literature of the period, some important data for a fuller understanding of the effect of the years on human experience may be gained. The dominant features of the time have found moving expression—the impact of the depression, the tragedy of impoverished land, with the desert on the march and the resulting odysseys of despair along the roads to nowhere, the rise and struggles of labor, the critical, skeptical spirit turned on hitherto accepted codes and traditions, the search for some sustaining faiths.

No attempt is made in this volume to distribute halos. The interest in the novels, poems and plays discussed is not purely literary or aesthetic. No judgment day is held, dividing authors into the sheep of the "great" and the goats of the "not great." The basis for selection and discussion is rather the closeness of impact and relationship to life as experienced during the decade.

Thanks are due to many publishers for permission to make quotations, as indicated and acknowledged. I am grateful to Mr. Harland Lewis and to Miss Gertrude Fraint for assistance in typing and to my daughter, Miss Marietta Luccock, for help in typing and indexing.

HALFORD E. LUCCOCK

Yale University
Divinity School

CONTENTS

AMERICAN MIRROR

CHAPTER I

THE VALLEY OF THE SHADOW

It is significant that at the beginning of their book, *America in Midpassage,* which gives a log book and history of the ten-year voyage of America from the 'summer solstice of normalcy' and prosperity, through perilous seas to faery lands forlorn, Charles and Mary Beard place the opening line of Dante's *Divine Comedy* as a motto for the story. They quote only the opening line, but there is a sharp pertinence in the whole first sentence to the history of the decade 1930–1940:

> In the midway of this our mortal life
> I found me in a gloomy wood, astray
> Gone from the path direct: and e'en to tell
> It were no easy task, how savage wild
> That forest, how robust and rough its growth,
> Which to remember only, my dismay
> Renews in bitterness, not far from death.

The record of the ten years is more than that of a voyage in mid passage to a destination unknown. It records a wandering in a 'gloomy wood,' a circling in dark confusion. It is also the record of a journey through an Inferno. And often, in the remembrance, there is, as with Dante, a 'bitterness not far from death.'

The 'valley of democracy' became, for millions, the valley of the shadow of death. It was the decade of the big D's—so many of the words used in attempts to describe the depression decade begin with D—depression, disaster, distress, disillusion, despair, dislocation, dole. These resounding dentals are not unlike a bombardment of big guns, booming and roaring, and reducing the countryside to devastation.

An obscure and forgotten item of the ecclesiastical calendar of the church may throw some light on the experience of ten years. June 28, 1914, the day on which the Archduke of Austria was killed at Sarajevo, Serbia, was St. Vitus' day. The world has had St. Vitus' dance ever since. That disease is marked by 'involuntary muscular twitchings.' In the second decade following the alleged end of the World War, involuntary 'twitchings' became more violent. Some indeed were literally muscular, the twitchings of hunger. Beyond that there were economic, social, international, moral and religious twitchings, that made up the chief plot of the years, culminating in another convulsion of war.

It is the aim of this book to consider some of the impact of the decade, 1930–1940, on American life as it has found expression in the literature of the years. Our particular interest is in attempting to understand what the recordings, in literature, in fiction, poetry and drama, principally, of this mind-churning stress have been saying. To make the focus more limited, we are especially interested in the social and ethical and religious emphasis and implications of this record of experience. The title "American Mirror" is far too pretentious and ambitious and misleading. The creative literature of any period is never an accurate mirror of its life. It is bound to be full of distortions. Many important features of life are not reflected back at all. It is easy to see, for instance, that the most widely acclaimed literature of England during the generation when the industrial revolution was gathering momentum made a very inaccurate and clouded mirror of the life of the people. Much nearer, we can now see that characteristic

American literature of the 1920's gave very inaccurate reflection of the gathering forces which burst into full power
in the 1930's.

For one thing, the present time is too soon to make an appraisal of permanent worth, either of the experience of the
decade or its literature. "Art," says Santayana, "is a delayed
echo." It is too early to listen for the fullest and clearest echo
of experience in art. More delay must intervene before that.
Again, the most accurate and vivid movements of the seismo-
graph recording the economic earthquake are not to be found
in what is called creative literature, not in fiction, drama, or
poetry. They are to be found in the reporting of the period;
the factual records; the history of the milling years; the mountainous records of the debates, political, economic and social;
the prodigious Federal exploits in the field of social welfare;
the history of scores of movements which made up the whirl-
pool after the Niagara of 1929.

Yet the creative literature of the 1930's preserves many
authentic portrayals of experience. And if, at the very beginning, we forswear any ambition to assess either the permanent
worth of the literature or the ultimate meaning of the history,
we will have much data for an understanding of the years as
they seized and shaped human life in America, and the experience they brought, economic, intellectual, moral, and religious. It will be a genuine, if limited, mirror, reflecting life
as no other glass can do. There is a real portrayal of the
genuine service which literature can render to an understanding of a time, in a device frequently used in the motion picture production of a novel. On the screen is shown a closed
book. Then the cover opens and characters, endowed with
life, come trooping out in procession. That is the authentic
miracle of great fiction. We can truly say that in some of the
literature of the depression decade, the years became flesh and

dwelt among us, full of truth, if not always of grace. Out from the economist's charts; from the banker's trial balance, those grim records of trial and error; out from industrial indices; from the tortuous jargon of legislative bills; from geologists' reports on the land itself; from the portals of the Supreme Court, and the doorways of thousands of homes, there step lives to dwell among us in our imagination and understanding. The ever-renewed wonder of fiction and drama is well expressed in a verse of the Psalms, 'one shall put ten thousand to flight.' That is, the story of one person, one family, one group, if the artist is able to re-enact the old miracle of Eden and breathe into their nostrils the breath of life so that they become living souls, will have a power that far exceeds the records of ten thousand cases buried in a mausoleum of statistics. We see this clearly in regard to war. No ten-volume history can compare in the power of emotional effect with the story of one man—*Sergeant Grischa,* or one group as in *All Quiet on the Western Front.* So in our present period when we have spent half an hour with Clifford Odets *Waiting for Lefty;* when we have driven from the dust bowl of Oklahoma to California with John Steinbeck and the Joad family; when we have lived on the inside of the Ford Factory with Wessel Smitter's 'Russ,' in *F.O.B. Detroit;* then we get the very feel of life and crawl under the skins of people.

Our field of interest is not aesthetic or literary criticism. There is no attempt to evaluate American literature of the last ten years. Much that deserves and will find an important place as pure literature in the record of the decade will find no mention here. That does not mean that we are blind to its literary excellences, or have failed to realize its existence. It is rather that our test here is not aesthetic. We are not seeking to divide books into a sheep-and-goats division of the 'great' and the 'not great.' The basis of selection is the closeness of impact and relationship to life as experienced in the present time. What does literature reveal of the effect of the dark decade on the minds and lives of people and their reaction to it? What does it have to say about the life of its time? The books selected for consideration are picked out on the basis of literature as a comment on and criticism of contemporary life. This undertaking of examining literature on a basis not purely literary, but frankly social, is not entirely unrelated to the judgment which time ultimately makes. The centuries are strewn with literary figures imposing in their day, forgotten now, forgotten because it was ultimately revealed that they did not have anything fundamental to say. Longfellow greatly outshone Herman Melville during their lifetime. A later century has completely reversed that judgment. Melville had much more to say, both to his own time and to all time.

This chapter is devoted to a very brief reminder of the events, the forces and trends of the 1930's, as the soil out of which the literature of the period grew. There is need to retell here the story of the rise and fall of Humpty-Dumpty, of the change from what the Beards call 'the golden glow' of the '20's to the leaden skies and pitiless winds of the '30's. That story is a painful rosary whose beads we have told over and over. There is more than a bit of accidental symbolism in the fact that one of the popular songs of the 1930's was entitled, 'The Merry-Go-Round Broke Down.' It did.

On October 29, 1929,

> The king was in his counting house
> Counting out his money.
> The queen was in the parlor
> Eating bread and honey.

Then the newsboy delivered the evening paper telling about the momentous stock slump. And they lived miserably ever after.

The foregoing three sentences contain a compressed history of the United States, and of a large part of the world, for the last ten years. Already in retrospect writers are searching for a descriptive adjective for the decade of the 1930's; the choice at present seems to lie between 'the dismal decade' and 'the doleful decade.' The latter has its points, for it was the decade of the 'dole.' The jazz party of the '20's, paralleled by the optimistic trust in automatic progress, broke up; the sound of revelry by night was interrupted by the subterranean rumble of an earthquake. The elevator loaded with humanity, due to shoot upwards to the sixty-fifth story of a skyscraper of man's own construction, jammed at about the tenth floor and then dropped. In that drop it was not only General Motors and A. T. & T. and other similar hopes of salvation that were deflated, but faiths as well.

The High Priests of Progress gave no indication of seeing any storms on the horizon. On New Year's Day 1929, Andrew Mellon, Secretary of the Treasury, prophesied that business was going forward on an even keel, that the gold standard was being established more firmly in Europe, and much similar soothsaying. On the same day, S. Parker Gilbert described Germany as so stabilized internally that she was paying the Dawes Plan reparations without difficulty, and the Kellogg-Briand Treaty had outlawed war. As if this were not enough of a guarantee for Paradise, Russia had made it sure by exiling Trotsky and the Trotskyites. Bliss was it then to be alive. It is literally impossible for us to think ourselves back to the day when the last enchantments of the nineteenth century were being whispered from the towers of the Coolidge era. Paul Engle has seized on the mood of the time in his lines:

"Because you had a date with a dame
Called Easy Money, for a thousand years,
You took the immeasurable cloth of time
And used it for a rag to shine your shoes." [1]

The widespread philosophy of the time, more folklore than philosophy, bore a curious resemblance to the worship of business as the solution of nearly every ill, which was put forth by Ed Howe, the 'Sage of Potato Hill,' Wichita, Kansas, in his later years. Ed Howe is remembered, if at all, as the author of one of the first 'realistic' novels of small town life in the Middle West, *The Story of a Country Town.* He was a forerunner of Edgar Lee Masters, Sherwood Anderson, and Sinclair Lewis in discovering and revealing the devilishness of the small town and country. But his later years, during the first two decades of the present century, were occupied in putting out syndicated remarks. In these he anticipated the wisdom of Calvin Coolidge to the effect that 'the business of America is business.' Ed Howe's aphorisms were collected in a book, published in 1919. No more abject and orthodox worship of the gods of business has been practiced. Howe spent much of his time spreading his prayer carpet and kneeling with his face toward the National Bank. "In thousands of years," he intones, "there has been no advance in public morals, in philosophy, religion, or politics, but the advance in business has been the greatest miracle the world has ever known." Again, "Every great improvement in the world's history is due directly or indirectly to the munificence of some man successful in the world's affairs." "Select the wisest and best man in your community, and he knows more than Adam Smith . . . Did Shakespeare, or Goethe, or Whitman, or Buddha, or Tolstoy, or Confucius, or Rousseau ever teach you as important lessons as you learned from your parents, from your

[1] *Break the Heart's Anger,* by Paul Engle. Doubleday Doran & Co.

worthy and intelligent neighbors, from the leading men of practical affairs in your own country and age?" [2]

How much deeper could genuflexion go? Howe grew lyrical over the virtues of thrift—a virtue which came to look suspiciously like economic insanity by 1933. This somewhat mystical devotion to business represented a large portion of the American people, and was one real element in the preparation for the crash.

William Allen White in his life of Calvin Coolidge, *A Puritan in Babylon,* has given the most important and engrossing picture of the Babylonian years of the 1920's. His book has a permanent worth, both as record and interpretation. The word "Babylon" is not fantastic as applied to the era. It was "the greatest orgy of wealth-begetting" ever known; a paradise, possibly the last paradise of capitalism. Mr. White writes, "The Chamber of Commerce was Coolidge's Alter Ego. In the booming stock market the President and the Chamber of Commerce were making one big noise in the same rain barrel." [3]

A stout Maginot line—to be exact, a Smoot-Hawley line of tariffs—guarded the enclosure. The sun of laissez-faire beamed brightly on the garden and wonderful growths of industrial monopolies, mergers, holding companies like the Insull Utilities, grew overnight like Jonah's gourd. The open shop was the symbol both of sound Americanism and of the Grace of God. The "greatest Secretary of the Treasury since Alexander Hamilton" was achieving a place in history by the reduction of taxes on high incomes. Speculation thrived under the alluring invitation of the Treasury-Federal Reserve policy of low

[2] Quoted by Wilbur L. Schramm in *Saturday Review of Literature,* Feb. 5, 1938.

[3] *A Puritan in Babylon,* by William Allen White. The Macmillan Co. 1939.

interest rates. Wall Street became a people's shrine, with a venerated sanctity hardly matched by any other holy spot on earth. That affords an interesting parallel to the situation created by the alliance of a religious hierarchy to economic and political power in the time of Jesus. The real Holy of Holies was not that empty room in the Temple which symbolized the presence of God. It was the Treasury. That was the truly sacred spot to the Temple monopoly who were making millions out of the traffic. When Jesus became a threat to the Treasury, he was guilty of an unforgivable blasphemy. Wall Street, to multitudes, as well as to the custodians of the shrine, was a Holy of Holies.

Yet, just when it was safest, there was a sunset touch. As has often happened in the history of pagan religions, the God fell down on the altar of the temple. The Holy Empire was revealed in the crash as a sort of tissue civilization, and billions in embossed bonds became waste paper. It was as though some titanic Alice in Wonderland had said with an angry sweep of the arm, "Why, you're nothing but a pack of cards!" In the single month of October 1929 over twenty billion dollars of so-called property in corporation shares was wiped out.

Ruell Denney, one of the younger poets, has pictured vividly the collapse of the house of paper:

Oh, where is the paper world, citizens, citizens?
  Where is the paper world, truckers and founders?
  It has been to the wars. Clerks, rest your pens now.
  The paper world's gone to the dogs and the flounders.

Where are the stocks now, bankers and brokers?
  Where are the promised, gilt-edged debentures?
  They're caught in the whirlwind; credit's a myth now.
  The wind through the banks flings the gold bills in capers.

Where are the treaties, you savers and burghers?
  And where are the seals of tail-coated signers?
  They have been to the fire: navies, call out your gunners,
  For the paper is bankrupt; the seas full of miners.

And where are those figures, you curt statisticians?
  Where are your records where men exist nameless?
  They've been to some ministry: all propaganda:
  And the mathematicians are not all quite blameless.

Oh, where is the paper world, councilmen, councilmen?
  Out of the courtroom the wind blows the dockets.
  And out of the schoolroom the wind blows the hoping
  As the wind blew the world's rent right out of our pockets.

The white leaves, the colored leaves man's lively tree has issued,
  The phrases of order and words for expectations,
  The wind blows through them like a gale down from the
    mountains
  And the old words, misused, are deserting the nations.

As the dead leaves at night in the sharp, sad November,
  The leaves of man's tree drop in gusts at the storming.
  The deigned, the unprinted, unsaid and unknown, raise a
    cyclone,
  And all tatter man's tree, its boughs not re-forming.

Oh, where will the tree, the green tree, get its leaves again?
  Not with leaves as eaters, not with leaves as spines,
  Not with leaves the color of its lice or of diseases,
  But green leaves, small leaves, close to the twig as a pine's? [4]

Yet while it was happening few wondered whether they
might not be witnessing the rapid erosion of a social system.
  To describe the collapse of that Holy Empire of financial
profit is no part of our theme. But the fact of the collapse is
as ever present in the life of America in the thirties as the

[4] *The Connecticut River*, by Ruell Denney. Yale University Press. 1939.

salt in the sea. It flavors, colors, embitters, dominates the whole. It put twelve to fourteen million people out of work, put twenty-five millions on relief, raised the national debt to forty billions, with vast consequences to every social institution in the land.

It is too early yet to know exactly what happened. A generation had to pass after the Civil War before the real nature and consequences of that struggle began to become clear. The depression was a far greater calamity than the Civil War, longer, wider, deeper. The present European War with its artificial and temporary dislocation of our economic life, with its illusory booms, will raise a dense smoke screen about the nineteen thirties, preventing accurate evaluation of the real nature of what happened. But for our purpose it is clear that it is a story of erosion. Even if we may not have been experiencing the steady and inevitable erosion of a social system, we have witnessed a massive erosion of property and of human life and resources. What happened in so many places on the land itself, a dribbling away of the soil, happened to property and human life.

No statistics can convey the property loss in human terms. Nothing has been urged with more pious emphasis than the sacred duty of owning your own home. Yet during the years 1929–1933 more than $3,000,000,000 of farm land was foreclosed, much of it for taxes. Between 1926 and 1936, 1,600,-000 lost their homes through foreclosure and 1,000,000 more would have done so if the government had not come to their rescue. The sheriff in Erskine Caldwell's play, *Tobacco Road*, who during the five-year run foreclosed the mortgage on Jeeter Lester's home twenty-five hundred times, was a national symbol.

The octopus of the mortgage, that national nightmare of generations, assumed a new omnipresence and omnipotence.

The mortgage was nothing new in American history. The Populist platform of the 1890's was largely built on the foundation of the mortgage; on the thralldom of the West to the bankers and insurance companies of the East. Vachel Lindsay voiced the grievance of the farmer, the real emotional drive of the Bryan Campaign of 1896, in a poem, in which he pictures the mortgage holder, not as the octopus but as the spider, spinning a web for catching prey, spreading out from the East to the West.

But the spider's web had never been so strong or so extensive as it was in the thirties; nor did it catch so many flies.

The erosion of life has been a national consequence. The economic black death of the twentieth century cannot be reckoned. In six years, three and a half billion dollars have been required to relieve actual want and wretchedness, right at the sources of the national food supply in agricultural districts. Some of the most significant literature of the decade portrays this human erosion at work.

To give a background for a summary of the expression in literature of some major influence of the decade, we may just list here a few outstanding features of the ten years.

A widespread experience of confusion might well be listed first, for it was reflected in most of the history. The opening lines of Archibald MacLeish's poem, so ironically called *Land of the Free*, portraying the westward push of the refugees from ruin on the road to nowhere, well express the mood of confusion:

"We don't know
We aren't sure
We cut our way in the bark of the big tree
'We hold these truths to be self evident
That all men are created equal'. . . .

We told ourselves that we had liberty. . . .

Now we don't know
We're wondering . . .

We wonder whether the great American dream was the singing
of locusts out of the grass to the West and the West is behind us now.[5]

It is significant that James Truslow Adams' *The Epic of
America*, the basic theme of which is the frustration of the
American dream, was published in 1931, when that frustration became for millions total eclipse. Maxwell Anderson
speaks for many through one of the characters in his play,
High Tor: "The very points of the compass grow doubtful
these latter years, partly because I'm none too sober, and
partly because the great master devil sets on top of the world,
stirring up north and south with a long spoon to confuse poor
mariners." [6] For millions of confused mariners on land the
compass went awry. The mountains were carried into the
midst of the sea. This mood of confusion was induced not only
by the uncertainties in the fortunes of individuals, families
and groups, but by the "stirring up of North and South" in
the succession of social and economic experiments. An oft-
repeated New Deal joke was to the effect that E Pluribus
Unum meant "We'll try anything once." The nation was
bewildered by the complexity of its problems; remedies for
dimly analyzed evils were sometimes chaotically planned. It is
not to be wondered that the view of the scene had, for many,
the fleeting and distorted and jumbled effect of a view of the
world from a moving car on a roller coaster. The sense of vast,
remote, impersonal forces operating to devastate the familiar

[5] *Land of the Free*, by Archibald MacLeish. Harcourt Brace & Co.
[6] *High Tor*, by Maxwell Anderson. Anderson House. Wash. D.C.

scene, induced not only bewilderment but also a sense of fatalism which found constant expression.

A sharpened social awareness and protest marked the years. Smashing blows were dealt to ordinary life in every nook and corner of the country, in agriculture and industry. There was the convulsive bludgeoning of a disintegrating system out of adjustment. The chief sound above all the babel of noises was the "melancholy long withdrawing roar" when the machine jammed. There was a fresh feeling of

> The long monstrousness of life,
> That most have suffered and a few been crowned for.[7]

Heywood Broun gave utterance to a judgment which expressed a main theme of the ten years, growing with a crescendo effect, "God help the United States or any other nation when the cry of hungry children, the grinding of gaunt men and the suffering of women can be classed as a local issue."

A mountain range in the landscape of the years, shouldering the whole sky, was the titanic government effort in the field of social welfare and recovery from 1933 on. The whole New Deal effort was on a scale and range never before remotely matched in history. The Beards' comment on the impotence of the Hoover administration to face the emergency up till 1933 by saying that the government had sent four million men to war but could not put five million men to work. It did finally put over seven million men to work on the W.P.A. There was a recognition that starvation was not a local issue. The latest years of the decade were marked by a growing recognition of the inadequacy of the New Deal efforts as a permanent solution. The 'spiritual crusade' of 1933 to drive the money changers out of the temple was toned down to a

[7] *King Jasper*, by Edwin Arlington Robinson. The Macmillan Company.

bivouac, and then became a retreat. The New Deal was not a planned effort to establish an economic order. It was rather a series of frantic, opportunistic and sometimes mutually antagonistic endeavours to meet emergencies. Lincoln Steffens' comment on Roosevelt I, Theodore, that "there was breadth rather than depth to his thinking," applies to many of the expedients of Roosevelt II. "There was breadth rather than depth," for instance, to the N.R.A. as a means of dealing with unemployment. Yet a new social service base line was established during the eight years of the New Deal, a line which should in general be held whatever the political changes.

The ten years were marked by the greatest advance of labor to real power in all American history. The story of the United States can be told more significantly in the terms of labor battles than of military ones. The battlefields of the Haymarket Riots of 1886, the Homestead Strike of 1892, Pullman in 1894, Lawrence in 1912, the Steel Strike of 1919—all these are fields which rival Bunker Hill, Vicksburg, San Juan Hill and the Argonne Forest.[8] The advance of Labor beginning with section 7a of the National Recovery Act, through the growth of the C.I.O., marked the greatest advance in the century's war. Under the N.R.A. the membership of the American Federation of Labor rose from 2,126,000 to more than three million in 1935, when the National Industrial Recovery Act was declared unconstitutional. The C.I.O., which was formed after the split over the principle of unions for a whole industry as opposed to merely craft unions, starting with the backing of over a million workers in the United Mine Workers, the Amalgamated Clothing Workers, and the International Ladies' Garment Workers Union, grew with a rapidity never matched in labor history. It reported an estimated membership of over three million in 1936.

[8] *American Labor Struggles,* by Samuel Yellen. Harcourt, Brace & Co.

In the midst of all changes, however, it should not be forgotten that the inertia of routine remained the prevailing force over large areas of life. This was reflected in the cry, recorded so often in *America in Midpassage*, "let us alone and rely on the automatic functioning of the market." Gerald Heard in an address in Los Angeles in 1939 drew a vivid comparison in speaking of the persistence of unthinking routine. He said:

"You have seen a cat catch a mouse and play with it for a while. Then a very interesting and terrible thing happens; it is given a mighty blow and thrown back but not killed. What does the poor little thing do when it recovers consciousness? It does the only thing it can do, sit up rather shakily and go through its toilet. Some will say, 'How brave, what a noble way to go to battle.' Not at all. The poor little thing's nervous system has been completely shattered. And all it can do is fall back on reflexes which are no longer applicable. That is what civilization is doing today. It is cornered, it knows it is cornered, and all it is doing is sitting up and brushing its whiskers."

There was a great deal of "brushing of whiskers" in the 1930's, going through the motions as though nothing of importance had happened. Newspapers, political speeches, business magazines and trade journals were full of it. The sense of complacency played a large part in the rolling up of the wave of reaction that marked the latter years of the decade.

A spirit of skeptical scrutiny and criticism was active, probably as never before in American history. The axioms of the owning class and the classical economics were met with challenges rather than genuflections. The sacred cows of business and respectability were roughly handled by large numbers, with marks of impious blasphemy. In a great body of criticism, reflecting a widespread mood, "the Lords of Creation" became the "hollow men" of the twentieth century—in a manner like that of T. S. Eliot's poem—

> We are the hollow men
> We are the stuffed men
> Leaning together
> Headpiece filled with straw.

It was as though the reverberations of a new prayer shook the land, not the traditional, "Lord, increase our faith," but "Lord, increase our doubt" about the pretentious defenses of privilege which were decked out as natural laws. This criticism sapped naive faith in many sanctities accepted before the 1930's. It looked at the concentrations of economic power; it labelled the courts, not as "antiseptic laboratories of objective justice," but as tools of economic power; it examined the economic domination of the school system and colleges, the press and radio; it saw civil liberties violated under the guise of veneration for the Constitution; it beheld an advancing fascism decked out in the garments of democracy. That scrutiny was in turn applied not merely to the contemporary scene but to the past as well.

This mood of impious skepticism toward the accepted gods of the pantheon of business was deepened by the revelations of the investigations of the Senate Banking and Currency Committee which were begun in January 1933, while the Hoover Administration had still two months to go. That committee was popularly known as the Pecora Committee from its counsel, Ferdinand Pecora. For seventeen months it dug deep into the ills in the financial structure of the country and laid the basis for the passage of the Banking Act of 1933, the Security and Exchange Commission Act and the Public Utility Holding Act. But the largest result of the investigation was undoubtedly in opening the eyes of the blind, in revealing the realities of the manipulation of stock and investment. "The Stock Exchange," wrote Justice Pecora in 1939, "was in reality nothing more or less than a glorified gambling casino where the odds were heavily weighted against the eager outsiders." [9] The investigation was like a vast peep show opened up to the public; and in the process the financial overlords of the decade after the World War suffered a severe deflation. Among the scenes presented were that of the bank president making four million dollars by selling short the stock of his own bank in the month that elapsed between the first market break in September 1929 and the final crash; a millionaire avoiding the payment of any income taxes when millions were losing everything; Samuel Insull in his dazzling stunt of financial sleight of hand, manipulating and losing $2,500 of other people's money for every dollar invested of his own. It was a thorough piece of education and contributed much to the attitude of an irreverent skepticism which so strongly marked the period and found its way into voluminous literary expression.

An outstanding mark of the latter years of the period, particularly since the election of 1936, was the wave of reaction in economics and politics which found very vocal expression. This has been lifted of course to full tide by the European War. Any liberal movement is always among the first casualties of a war. In the scare of 1933, a large section of business was kneeling at the mourner's bench, asking "what shall we do to be saved?" Ten years later, after the pattern of many a convert at an emotional revival, the backslide was complete, and the seekers for salvation were saying, "Just skip it—we were a bit jittery, that is all." While it is true to say that the early years of the depression were marked by a widespread loss of confidence in the economic system, the latter years featured a spirited rally of conservative forces. For instance, in 1932, Henry Seidel Canby wrote, "the rentier class has lost confidence in the economic system upon which it lives." That could not be written with assurance seven years later. This

[9] *Wall Street Under Oath*, by Ferdinand Pecora. Simon and Schuster.

was partly due to the shock of seeing labor gain genuine power—the same cause and result as in the history of Italian fascism. The motto of Big Business was the slogan of General Sheridan at the Battle of Winchester, "Turn, Boys, turn, we're going back!" The object was not to reform; it was to re-form the defenses of economic power. The New York Stock Exchange was perhaps the clearest illustration of this rally. In the language of John T. Flynn:

"The Exchange was frightened in 1932. It was again profoundly frightened in 1934. But these men are gamblers. They have an unshakable faith in the permanence of human greed and human credulity. They invariably came out of their terrors feeling that things have always been thus and always will be, and the good old earthy Earth will presently get back to its dollar-chasing and its wagering and we shall be on top again."

This spirit of blind and frightened reaction has been well dubbed a sort of political lockjaw. Like the League of Nations, most of the business rulers of the country were equipped to resist change, but not to produce it.

The very policies under which the country sank deeper and deeper into general disaster were solemnly dusted off in 1938 and 1939 and trotted out as the means of sure-fire economic salvation. There is an interesting psychological symptom here. A typical senile defect is the dropping out of recent memories, though the past long ago may be preserved in its entirety. A disturbing case could be made for the diagnosis that our civilization has entered into a period of senile decay. For what seems to have happened in the minds of large numbers of business and economic leaders is the dropping out of any vivid memories of the recent past. Areas of recent experience which are full of guidance for future action seemed to have dropped out entirely, leaving only a sentimental nostalgic memory of a far distant past. This is strikingly true in the economic realm.

There has been a remarkable Freudian loss of memory on the part of Chambers of Commerce. Harold J. Laski, revisiting America in the summer of 1939, thus comments on the trick of memory in forgetting things not convenient to remember;

"He (the business man) has forgotten, or does not choose to remember, why Mr. Roosevelt was returned in 1932, and triumphantly reelected in 1936. He suppresses his memories of investigations like those of Judge Pecora and Senator La Follette. He is largely ignorant of the facts about how the National Labor Relations Board has actually operated, and is eager to believe anything that might discredit it; one large employer, to whom, after a discussion, I gave a copy of Professor Brooks' 'Unions of Their Own Choosing,' frankly denied that it was true. They both fear and dislike the unemployed; and they repeat to nauseation the kind of tale current in England fifteen years ago about their unwillingness to look for jobs. They resent experiments like the TVA; and they reecho most of the old shibboleths about the inefficiency of governmental operation without regard to the massive body of facts which now exist on the other side." [10]

A constant cry has been that of Denver in *The Silver King,* "O God, put back Thy Universe, and give me yesterday." Often the most profound economic understanding has been that of the song, "How dear to my heart are the scenes of my childhood." There is a powerful delusion to the effect that the United States can do what is called "restore prosperity" without making a single major change in the conditions which brought on the depression.

Odette Kahn, a European visitor, thus comments on the mentality displayed:

"They move in a world of illusion of which, outside the lunatic asylums, there is no longer the faintest trace in Europe. In this

[10] *New Republic,* July 19, 1939.

world of theirs, wealth has moral merit; poverty is a deliberate perverseness, what you go and wallow in . . . and out of which your can leap in a jiffy by means of a minimum of search for, and perseverance in, employment." [11]

Santayana has said that those who disregard the past are bound to repeat it. The whole dismal history of 1929–1932 has been forgotten by many as though it had never been. The policies for which many economic overlords and manufacturers' associations clamored for the last three years of the decade were the very ones in operation from 1922 through 1932. In 1929 there were thousands of voices crying from counting rooms, "If Congress will only leave us alone, business will go forward." The United States Chamber of Commerce has lately been crying for that very thing as though for a new divine messiah. Yet Congress did that very thing—and we know what happened. Bread lines grew longer and longer. The digging in of economic reaction on the old front line of battle has been a major feature of the last few years.

From this brief, inadequate glimpse of some of the features of the ten years in American experience, we turn to the literature produced during the period.

[11] *I Think Aloud in America*, by Odette Kahn. Longmans, Green & Co.

CHAPTER 2

SOME LITERARY TRENDS OF THE NINETEEN-THIRTIES

ANY SORT of a trial balance of the literature of a period, taken when the period has just closed, and while the forces finding expression in the years under review are still operating or merely coming to full strength, is not only a risky, but an impossible task. Any one essaying it must be content with the inglorious role of a fool rushing in where the angels of literary criticism tread softly, and wisely wait for fuller returns. Obvious reservations must be made to permit the trip at all.

It is too early for any judgments or generalizations aspiring to any permanent validity to be made. The only job that can be attempted without impertinence is that of an unpretentious bit of journalistic reporting and not the building of a literary pantheon. The evaluation of literature seems to follow a recognized pattern of three stages. There is first the immediate reception, either of welcoming appreciation or dissent, usually mixed; then follows the inevitable devaluation of the generation immediately following, and then the appraisal of a still later generation when the tumults and creations of a particular time have passed into the stream of history, far enough away to allow perspective. Thus the savage manhandling of the great Victorian figures which was so constant and joyous an excitement of 1900–1920, has given way to a new scrutiny and appreciation.

A great many quagmires can be avoided if the aim is not that of distributing halos, nor the determining of whether or not it was a poor era for great literature, but rather that of trying to observe where and in what degree it was notable as an expression of the life of the time, its experience, its moods, its responses to the forces operating on it.

To be kept in mind also is the seeming paradox that some of the most characteristic literature of one decade does not appear until the next. Here the "delayed echo" nature of art, already mentioned, comes in. Time is required for the distillation of experience into art. An instance of this is to be found in Meyer Levin's *Citizens* published in the spring of 1940, dealing with the Memorial Day "massacre" of 1937 in South Chicago, a novel dealing with labor conflict, a welcome variation from a pattern grown too standardized and mechanical, a novel which grew out of the soil of the nineteen thirties.

The whole new area of experience in America which might be called "life on relief" is just beginning to come through in fictional treatment and a large amount will doubtless follow. Caroline Slade's *The Triumph of Willie Pond,* a book of the spring of 1940, the story of a man on W.P.A. and also later on public care in a tuberculosis sanitarium, is an instance.

Another needed caution, which has often been made, and which has continual relevance, is that the primary source for data in the period is not in its creative literature, fiction, poetry, and drama, but in its factual reporting. This is true of any time; but it is to be doubted whether any decade ever showed such a demand for information and comment as marked the nineteen thirties, or such a full and varied supply. Fiction had sharper competition from non-fiction than ever before. The picture magazines made their advent, digests spawned like the fish of the sea, radio commentators explained the heavens above, (including both bombers and cosmic rays), the earth beneath, (including tanks and the dust bowl), and the waters beneath, (submarines and floods). "All I need for breakfast" exclaimed the woman in the famous cartoon, early in the decade, "is coffee and Walter Lippmann."

One obvious mark of much literature of the time stems from the confusion of a distracted era, and also has close relation to ethics and religion. Variety and confusion, and experimentation at times chaotic, are natural effects of the absence of a common body of convictions and faith. In such a time it is inevitable that there should be a confused lack of pattern, and of common outlook. If we are disappointed in finding what might be called "great art" in the decade, as we conduct a Diogenes search, we may well remember that while there was a ferment like that out of which great literature has come in the past, the actual literature has followed rather than paralleled in time the trend of the most violent ferment. And if the literature is confused in its report, that very quality must be a mark of validity.

"The writer who is absolutely clear in his point of view and knows all the answers without fear or hesitation will most likely write tracts for the times. The fact remains that life is confused and confusing and the great writer who is perhaps the most sensitive film for recording the conflict of principles in the surrounding world is himself a battle ground for them." [1]

The whole impact of life was too big and mysterious to analyze and understand. Again and again in fiction we get a bewildered feeling that life was steered from some far point. That numbed wonder is voiced in Archibald MacLeish's *Panic*. No one knows where the new, strange doom is coming from, the banker no more than the fear-stricken crowd.

[1] John Gassner, in Flexner, *The American Playwright, 1928–1935.* Simon and Schuster.

Blight—not on the grain!
Drought—not in the springs!
Rot—not from the rain!

What shadow hidden or
Unseen Hand in our midst
Ceaselessly touches our faces? [2]

The same puzzled bewilderment finds constant expression
in prose. It is found sharply and vividly in various spots in
Albert Bein's play *Let Freedom Ring*, a dramatization of
Grace Lumpkin's *To Make My Bread*, and in Steinbeck's
Grapes of Wrath.

The remote impersonality is bewildering. The lines of
Geoffrey Scott might well stand as a motto for a great deal of
fiction, poetry and drama of the 30's.

I go
Lost in a landscape of the mind,
A country where the lights are low
And where the ways are hard to find. [3]

It was an era of cruising in a world of low visibility.

The manifest confusion comes also from a lack of common
body of accepted belief. There was no fixed and continuing
center to serve as a common standing ground. John Chamberlain uses a picturesque and accurate figure in discussing the
absence of fixed values, when he says that the time called for
"cruising where the channel buoys took part in the cruise."
This was true of a whole generation of writers; it was also
true of the individuals themselves. There was war among the
members. A British poet, Louis MacNeice, himself very sensitive to this inner war, writes:

"the unconscious collaboration between Jekyll and Hyde, Jekyll

[2] *Panic*, by Archibald MacLeish. Houghton, Mifflin & Co. 1935.
[3] *Poems by Geoffrey Scott*, Oxford University Press. 1931.

being 'the poet as he thinks he is or consciously wishes to be', Hyde 'his suppressed and subordinate self'. In T. S. Eliot Hyde is the yogi-man, but in Yeats Hyde is Common Sense." [4]

Edna St. Vincent Millay during the decade has been a dialogue between Miss Jekyll and Miss Hyde. To demand of the writers of such a time that they see life steadily and see it whole when from lack of such an accepted body of conviction they saw life in flickers and in disjointed pieces, would be to expect the impossible. Periods of great literature make it clear that it springs more readily in a time dominated by a common outlook than in a time, such as in the 1930's, when it was lacking. The fact has a close bearing on the relation of religion to literature, as we shall later examine. Martin Turnell has well expressed it in relation to poetry: "While the medieval poet was living in a ready made world and was provided by the theologian and the philosopher with his subject matter, the modern poet having no such advantage, has tended to create a world of his own." [5] This accounts in part for the distressingly "private language" like a telegram in code, that has made much very modern poetry so baffling to the reader. That "private speech," a sort of soliloquy in an unknown tongue, is well satirized in verse in The New Yorker:

> What poets mean by what they mean
> Is toughter than it's ever been.
> Some swear that Ezra Pound's the ticket;
> I get lost in Ezra's thicket.
> I'm stumped by what the lilacs bring
> To T. S. Eliot in the spring.
> I sit up late at night deciding
> What goes on in Laura Riding.
> Ah, never will the masses know
> What Auden means who loves them so. [6]

[4] Modern Poetry, by Louis MacNeice. Oxford University Press.
[5] Poetry and Crisis, by Martin Turnell. The Paladin Press, London.
[6] The New Yorker, July 8, 1939.

The failure of a large amount of contemporary poetry to win either attention or appreciation is partly due to the cult of wilful obscurity or the private telegraph code. C. Day Lewis has expressed a well-founded misgiving:

> I fear this careful art
> Would never storm the sense.

Much "careful art" has never gotten within storming distance of the sense.

The advice of St. Paul, "Be not carried about with every word of doctrine," sounds strangely perfectionist in a world where forty mile gales of opinion, rising often to near-hurricanes of ideology, have made the solidest land marks bend and sway.

C. Day Lewis himself is one of the newer poets, and puts the fact clearly: "To tell the truth literature is never put by for long without a master; it needs a settled background. Even now it is trying to decide which master to serve, the revolutionary mass movement or the liberalism of Freud."

An outstanding mark of the period has been the emergence of literature into the realm of public questions. The vacuum in which so many characters in fiction moved has been vanishing. Edward Weeks used a sea figure in describing the change —"The lighthouse writer is out. The day is past when a writer could live in a lighthouse untouched by the world's events." Or to move back to land for a metaphor, a common noise of the 1930's was the collapse of ivory towers. It is significant that the title of one of Archibald MacLeish's books of poems was entitled *Public Speech*. Fiction and drama became more and more "public speech," a speech related to public affairs. MacLeish contends that was always true of the greatest poetry. He brands the 19th century poet as a "ridiculous and pathetic figure" (rather sweeping epithets!) because he was incapable of writing of the economies and politics of the 19th century as his predecessors Milton and Dante wrote of theirs. "The nineteenth century poet," Mr. MacLeish says, "would have considered himself no poet had he seen and understood the furnaces and coal pits and starving children of the midlands. And yet his predecessors in Greece had written very little of flowers and maidens, writing instead of governments, of wars, of policies, of love, of Gods, and death." Granting a poetic license of exaggeration in these words, they nevertheless do interpret a chief change in the literature of the 30's as compared to earlier periods, a change which has made for a greater closeness of contact of literature with the life problems of its time, a greater relevance to the environment, a gain in authentic portrayal of forces bearing on people.

Whitman called loudly for a poet who would "flood himself with the immediate age." That call has been answered in Sandburg, MacLeish, Stephen Benét, Edna St. Vincent Millay, and many others. The title of one of Joy Davidman's poems, *Prayer Against Indifference*, might fairly stand at the head of a large amount of poetry of the present, as it moves into the realm of public questions, and scorns social apathy. The opening stanza conveys the mood of the prayer:

> Knock music at the templed skull
> And say the world is beautiful.
> But never let the dweller lock
> Its house against another knock;
> Never shut out the gun, the scream;
> Never lie blind with the dream.[7]

Incidentally it may be noted that this strong concern for public speech on great questions has posed anew an old

[7] *Letter to a Comrade*, by Joy Davidman. Yale University Press.

dilemma of the poet—and for the novelist and dramatist also
—a dilemma which is continually evident in the writing of
these years. It is the dilemma that talents which are dedicated
to the specific ills of any year often do not survive the immediate situation; while on the other hand, writing in a social
vacuum, which does not have any relationship to the major
questions and experiences of a time, lacks depth and pertinence.

In our interest for the new in the period, for that which reveals and interprets the time, we must not forget that a large
bulk of merely traditional fiction was continually produced
and read: stories with not much vital relationship to contemporary experience. There was an unfailing stream of fiction
and drama to which could fittingly be applied the most withering noun in the leftist critic's vocabulary, "escape." There
has been much running to sanctuary in reading. Ted Olson
has pictured the safe "hide-out" of the mind in his poem entitled "Rental Library":

> The mind lies snug, and sniffs no hint
> Of danger in this copse of print.
> The mind sleeps sound; his dreams are free
> From even a nightmare memory
> Of the time when he was caught
> Briefly on the moors of thought,
> And heard the hounds, and the hunter's shout,
> And saw the hovering hawks of doubt.[8]

"Escape" is a word thrown around as a deadly missile. Yet,
while recognizing its validity in regard to a host of best sellers
(and "much-less-than-best" sellers) we need to be on guard
against the complacent sneer in that word "escape" as frequently used. For instance, in regard to the modern "opium

[8] *The New Republic*, April 1, 1940.

of the people," the mystery novel, we might with considerable justice paraphrase Wordsworth:

> Scorn not the thriller; critic, you have frowned,
> Mindless of its just honors.

It has been a means of recreation and legitimate entertainment, often making no more pretension to be literature than does chess or a crossword puzzle. The reader of crime and mystery stories does not necessarily incur the charge of "refusing to face reality" any more than does the man who retires from the battle of life by going to sleep every night. The mind, fortunately, in self-defense has a saturation point for social tragedy. There is a marginal utility even for the most honest treatment of contemporary realities. This will doubtless be even more evident in the immediate future than in the past, when the mind will need sanctuary if it is to keep balance and sanity. Fiction is not quite the same thing as piano tuning. The continued banging on one string brings diminishing returns, as has been amply demonstrated by a too long parade of novels dealing with life under the Nazi terror and strike novels, following a pattern almost as rigid as that of the sonnet.

Most readers can have a warm sympathy with the helpless victim of Mr. Opal's benefactions of books, as feelingly described:

"Mr. Opal had been sent books as well as flowers, those rather dismal books the literary people seem to be turning out these days. Not one of them was characterized by any suggestion of good cheer, not one occupied with the happier phases of existence. There was the long volume concerning the abuses of the Armenians by the Turks, and there was the even longer one about the sufferings and aspirations of the poor Jewish immigrants on the lower East Side, written by a young man with a marked predilection for detailed description of the ugliest people he chanced to see. From a scholar acquaintance came two lives of Philip II and one of Ignatius Loyola. Mr. Opal spent several lengthy days on the fall of capitalism and the inevitability of Communism after years of bloodshed. He refreshed himself with a study of the poor whites of the South and their deplorable degradation." [9]

Mr. Opal is a synthetic character, but his range of book selection is a rather fair sample of the product of the nineteen thirties. Ambition to master it all must be made of sterner stuff than a vast number of readers can supply.

Another valid reason for the persistence of novels of conventional pattern and theme, in fields distant from "the class struggle" is found in the words of Henry Seidel Canby, when he writes of "a reading public which has a pardonable liking for books they could understand about people that appealed to them." He adds wistfully that he is "sorry that tradition went underground." [10] Man shall not live by Studs Lonigan alone, nor by Jeeter Lester.

Yet there is a far deeper reason for what is often too ignorantly and snobbishly called "escape literature," when that term of disdain is made to cover writing not dealing explicitly with social or economic questions or centering in the contemporaneous. Escape is a legitimate function of genuine literature, escape from the provincial into the universal, from the here to the there, from today to yesterday. Much of the finest in literature has been escape, as has been much genuine religion. There is a specious tendency to label anything not dealing with the economic struggle as "escapist." Literary criticism from the Marxian viewpoint is particularly liable to this astigmatism. However, the word may cover what may be called an illicit shelter for the mind. A great many novelists and playwrights have been refugees from reality. The pattern

[9] *The New Yorker*, April 27, 1935.
[10] *Seven Years' Harvest*, by Henry Seidel Canby. Farrar and Rinehart.

of flight, of running away from actual life is a recurring one. Hollywood has been the Holy Mecca of this cult of escape, as Flexner says:

"Hollywood has one word which seems to damn anything which may lead people to think in a manner displeasing to the men who control the industry. Labor questions, politics, racial prejudice, social injustice and inequality are 'controversial.' They must either be avoided completely or subjected to reactionary distortion." [11]

Yet even the most complete escape into romanticism may have real social value in its unintentional indications of what an era lacked. The nostalgic evocation of honeysuckle and roses may have worth as an indication of a real dissatisfaction with the time and moment from which author and reader escape together. In making any estimate of the reading of a people, it must be remembered that the greatest bulk of the reading was done in this field. Literature has been sought as entertainment rather than as interpretation or criticism of life and society. Few of the best sellers from 1900 on have been books of ideas. Novels like *The Late George Apley* and *Grapes of Wrath* are striking exceptions. *Mrs. Wiggs of the Cabbage Patch, The Little Shepherd of Kingdom Come, So Red the Rose* are far more typical. In part, of course, the continuation of romantic escapist fiction is due to the mechanical principle of inertia—the carrying on of tradition. There is a real wisdom in regard to the lag between conditions and social thinking and literary expression, in the little verse:

> There was a dachshund once so long
> He hadn't any notion
> How long it took to notify
> His tail of an emotion;

[11] *Op. cit.*

And so it happened, while his eyes
Were full of woe and sadness,
His tail went wagging on
Because of previous gladness.

Many tales went wagging on!

The emergence of hunger into literature as well as into American life is one of the major differences between the 1930's and 1920's. In S. N. Behrman's comedy, *End of Summer*, the leading character, a rich woman, says to a young college graduate looking for a job, "Whatever you say it is an exciting time to be alive." He answers, "That's because your abnormal situation renders you free from its major excitement." She asks, "And what's that?" He gives the grim answer, "The race with malnutrition." The "race with malnutrition" has been a major excitement for millions and in various forms a major theme of the decade. In one of the most painful short stories of recent years, *Daughter*, by Erskine Caldwell,[12] a sharecropper is put in jail for shooting his young daughter. A kindly sheriff endeavors to establish that it was an accident. But the man insists on telling just how it happened:

"Daughter said she was hungry," he exclaims doggedly, "I just couldn't stand it no more. I just couldn't stand to hear her say it."

"I made enough working on shares," he says, "but they came and took it all away from me. I couldn't go around begging after I'd made enough to keep us. They just came and took it all off. Then daughter woke up this morning saying she was hungry, and I just couldn't stand it no longer."

The force of the story lies in the tragic repetition, "Daughter said she was hungry." The force of some of the most char-

[12] *Kneel to the Rising Sun*, by Erskine Caldwell. Viking Press.

acteristic literature of the dark years comes from the same
elemental fact—hunger. A recent historical survey bears the
title, *Hunger and History*. Hunger entered literature in America in an unprecendented way. Carl Van Doren's statement
that *Tobacco Road* became for the '30's what *Main Street* was
for the '20's is not too exaggerated to represent this basic
difference. An often repeated theme has been exactly that
proposed by George Meredith in his recording that "there is
hardly any situation so interesting to reflect upon as a man
without a penny in his pocket and a gizzard full of hide."
And authors reflected on it volubly! Donald Ogden Stewart
has described this emergence of hunger as a dominant theme:

"We of the long-lost younger generation began, as you may
remember, by being very disillusioned by the War and disregard-
ing any interest in things political as being of minor importance.
We announced ourselves as determined to get down to the funda-
mentals of life and tell about them. Well, as you know, the funda-
mentals of life are generally supposed to be Hunger and Sex and
I'll leave it to you to guess which one we chose to work on. Well
—we took Sex—and a very pretty little trip it was, too. But trouble
was that we were on the merry-go-round and didn't know it—
a merry-go-round that played a very pleasant tune, in fact such
a pleasant tune that it took us a long time to notice that it was
always the same tune and that we weren't getting anywhere. Of
course, most of America was on the same merry-go-round and we
couldn't be entirely blamed for our neglect of that other fundamental of human life—Hunger. Everybody, including writers, was
making money—everybody was enjoying the ride—and the supply
of gold rings seemed to be endless. Then came what is now laugh-
ingly referred to as the Crash and a lot of people suddenly discovered Hunger." [13]

Two features of novels, short stories and drama come from
this role played by hunger. New, unfamiliar types walked on

[13] *The Writer in a Changing World*. Edited by Henry Hart. Equinox
Cooperative Press. 1937.

the stage in large numbers. The sharpened awareness of
want, the freshly stirred conscience, the insistence of the relief problem, the volume of heated political discussion, have
immensely widened the cast of characters. The "ill fed, ill
clothed, ill housed" have supplied a proportionately greater
number of subjects for literary treatment than in any previous
time. A second feature is the steady weakening of the American tradition of the happy ending. That tradition is not, of
course, exclusively American. Journeys end in lovers' meetings
far more often than in the tombs of Romeo and Juliet. Yet
there is a real rootage of the happy-ending tradition in the
American soil, in the sanguine and hopeful nature of the
American people. Yet in the midst of so many case histories,
where in spite of the Stars and Stripes and "The American
Way" they did not "live happily ever after," there is small
wonder that novels and short stories began to reflect (outside
of the coated paper magazines) on the realities of American
life.

There was also what might be called a movement from
Freud to Marx. There was a shift in fiction and drama and
poetry from a preoccupation with the psyche of the individual
to the impact of economic forces on the mass. This does not
mean that fiction in general gave up its function of the portrayal of character or explanations of personality. It is very
evident that there was a continued and deepened interested
in that field of the inner life. A later chapter will deal in
particular with that. Psychology was a much explored field.
Psychiatry and abnormal psychology formed their way into
fiction and poetry, as in the novels of William Faulkner and
the poems of Robinson Jeffers; Millen Brand's *The Outward
Room* is a typical instance. The mysterious regions opened up
by Freud were not neglected. And, as we shall see, later, the
personal revelation type of story flourished as never before.

Yet it remains true that the name of Marx furnishes a better clue to the decade than that of Freud. The economic earthquake was so great and far reaching that it compelled attention. What might be called the Scott Fitzgerald era of the twenties seemed, from the deep valley of the depression, to be as far away as the middle of the nineteenth century. As has been observed often, many of the "big excitements" of the nineteen twenties seemed to be luxuries in the depression times.

The change might be expressed by saying that the most characteristic literature got far beyond the disillusion which was so frequently the stock in trade of the nineteen twenties. Someone has said of the group known as "Georgian poets" in England that they were "more eloquent in their disillusions than in their visions." That was largely true of the literature of the boom days. After 1931 millions of people, including many authors, who had also contracted the habit of eating, found that picturesque and romantic disillusions were rather thin and empty stuff when confronted with disaster. Empty stomachs became more important than hurt sensibilities. The vexations and hurt feelings of a Carol Kennecott or the spiritual frustration of an Amory Blaine in *This Side of Paradise,* or the frantic dash for personal freedom of a Janet Marsh seemed trifling themes when the dominant feature of the national scene was twelve million unemployed.

It is not enough to dismiss this body of writing as "propaganda." There are those, of course, who dismiss as propaganda anything dealing with social questions. And, of course, by a far stretching of the word, any literature setting forth a definite point of view is propaganda. A labor novel such as William Rollins', *The Shadow Before,* is propaganda; but, then, so were the Alger books. The largest proportion of fiction and poetry dealing with economic and social conditions was quite free from any definite ideological "loading."

One of the most sharply and briefly expressed descriptions of the new area of interest is to be found in the statement of a British novelist, J. B. Priestley. His words apply with equal force to the United States. Writing an introduction to a new edition of *Angel Pavement*, he says:

"If I wrote this novel now, I doubt if I could preserve what seems to me a certain air of detachment, not perhaps in the eager bustling narrator, who is probably too anxious to make all his little points, but in the creator of the general scene. I should tend now to stress the heart-breaking dependence of these decent people on a rotten system. I could not help doing this because I find now even an apparent air of detachment almost impossible to attain. The reason is of course that our contemporary world problems have such a terrible urgency, and it is my experience that no writer with a considerable public is allowed to forget the existence of such problems for a single morning, even if he could forget them when left to himself."

The movement in literature treating economic questions moved much more specifically in a Marxian direction at the beginning than at the end. John Chamberlain published in 1931 his swan song for the progressive movement, *Farewell to Reform*. It is a book of permanent historical value, a history of the rise and fall of the reform movement, the failure of mere political good government crusades, a dirge and a farewell. Reform like patriotism was not enough. The need for structural economic change was evident. The following year Lincoln Steffens published his *Autobiography*, one of the most important books written in America in the twentieth century. Covering approximately the same period as Chamberlain's book, Steffens reached a similar conclusion, that the real serpent in our possible Garden of Eden was not corrupt politicians but the large financial prizes offered to business. Some socialistic elimination of such prizes was necessary to salvation. Writing in a lyric strain of his observation of early stages of the Russian Revolution he sang, "I have seen the future and it works."

But at the close of the decade John Chamberlain published another book, *The American Stakes*, which in the opinion of one reviewer might well have been called *Hello to Reform*. For in it he forswears absolute Marxianism or any other variety, and puts his trust in the much less radical "broker state." That particular change of view and ideal is significant of the change reflected in many other works. The "red dawn" which shed such rosy light over the landscape in proletarian fiction, in radical poetry, went down into a dull dusk, particularly after Stalin's embrace with Hitler let the comrades down so badly. Yet the change of emotional climate at the end of the decade must not be allowed to dim the historical fact that during the period a large amount of both fiction and poetry reflected an increasing interest in economic remedies veering toward the left.

The movement might be expressed, somewhat inaccurately, as a shift in interest from the inward to the outward. Holding one's own pulse, charting one's emotions, turning the eyes inward, gave way in vast multitudes of people to a necessary examination of the outward scene, the concrete and often terrible realities of cause and effect in the world outside the private skull. Many palpitating little egoisms were brought outdoors into a larger world of thought and turmoil. Any generalization is dangerous and to take this one about the movement from inward concerns to outward forces as being a complete picture would leave out of view some of the most important work done in recent years. It is not too much to say that there has been a preference on the part of many readers for novels of inward drama over those of mere outward adventure. Santayana's *The Last Puritan* testifies to this interest. Thomas Wolfe, whose self-revelation in three gigantic novels threatened to outweigh in bulk the *Encyclopedia Britannica,* is an even better example of concern with the inner personal world. There are many memorable panoramas of the outward America in Wolfe. But the major theme is the psychological insides of the author himself. The two cannot be sharply separated. It is not so much a movement toward outward adventure that has been evident as it is interest in social and political forces as they affect the individual. The whole trend is well expressed in the words of John Jay Chapman:

"The unquietness of the universe which will not leave us alone, but keeps thrusting itself in and booming and banging. It never leaves the room without banging the door or enters except by falling into the center of the room and raising a howl."

Again this dominant feature may be regarded as a shift from the individual as a center of focused interest to collective life and activity. Collective destiny, as well as collective life, has become a new concern. Experience has been reading a ten year sermon on the text, "We are members one of another." An absorption with the problems of individual destiny has had to make room for an awareness of economic tidal waves that engulf the whole. The first World War taught that nations go to war with the last man, woman and child tied together. The depression made it evident as never before that the same stout ropes hold in peace. The ancient Cimbri, when going into battle, would tie all the people together in the most solid formation imaginable. The realization of those ties has found fresh expression in a thousand poems. "The incorrigibly plural world," to use Louis MacNeice's phrase, "has broken in." The dictum of Arthur Symons that "the artist has no more part in society than a monk in domestic life" has been put into an historical museum. In the center of the stage have been the adventures of individuals trying to get along with a collective world. It was an adventure often like that of Babes in the Woods. We see this sharply in a wide variety of works; in a book of case histories of people on relief such as Mrs. Armstrong's *We Too Are the People*, dealing with Northern Michigan, in the agricultural South as in Munz's *Land Without Moses*, in a mass production factory as in Smitter's, *F.O.B. Detroit*. This very awareness of the collective nature of our present world, has both given strength to fiction and taken it away. Insofar as the common man has become the hero, even though often the tragic hero, fiction has not created a gallery of notable individual characters. When a person who has read widely in the field tries to recall the sharply delineated characters, into whose nostrils the author has managed to breathe the breath of life, the list is short and the figures blur into one another. For instance, there have been six novels dealing with the Gastonia Strike in North Carolina in 1930. It is greatly to be doubted whether the casual reader of them all could recall a single character except Ishma, the central figure of Fielding Burke's *Call Home the Heart*. That has been a great artistic deficiency of both regional and labor fiction; the hero has been the region, often the land itself, or the workers seen as a group. Possibly that is why in these years we find so few novels whose characters we love and turn back to as the people of Jane Austen, Dickens, Thackeray, who have become personal friends. On the other hand, in a sharpened comprehension of the forces which do exert pressure on the tied-together life of people, fiction has touched the ground on which life is lived and gains strength as in the old Antæus of mythology, who gained strength when his feet touched the earth.

These are some of the reasons for the sense of strange sterility and remoteness which has come over some of the leading literary figures of the 1920's. It seems incredible that only a few years separate us from the time when Mencken lay about him with a slapstick act which seemed so funny at the time, but so thin when viewed in retrospect today; when "bed and booze" fiction was a headliner; when "debunking" was the most applauded exercise of literary skill; when the gods of the late 1920's, such as Lippmann and Krutch, seemed so infallible. Social upheavals have always had a bad effect on established writers. The present upheaval has run true to form in that respect. Sherwood Anderson, Theodore Dreiser, Sinclair Lewis, Scott Fitzgerald, Joseph Hergesheimer, Branch Cabell, Willa Cather, are only a few who for various reasons have become "dated." H. L. Mencken, as a literary figure, has gone into "the lean and slippered pantaloon" stage. Sinclair Lewis, the creator of Babbitt, becomes, as the loving designer of Fred Cornplow in *The Prodigal Parents,* close to being the country's Babbitt No. 1. The novels of Sherwood Anderson and Theodore Dreiser, written during the thirties, seemed like awkward burlesques of their earlier works. Ernest Hemingway's endeavor to deal with economic problems in *To Have and To Have Not* reminds us of the words written about Byron, "When he tries to think he is a child." The new struggle gave to many literary figures, as it gave to many business pundits and economic wizards, the appearance of dust-covered antiques.

One steadily recurring note is the sense of waste. Floods and dust storms sounded the shrill alarm that the land was being wasted. It had been misused, wasted in riotous living and the bill was being presented to this generation. It was deforested, burned, blighted, eroded, the soil blown away. Our sharp national consciousness of the land came naturally at the time when we were losing it. The tragic story was covered in two remarkable documentary films, *The Plow that Broke the Plains,* and *The River.* In the latter film Pare Lorentz speaks in a blank verse sort of prose that has the cadence of doom.

With the waste of land, went the waste of life, the tragedy of sub-marginal people on sub-marginal land.

This sense of waste carried over into other wastes, of life, of youth, of promise. Throughout a large part of the characteristic literature this note sounds.

Labor walked on to the stage of literature, as on to the stage of national life, as never before. The growth of the organized labor movement is not adequately represented by the literature of the time in which the growth was taking place. Here again the "delayed echo" nature of art comes in. But certainly never before was such an accurate, detailed and sympathetic picture of the actual processes of labor in scores of occupations and regions set forth. The sign we see on roadways, "men at work," could fairly stand as the fitting inscription over a vast library of fiction, drama, and poetry. From the foreign-born laborers in cranberry bogs in New England in *Sun on Their Shoulders* and *Cranberry Red,* to *Marginal Land* in the Dakotas; from the swamps of Florida in *The Yearling* to the conveyor belts in Detroit in *Nobody Starves* and *F.O.B. Detroit;* from a dizzy mail order house in Chicago in *The Chute* to the textile mills of North Carolina in *A Sign for Cain* and *A Stone Came Rolling,* men and women at work are portrayed. This impressive gallery not only leads into a new understanding of America but also, for the overwhelming part, to a new appreciation of the worth and dignity of the men and women on the jobs, and of the pressures upon them.

The reverse side of the picture is the plight of unemployment in youth, middle age and old age. Indeed, never has the thought of John Masefield's poem *Consecration* been so fully and variously fulfilled as in the last ten years in America.

"Not the ruler for me but the ranker, the tramp of the road,
The slave with the sack on his shoulders, pricked on with the
   goad,
The man with too weighty a burden, too heavy a load.

The sailor, the stoker of steamers, the man with the clout,
The chantey man bent at the halliards, putting a tune to the
   shout,
The drowsy man at the wheel and the tired lookout." [14]

There have been notable extensions of experience, ranging all the way from the mechanical processes by which products are made, transported and sold, to a revelation of what mass production under pressure, whether in automobile assembly lines or the stretchout in a textile mill, means in terms of the life of the operators. How it feels to be jobless, what the terror of losing a job does to a person, what the economic jungle is like to those caught in it—all these are memorable excursions in sympathy and have had a high potential moral value in promoting the social use of imagination. In the scores of novels of labor conflict, entirely apart from the bitter futile battle about what a pure, orthodox "proletarian" novel is, the case for organization and solidarity has been presented.

A new consciousness of America itself is strongly felt in the ten years' record. This began after the World War, for one effect of the war was the sure awakening of the writers to a strong concern with this country. That awakening was augmented by the depression. It was further strengthened by the rise of dictatorships in Europe, the overthrow of democracies,

[14] *Collected Poems* by John Masefield. The Macmillan Company.

and the threat to American institutions by conditions which produced fascism in Europe. This is true not only of the interest in the United States of the present. It has extended to the past. It is not too much to say that more interest in American history is being shown today than in any previous generation. We are asking, "How did we get that way?" The person who is ready with the magic word "escape" as a sure explanation of most literary trends would doubtless point out that the vogue of historical novels about America comes from the desire to escape from the insecurity and fear of the present to the calm security of the past. There is no doubt much truth in this explanation. But it is too small to contain all the truth. The interest in the American scene is not entirely unrelated to what has just been said about the new consciousness of the land. There has been a very real development of an intense nationalism in America, not the immature bombastic spread-eagle type, but of a deepened concern for American interests. The historical novel and the interest in it, so far from being mere retreat from the present day or escape from it, are often expressions of the ideas of today which are read back into the past.

In all this there was an answer to the persistent need for entertainment. But there was far more in it. The popularity of the particular type of entertainment in the historical novel was in part due to its being a shelter for the mind in a time of storm, a sense of solidity in an increasingly chaotic time. Its service was somewhat parallel to that of a religious faith in an hour of crisis. Indeed this "literary nationalism" had some of the aspects of religion, the most vital religion which many people possessed. Alfred Kazin has well expressed this boon provided: "Where the generation of the twenties wanted to revenge themselves on their fathers, the generation of the

thirties needed the comfort of their grandfathers." [15] In 1940
even the postage stamps went nostalgic, presenting an array
of faces with luxuriant growths of whiskers, reminders of
other days and other styles of facial decoration: Lowell, Longfellow, Whitman. "Backward, O backward, turn time in your
flight," became a national industry with such varied forms
as ransacking attics for antique furniture and old pictures, to
fighting the Civil War again on every battlefield, and blazing
the wilderness trails of pre-revolutionary times. The era of
debunking, when biographers searched frantically for some
respected figure who had not already been turned into a
stuffed shirt in the modern manner, was ended and the days
of solid reverential four volume biographies of Abraham Lincoln and Robert E. Lee succeeded them. Wide acclaim
awaited the personal story of the past. Hertzler's *The Horse
and Buggy Doctor* and Partridge's *Country Lawyer* are only
two of scores of books with the same attraction of remembrance of things past. "We're out to find the United States,"
declares a character in a pre-depression play of John Dos
Passos, *Fortune Heights*. His declaration of purpose interprets the connection which frequently existed between this
interest in the past and the present. He says:

"We stand on the Declaration of Independence. In school they
taught us a citizen of these United States had inalienable rights.
How can you have life, liberty, or the pursuit of happiness if
you're thrown out of your job and out of your home? A country
where a man wants to work and can't earn his own livin' ain't
the United States. We're out to find the United States." [16]

Not even the most cursory survey of national moods and
forces could leave out fear as a leading mark of the decade

[15] *New York Herald Tribune*, Dec. 31, 1939.
[16] *Three Plays* by John Dos Passos. Harcourt, Brace & Co.

under review. The terror that stalks at midday has been abroad in the land. It is impossible to compute the amount of sheer fear represented in the phrase that can be said in the fraction of a second, "ten million unemployed"; fear for the job on the part of the worker, the frame of fear in which the unemployed walk, fear of old age. At the other end of the scale, the shadow of fear rests also, fear of change, fear for the undermining of privilege, fear of bankruptcy, fear of "subversive" influences. Henry Seidel Canby writes:

"What if anything does literature show to be the prevailing time current of the thirties? I believe it to be fear, though fear is too strong a word for its quiet margins and panic would better describe some of its hurrying tides. This fear sometimes is conscious, sometimes unconscious. It ranges from skeptical inquiry into the possible disintegration of culture as we have known it to the deep pessimism of convinced alarm." [17]

Fear is like a poison in the veins. Its effects are carried everywhere. They were carried everywhere during what have been called 'the threatening thirties.' Violence and intolerance, and there was much of both, were increased by fear. The violence of the strike in Little Steel in 1937, with its Memorial Day Massacre in Chicago, the voice of Father Coughlin over the radio, the hysteria expressed and produced by the Dies Committee, and anti-alien agitation and legislation, these are only a few of the more violent expressions of fear. It has been freshly demonstrated that tolerance is, to a degree we do not like to admit, a product of prosperity. Fright not only congeals the blood, but tends to congeal the humanity of people. The national jitters were well represented in the nation's books.

Violence is an easily discernible mark of some fiction and poetry. It appears more in intensity than in extent, being so

[17] *Saturday Review of Literature*, May 22, 1937.

strongly manifest in the work of a few writers that they have been referred to as a "cult of violence." Hemingway, Faulkner, Robinson Jeffers, Erskine Caldwell, are the names most associated with the preoccupation with violence, brutality, and cruelty, though the trend is evident in many others, in O'Neill, in Farrell, John O'Hara and W. R. Burnett. That there should be a literary celebration of violence is a natural result of the thorough tuition of that great school of violence, the first World War. Yet that is not an adequate explanation of such writers as Jeffers and Faulkner. The delight of big muscles and violent action as a heritage of the war is seen most clearly in Hemingway. A comparable figure in England, regarded by some critics at least, as a war casualty, is Richard Aldington. He was a particularly sensitive poet, an idealist, who turned after serving in the war, to writing novels which seemed to be idealism gone into reverse in their portrayal of the hard and ugly and the brutal. A frequent diagnosis made is that in his novels he tried to hide the real depth of the hurt which the war brought to his poetic idealism, by a protective covering of hard-boiled cynicism. Something of the same sort may well be, in part at least, the explanation of Hemingway and his loving and technically skilled portrayals of "tough guys" in action. Here is the clinical report given by Max Eastman:

"We took this young man with his sensitive genius for experience, for living all the qualities of life and finding a balance among them—and with that too obvious fear in him of proving inadequate—and we shoved him into our pit of slaughter, and told him to be courageous about killing. And we thought he would come out weeping and jittering. Well, he came out roaring for blood, shouting to the skies the joy of killing, the 'religious ecstasy' of killing—and most pathetic, most pitiable, killing as a protest against death."

Where in any author before was such a parade of violence, hangings, shootings, suicides, caesarian operations with jack knives, abortions, gangrene, bullfights, prize fights, all preserved in alcohol? The style in which these epics of assault and battery were written has been the most widely imitated style of our time, giving rise to what has been called "the Joe Muscle School" of writing.

The simple explanation of the war, too simple to account for Hemingway, is far less adequate to explain Faulkner, with his extensive portrayal of abnormal personalities of the South, and the poet Jeffers, with his preoccupation with incest and homicide as symbolic themes. The two are by no means to be bracketed together. Each in a different way seems to be expressing a sense of "the abyss" under the covering of life, the horror, the malignant element in man, that supplies relevant data for any inquiry into the religious aspects of our time and literature.

Here, then, are some main lines of the portrait, albeit a very sketchy and impressionistic one. Where does it affect our particular interest, that of the ethical and religious emphases of the time? Indeed, we may well ask, where are the ethical and religious elements in all this varied expression? Why search for the ethical in a time when most writers carefully avoided the very appearance of ethical purpose or preoccupation? Why concern with any religious implications in a body of literature in which explicit religion as a subject or indeed as a part of the life portrayed in fiction was faint and blurred, when it is found at all?

The answer, of course, is that the ethical qualities of experience and the transcript of it are inherent in the thing itself. They do not depend on labelling. They do not depend on any consciousness of ethical purpose. There is no such thing as literature divorced from moral or religious implications. R. Ellis Roberts argues this in an extreme form, but with recognizable cogency, when he says that the nonsense of Edmund Lear and Lewis Carroll, and the simple lyrics of many nature poets, presuppose both in author and reader the profoundly ethical thesis that mere joyfulness and gaiety are right for men. If that be true there is in such portraits of the life of the Negro in the United States as are found in *Uncle Tom's Children,* and the drama *Stevedore,* the profoundly ethical thesis that such life is profoundly wrong for men. If we pause, in a deserved attention, reverence even, for the thing that is, pause to see what is portrayed and to listen to what honest voices of our time are saying, we will find that they are full of ethical interest, insight and judgment, and valid religious implications. Often the very absence of religion in the life recorded and in the recorders themselves is negative testimony of the first importance to service of religion to life. It will be the task of the succeeding chapters to trace out these affirmations with as convincing detail as may be possible. Here are merely listed some obvious trails of exploration.

There is moral insight and value in the continued judgment of an area, such as the 1930's make on the 1920's. That judgment is given prophetic expression in the words of William Allen White:

"What a sordid decade is passing! . . . The spirit of our democracy has turned away from the things of the spirit, got its share of its patrimony ruthlessly, and has gone out and lived riotously and ended up by feeding it to the swine . . . What a joy it would be to get out and raise the flaming banner of righteousness! Instead of which we sit in our offices and do unimportant things and go home at night and think humdrum thoughts, with the gorge in us kicking like a mule all the time."

There was a great deal of "kicking like a mule," to use Mr. White's barnyard figure of speech. The very tragedies of the 1930's were a weighing in the balance of the decade which preceded. A profit-centered materialistic way of life had led to economic and social damnation. That judgment was a distinct moral asset.

The very confusion, already indicated and so readily apparent, has a clear word on the service of religion as a background of life. The vigorous and often bitter protest against exploitation, against the mangling and waste of life, was an assertion of the dignity of man, the undebatable worth of human stuff. This had very audible and genuine overtones concerning the actual nature of man. Many books from which many people turn away in shock, their ears and minds offended by the coarseness of speech, have carried in the voice of today the spirit and content of a definitely religious prophecy—that of Lamentations—"The young children ask bread and no man breaketh it unto them," or of Amos, "Who buy the poor for silver and sell the needy for a pair of shoes and sell the refuse of the wheat."

The very struggle depicted in scores of labor novels and plays has an ethical and religious value in that it is an alternative to a limp fatalism and defeatism. It is the bass note found in Clough's "Say not the struggle naught availeth." There is a definite messianic strain in the call to organization, an experience of solidarity and brotherhood.

The very consciousness of waste both of land and people marks a stirring of conscience. It is the beginning of a sense of stewardship, of trusteeship. That widespread awakening to the prodigal waste of a great American heritage in the land, and in the frustration of the American dream, follows rather closely the lines of the story of the prodigal son. After the wild waste, then "he began to be in want." Then he came to himself. That is a moral and religious asset.

Finally, as we shall examine more closely, there is a striking parallel between the most significant religious and theological thinking of the period and much literary interpretation of life and the world. In both there has been a forswearing of an easy and superficial optimism. There has been a sense of the evil forces under the surface of life. Theology has taken a clearer look at evil; it has escaped from the bog of romantic sentimentalism into a religiously realistic appraisal of the evil in man and in society. There is nothing in the spiritual life of our time more interesting than this double exploration by religion and literature of the deeper and darker aspects of life beneath the surface. This new sense of the fearful aspects of mind and society and the universe is found in religious thinking. It is also found in cruelty, the violence of O'Neill, Jeffers, Hemingway, Faulkner. It is no accident that our time has rediscovered and reappraised Herman Melville and the tragic sense of life that he profoundly felt.

CHAPTER 3

THE CANDID CAMERA AT WORK

ONE OF THE NEW terrors of life is unquestionably the candid camera. In other years and in other places a terrifying bogey man was Jack the Ripper. Today he is Jack the photographer. We may exclaim in despair in scriptural language, "Whither may I flee from thy presence? If I go abroad in the street, thou art there, and if I hide at home, thou art there. And if I take the wings of the morning and fly to the uttermost part of the earth, thou art in the midst of me." Relentlessly candid cameras are clicking all over the land.

Some of the most valuable parts of the literature of our time can be brought under the head of "the candid camera at work." Never have clearer lenses been trained on all the nooks and corners of the life of America. Emerson once wrote that the important thing was to get the American genius to work on "the great, listless, dumb, lifeless America." America has not been listless, dumb or lifeless. But certainly his hope has been realized beyond his dream, for much talent and some genius have worked on America. The result has been the production of literary photographs of great range, variety and truth. No better picture of that achievement can be drawn than that in another exhortation of Emerson given in 1837: "It is time the sluggard intellect of this continent should look out from under its iron lids and fulfill the postponed expectations of the world with something better than the exhortations of mechanical skill. The millions that around us are rushing into life cannot be fed on the sere remains of foreign harvest. The literature, the feelings of the child, the philosophy of the streets, of the meaning of household life are the topics of the times."

The call fell on deaf ears in Emerson's day. But it has had an increasingly abundant response in the line that began with Frank Norris and Howells, the early Hamlin Garland and Robert Herrick. A large part of the fiction of the past ten years has been occupied with exploration of distinctly American fields. The phrase used as the title of a book of essays by Stuart Sherman in 1932, "The Emotional Discovery of America," describes the process which has been going on opening up new paths to the understanding of American life.

Indeed, the word "camera" in the title of this chapter has far more than a figurative meaning. Photography in the last decade has furnished data for a mirror such as no other generation has had. Photography has not only entered the field of an authentic art, but it seems at times to be literature as well. Such a book as Archibald MacLeish's with the ironical title, *Land of the Free*, is hard to classify. It is a book of pictures with a "soundtrack" of poetry and prose, presenting in both the bewilderment of a homeless America, driven off the fields, taken to the roads, roads leading nowhere. Erskine Caldwell and Margaret Bourke-White have combined text and camera in a deeply moving Exhibit A of the share cropper, *You Have Seen Their Faces*. Government agencies have produced many of the pictures. Here were portraits drawn by the sun on celluloid, a few evidences of the cost of raising cotton paid for by lives blighted and wasted, a few indications of what it means when ten million persons live in degradation and defeat. Another group of photographic discoveries of America is the series of films produced by Pare Lorenz which have had a high value as social documents, *The Plow that Broke the Plains, The River* and *The Fight for Life.* The *River* has been published as a group of still pictures with text in the sonorous metre and beat of poetry. It is the story of the Mississippi, attempting to suggest what the ramifications of that great water system mean to the physical, economic and spiritual life of the country. It is a story of sin, unfolding with the relentless inevitability of a Greek tragedy, with soil erosion, dust storms, slaughter of forests and flood chanting, "Be sure your sin will find you out."

The Fight for Life is a government sponsored motion picture, based partially on Paul de Kruif's book of the same name, and dramatizes vividly the preventable waste of life in childbirth, and the social effects when proper care is made an unattainable luxury for large numbers of people.

Another example of the camera as a new medium of social interpretation is to be found in *American Photographs* by Walker Evans. It presents more than eighty photographs taken in the eastern part of the United States, pictures which reveal little of conventional beauty or trick professional technique. Lincoln Kirstein, the poet, who contributes the introduction, says they represent a "straight puritanical stare." It is that "straight stare" which gives them their social and moral value. It is not the record of a photographer's holiday, so much as sharp data on a social upheaval. Granted that these photographs do not fairly portray America, the charge could easily be brought to the photographer, as is brought to many writers, that they belong to "the cult of the ugly." But he has fulfilled his commission given by the Farm Security Administration to take his candid camera to the impoverished area and report what he saw. The pictures speak—even scream at times—eloquently, of some things which lie behind the show window.

Here again, at the risk of repetition, it is necessary to emphasize the predominant interest of this book, which necessarily limits the range of view. That purpose is not to furnish even a cursory glance at the whole body of American literature during the period. Large numbers of widely read books, many of them the most widely discussed, are not considered at all. One such group is that which frankly aims at entertainment, having no purpose of holding a mirror up to nature or the contemporary world or to its conditioning influences. Much of it is on a not much higher level than that of being, in Browning's phrase, a substitute for a cigar. Some of it deserves the description, "artistic sand piles in which the ostrich author hides his head." Such omissions do not imply the least disdain of entertainment. The reason is simply that such writing does not fall within the boundaries of our present interest.

The large function of "escape" literature, not using that term as a phrase of contempt, but as a description of a large and legitimate service, is movingly portrayed in a poem by Lawrence Lee, entitled, *Evening Cinema*:

> Here are the meadows where we may forget.
> Wake not the faces lifted to a dream,
> For of the world we bear some likeness yet,
> Shadow beside shadows let the heart take root,
> The fallow mind send up its tendril wish,
> The body be of air from head to foot.
>
> The passing to Elysium is swift:
> For two starred hours the lotus holds the soul;
> Then, in the light, the soft illusions lift,
> And with some look of dream still in their eyes
> The wakers stand upon real streets and see
> Toward what dark rooms the homeward turning lies.[1]

[1] *Monticello and Other Poems*, by Lawrence Lee. Charles Scribner's Sons.

A large boon to life is here portrayed. Yet the last three lines show the essential futility of mere escape when it has no relation to "real streets" and "dark rooms," when it brings no interpretation of the world outside of the temporary illusion. Our concern is with the writing which comes out into the street from the darkened room of magic, and goes with the beholder on "the homeward turning." It is with the fiction and poetry and drama which essay to give some path to the understanding of life and its environment. It occasions no surprise that such literature is on the forbidden list of great hosts who are addicted to painless romance. They are well described by Lincoln Steffens, "Thinking is an agony for them. I feel like massaging their hams after a brief conversation." [2]

Lord David Cecil has strikingly described the service of literature which does bring genuine understanding of experience. He writes of what the *Old Wives' Tale*, which he considers the best English novel written in England, had done for him:

"He sometimes has to pass through those Midland towns from which Arnold Bennett drew his setting. Before he had read that book he used to avert his eyes from the landscapes outside the train windows, as from the epitome of all that was humdrum and uninspiring. But now the black factory chimneys, the clanging tramways, the red villas, even the hideous public buildings loom up before him hallowed by romance. Literature, he adds, can do no greater service than this—to teach men that no form of life is to be despised." [3]

One mark of most of the fiction and some of the drama considered under the head of the "candid camera" is just what

[2] *Letters of Lincoln Steffens*, Harcourt, Brace & Co.
[3] *New York Times*, July 9, 1939.

the adjective implies, "realism." That word, which has been fought and refought over like a battlefield in Belgium, is here taken arbitrarily to imply correspondence to actual life. Let it be freely granted that much of it has the artistic aspects associated with photography, but not in great painting. A camera gives equal attention to all objects within its view. It cannot be interested only in a head and neglect the background. The sin of photography is its coldness, its lack of human touch. Much of the fiction lacks the deep plumbing of character. But it does report, "Here is where people live; here is what we have made of America: these are the places where the burdens of our day rest heavily and cut cruelly."

Aldous Huxley in *Ends and Means* has argued that the two primary essential virtues are love and awareness. Now love without awareness may easily degenerate into sentimentalism, superficial or mawkish. Awareness and intelligence without love may be the scrutiny of indifference or contempt, like the impersonal examination of a laboratory microscope. Together they are major virtues of the good life. Many scores of novels of the ten years have awareness of social environment, and personality, and love in the sense of sympathetic understanding in their presentation. There is frequently a realism that may well be called ruthless. Authors get behind the finely painted billboards to the waste heap they hide. This may degenerate into a cult of the ugly and by its biased selection, as in Faulkner and Caldwell, may present a picture as grotesquely unreal to the whole spread of life as the most confectionery romanticism. Muddy water may be just as shallow as clear, though mud is often mistaken for depth and honesty. Robert Frost spoke a penetrating word on that subject when he said he is not the kind of realist who offers a good deal of dirt on his potato to show it is a real one—but rather one who is satisfied with the potato brushed clean. The great point in literature is to have a real potato. There have been plenty of real potatoes.

The first group of pictures, the product of the candid camera, is what is called regional fiction. In general, it is marked by the region itself being the hero or principal character. Novelists have covered the country with the diligent thoroughness of the United States Geologic Survey. They have swarmed over our national landscape with the eagerness, and often with the haste, of Forty Niners staking out a claim to a gold mine. Of course, this is nothing new in our literature. Mark Twain, Mary E. Wilkins, Bret Harte, Sarah Orne Jewett, George W. Cable are in the line of regional novelists. Much recent fiction has been a full rendition of the hymn

> I love thy rocks and rills
> Thy woods and templed hills.

Pearl Buck is doubtless right when she says that the people portrayed are the least effective part of the regional novels. There has undoubtedly been much more successful description of surfaces than there has of imaginative creation of character. In large part, environment and incident come first, character comes second. There is a great deal to be said for the remark of a woman sent out from a New York tenement district as a fresh air farm guest. She returned after a very few days, and when asked the reason, she replied, "I like to look at people better than stumps." Most of us do, and the novelist had better remember it.

Yet there is large value in the life of a region. There has been a robust quality to the portrayals. The secret of many of them is to be found in the words of Chanticleer, who explained how he planted his feet on his native soil, waited for the strength of the earth to rise up through his body to his throat, and then he announced the coming of the dawn to his own valley. That is a rather exact description of a great deal of regional fiction—the feet of the author are planted on his native soil and the strength of the earth rises up through him.

Our method must be the selection of a few of the many works which bear on our main interest, taken as samples. Otherwise there will be a mere list like Homer's catalog of ships, without its rhythm and cadence. Much of this regional literature is prose in the tradition of the English poet, George Crabbe, to whom the high tribute has been paid, "He didn't lie about life." Here is his own artistic creed:

> I paint the Cot,
> As Truth will paint it, and as Bards will not.
> Yet Gentle souls, who dream of rural ease,
> Whom the smooth stream and smoother sonnet please;
> Go! if the peaceful cot your praises share,
> Go look within and ask if peace be there;
> If peace be his, that drooping weary sire;
> Or theirs, that offspring round their feeble fire;
> Or hers, that matron pale, whose trembling hand
> Turns on the wretched hearth the expiring brand.

This quotation from Crabbe, however, gives only a small part, and not the most characteristic part, of the attitudes shown toward America in the thirties. A fresh love for the land was evidenced, a love which seemed to deepen as it became progressively evident that the land was desperately sick. At times it bore resemblances to love for a mother, stricken with a fatal disease. There was an affection for the earth and for the life which it supported which would have seemed sentimental and naive to some dominant moods of the nineteen twenties, when spleen was in the ascendent and minor irritations rapidly became cosmic themes. A symbolic picture of this feeling is that of Tom Joad's father in *Grapes of Wrath*, picking up and pouring through his hands the earth of his own farm yard, handling it with love and grief at leaving it, as the very stuff of life. Thomas Wolfe gives a massive picture gallery scattered throughout his novels, both giant murals and miniatures of a beloved America. Many of these passages have been gathered together in a volume of selections entitled, *The Face of a Nation*. There are hundreds of vivid and loving memories touched with nostalgia, such as, "The slow thick yellow wash of an American river"; the moonlight which he describes as "filling the cat's cold eye with blazing yellow"; "the sound an American train makes going across an old iron bridge"; "the color of North Carolina Mountains." [4] It is an America of the senses, sound, sight, taste, that Wolfe celebrates in the Whitman tradition. In similar manner, Frederick Prokosch has filled his *Night of the Poor* with swift compressed evocations expressing the same feeling:

". . . cold pine-shadowed lakes," "the trains . . . echoing through the hills . . . and the trucks rumbling down the state highways," "wooden bridges and old cars left in the woods to rust and rot away," "Poles and Italians sweating at the forge, faces lit by the red furnace blaze."

Now in November by Josephine Johnson, published in mid-depression, is authentic American earth. She is an unusual combination of poet and realistic reporter. She thus defined her aim, "I wanted to give a beautiful and yet not incongruous form to the ordinary living of life—to write, as I once said, poetry with its feet on the ground. I wanted to sketch these characters in a sort of plain idyl, beautiful only in so far as life itself is beautiful." *Now in November* succeeds in being "poetry with its feet on the ground." The region is Missouri, the epic is the familiar one of ten years' struggle with the land, culminating in a drought. One of

[4] *The Story of a Novel,* by Thomas Wolfe. Charles Scribner's Sons.

three daughters, Margaret Hardlame, tells the story, looking back after the disaster which engulfed the family, including drought, fire, frustrated love, insanity and the suicide of one of the sisters, foreclosure of the mortgage, eviction of Negro share croppers. It is not primarily a horror tale, but rather an artistic reflection of the whole experience. The first sentence of the novel gives the theme and method, "Now in November I can see our years as a whole." It ends with nothing left but courage and youth which expects little or nothing. Written with more feeling for beauty than of stark realism, it gets under the surface more than the familiar saga of backbreaking days on the farm could have done. The central theme is inner as well as outward, the effect on character and personality of the struggle to wring a living out of the soil under adverse conditions.

"I do not see in our lives," she says, "any great ebb and flow or rhythm of earth. There is nothing majestic in our living. The earth turns in great movements, but we jerk about on its surface like gnats, our days absorbed and overwhelmed by a mass of little things—that confusion which is our living and which prevents us from being really alive."

The novel is marked with a sensitive love of the earth, the excitement kindled by a flowering bush, the strange beauty of a snake shedding its skin, "air that came sweet and stale and full of a grassy smell"; as she writes, "beauty in all its twisted forms, not pure unadulterated, but mixed always with sour potato peelings or an August sun."

The Folks by Ruth Suckow, another 1934 novel, is a friendly camera moved up close to Mid-America, with the account of changes in the texture of living doing a real service in explaining what has happened to America since the World War. Miss Suckow had in her early years a good vantage point for observation, the front porch of several Iowa parsonages. No novel is more valuable for a presentation of what happens to families whose way of life has been centered in the church and largely moulded by Christian and Puritan tradition, when a settled and old order is undermined by the confusions and frustrations of a new day. The background is a small town, the sort familiar to millions as real as potatoes and oatmeal. The effect of the skillful drawing of this background is thus given by Horace Gregory, the poet, himself a Middle Westerner:

"I know the Fergusons a shade too well; they are the folks back home, living at the very heart of a countryside that is America, and when they speak their homely dialect, long sleeping loyalties are roused again."

Outwardly it is the familiar story of "local boy makes good." Fred Ferguson comes into the little town of Belmont from his father's nearby farm, gets a job in a bank and rises in the world. The theme of the novel is the changes which his own increasing prosperity and the social and economic changes of the years bring to the family life, its faith, conduct and mores. The old world had its unshaken simplicities, as reflected in the advice given by the grandfather to his grandson, Carl: "Take to yourself a good wife, and don't drink nor smoke nor gamble your money at cards, and work hard at whatever your work is,—then you'll get along, my boy. These are the principles I've always stuck to and uphold the Lord and His Holy Works." Such a prescription had been enough for Grandpa's day. But for the third generation or even the second, it proved unduly simplified. And yet doesn't it sound like the voice of Calvin Coolidge? With increasing means, social ambitions rouse in Mrs. Ferguson, dreaming of greater worlds to conquer than the Presbyterian Ladies' Aid Society. The taboos against dancing and card playing lose their force. No longer does it seem a bit immoral, or a disintegration of character to get a woman to help in the dishwashing and housework. The greatest impact of the change, however, falls on the children. One, the eldest, is a "good boy" accepting the parental shaping, only to find a thwarted life. One girl escapes to Greenwich Village, but never escapes the Puritan heritage of guilt over the promiscuous love making which she takes up from a stern duty of asserting independence. The youngest shocks the family by marrying a Communist. Fred Ferguson and his wife go where all good Iowans go—Southern California. But the pull of the familiar was too strong and they returned to Iowa. The storm of the depression leaves him with the threat of poverty—and a bewildered wondering whether the Communist son and daughter-in-law may not be on the right track after all. No more effectively detailed picture of an America drifting past old landmarks can be found. Nor one containing more trustworthy data for a study of religious changes in the twentieth century.

Some novelists have highlighted the interest in the land by the device of taking a piece of land itself as the hero of a story. Louis Bromfield did this in *The Farm*, tracing the history of an Ohio farm through several generations, thus making it the thread on which is hung a succession of agricultural, economic and social changes.

Peattie has done the same thing in *American Acre*. Paul Corey's *Three Miles Square* uses the same pattern in dealing with agricultural life in Iowa, though his time frame is not nearly so long—only from 1910 to 1939—as in the novels of Bromfield and Peattie.

On all America, the time exposure of the lens has been turned. As goes Maine, so goes the Union, as far as fictional presentation is concerned. Novel writing has become a leading industry in Maine, due, someone has suggested, to literary properties of the iodine on the seacoast. Rachel Field's *Time Out of Mind;* Mary Ellen Chase's *Mary Peters* and *Silas Crockett;* Gladys Hasty Carroll's *As the Earth Turns* are only a few. Vermont has Dorothy Canfield, with the *Deepening Stream* in 1931, *Bonfire* in 1933, and *Seasoned Timber* in 1939. It is an arbitrary matter whether one chooses to regard novels such as those of Dorothy Canfield's as primarily novels of a region, or novels of character and personality. They are, of course, both. They will be noted more fully in the following chapter, as will Ellen Glasgow's *Vein of Iron* and Marjorie Kinnan Rawlings' *The Yearling.* Typical of many novels dealing with the land are two portraying South Dakota and Minnesota, Horace Kramer's *Marginal Land* and Herbert Krause's *Wind without Rain.* Both center in the struggle with a grudging land, Kramer's novel telling once more of the fight for wheat.

If the South, as President Roosevelt asserted to much annoyance south of the Mason and Dixon line, is the country's No. 1 economic problem, it has also been the No. 1 hunting ground of fiction. A whole regiment of novelists have stepped to the music of "We're Marching through Georgia"—and through Mississippi, Alabama, Tennessee, Florida, and North Carolina. This work ranges from such sympathetic pictures of what might be called more normal life such as Hamilton Basso's *Court House Square,* where the best of an old tradition confronts a new world, and Bernice Harris' *Purslane,* to such savage explorations as in T. S. Stribling's trilogy of Alabama, *The Store, The Forge,* and *Unfinished Cathedral. Court House Square* seems as fair a sample as we can get of the honest portrayal of the life of a region, in which realism is not confused with ugliness and degeneracy, and in which the genuine moral values of the South find expression. A

young writer, David Barondness, returns to his native Mace-
don, South Carolina, drawn by homesickness. Once home,
he discovers that by temperament and liberal spirit he is more
of an exile at home than he was in New York. The town is
seething with bigotry, prejudice, suspicion, and reactionary
spirit. The Barondness family have had, for several generations, a representative who at the command of conscience de-
fied the code of the community. David does this in his generation by defending a Negro dentist, bringing down on himself
the hate and savagery of a large part of the town. The novel
traces perception on the part of the hero of the gap between
the romantic tradition and the actual present, with its economic and racial problems, the lack of education and the
paralysis of reason by emotion and inbred prejudice. Somewhat similar in theme, set in Mississippi, is Robert Rylee's
Deep, Dark River. It is a novel of the deep South notable for
three things among others. It entirely avoids the grotesqueness of the horror school of Faulkner and Caldwell; it draws
a Negro character who is not a stage property, neither a clown
nor a lay figure to demonstrate an economic thesis, but a
notable person, observed with sensitiveness and sympathy; it
tells a story of cooperation between black and white which
results in a real spiritual victory without becoming in the least
didactic or sentimental. Mose Southwick, an exploited Negro
sharecropper, a man of high personal integrity, and religious
feeling, has shot in self-defense another Negro hired by the
planation manager to kill him. A woman lawyer at her own
great risk comes to his defense. The trial reveals the whole
economic and social situation. In view of the clear detail of
the injustices under which the Negroes are held, and the
economic power of the landlords, the happy ending of the
acquittal and victory may seem unreal and forced. Love for
the South glows through the novel, with a sense of shame

over the wrongs it tolerates. That deep love appears in the words of the woman lawyer, Mary Winston, to an old man:

"I'm a woman coming to the old strength of this country for help because I love what you were and what you and my father built and then neglected while it rotted away. It's that neglect I can't forgive. It's like God had gone back to the swamps to live with snakes." He replies: "You tell me that you think I have sat here these years without knowing it. It's been creeping, crawling over the fields. No wonder the niggers chain the doors and shutters at night. Sometimes I feel like doing it myself. To look at my own monstrous children. What strange ends a man comes to." She says, "Then you do love this country as I do, the greatness of it and how it holds you. The black sloping down to the walled river. And sometimes I hate it, too."

Another type of novel, warm with love of the land and of people, a regional novel with a mixture of poetic imagination and realism, is James Still's *River of Earth*. Its location is the mines and hills of Kentucky seen through the eyes of a boy. It is neither the exploitation of a quaintness which has become a stereotype or a proletarian novel about underpaid miners, though it does reveal the poetic thought and speech of a people close to primitive life and it does have in the foreground the collapse of the economic base of life, when the mines reach marginal utility and unemployment plunges the men into a baffled bewilderment. The weight of this on the women is expressed by the boy's mother:

"Since I married I've been driv from one coal camp to another. I've lived hard as nails. I've lived at Blue Diamond. I've lived at Chavies, Tribbey, Butterfly Two, Elkhorn and Lackey. We moved to Hardburly twice and to Blackjack beyond counting. I reckon I've lived everywhere on God's green earth. Now I want to set me down and rest."

Paul Green's *This Body the Earth*, one of the strongest novels of the South, is so predominantly centered on the struggle against an agricultural system that it is considered later in the chapter on labor literature.

The foregoing three novels are chosen from a large number. They are important in themselves. They are also important as necessary counterbalances to the two men who have received the largest amount of critical attention as portrayers of the South, Erskine Caldwell and William Faulkner. Among the many troubles the South has endured must be listed the fact that, largely through the unprecedented popularity of the stage presentation of Caldwell's *Tobacco Road*, large numbers of people, who do not know the South at all, have accepted Jeeter Lester and his gallery of degenerates as fair samples of the *dramatis personae* below the Mason and Dixon line. That fact, in itself, ought to be grievance enough to cause another civil war. Caldwell has written prolifically during the decade, publishing four novels, *Tobacco Road*, in 1932, *God's Little Acre*, in 1933, *Journeyman*, in 1935, and *Trouble in July*, in 1940. He has also four major books of short stories, *American Earth*, in 1931, *We Are the Living*, in 1933, *Kneel to the Rising Sun*, in 1935, and *Southways*, in 1938. The predominant quality of his work gives him little or no claim to be classified as a realist, in spite of the fact that at the trial resulting from the charges that *God's Little Acre* was obscene, the judge decided that the novel was a sincere effort to tell the truth. Most of Caldwell's subjects are mentally sub-normal or abnormal, and frequently amoral. That bias of selection prevents anything like a fair picture of a region or a way of life. Kenneth Burke calls his people "grotesques," suggesting that the author, before presenting them, has performed on them an operation like that in which the higher centers of an animal's brain have been removed, leaving the animal responses greatly simplified.[5] A gathering of Caldwell characters such as have walked on the stage in the five-year run of *Tobacco Road,* is like the Pool of Bethesda, at which were gathered "the sick, halt, blind, withered" (John 5:3). It is a convention of the distorted, the moronic, a laboratory demonstration of evolution in reverse.

During the ten years there has been evidence of two men in the author. One is the observer and humorist. The other is the social diagnostician, who in the later books is overshadowing the observer. Caldwell's early life in Georgia and other parts of the South, his experience in all sorts of occupations, mill worker, farm hand, cook, cab driver, gave him ample opportunity to observe the human results of an agricultural system in decay. But his earlier work had little explicit social implication, his recording of the life of people in wretched conditions being given with a perverse humor and gusto. The sense of comedy served to "take the curse off" so much piled up horror, with its multiplied cases of rape, brutality, murder, and lynching. This continued assault of the physically and mentally unpleasant gives the effect of a war of nerves, a sort of literary "blitzkrieg." Readers and audience have thus had a mingled effect of shock and comedy, which is one element accounting for the long run of the play.

That there are such dregs at the bottom of a maladjusted agricultural order is hardly to be doubted. A man who knows the South thoroughly, Jonathan Daniels, says of the characters in *Southways,* "They rise in Georgia as indigenous as a Georgia hill. That they are Southern folk, clearly, honestly, and vividly drawn is certain." Calling attention to them, however unpleasant or disgusting the process, is a contribution of real moral and social value. Much more definitely in his re-

[5] *The New Republic,* April 10, 1935.

cent work, notably in the stories in *Southways* and in the novel *Trouble in July,* Caldwell traces the decay of morality and character to economic oppression, as a natural result. Even in *Tobacco Road* the economic basis of degeneracy emerges clearly. It has been estimated that the companies playing the drama have eaten 50,000 turnips. Turnips are important. Jeeter wails continually that his turnips have "damn-blasted, green-gutted turnip worms." A way of life reduced to rotten turnips is bound to show personal decay. *Trouble in July* is the story of a lynching, in which a whole community passes in review with its corruption, its cowardice and decay, like the report from a cancer clinic. The author never allows indignation to burst into flame, but its presence is strongly felt.

William Faulkner's work, though specializing in degenerates and horror and shock, is very different from Caldwell's. There is an absence of humor; it is more straight sodden stuff. It is also true undoubtedly that his audience is much more limited than Caldwell's. Faulkner is a critic's novelist, rather than a popular one. One wonders also whether he is not more of a "fad" among the intelligentsia. Just as "Everybody talkin' about Hebben, ain't goin' there," in the words of the Negro spiritual, so everybody talking about Faulkner "ain't" read him. The figure of 60,000 as a total sale of all of Faulkner's novels and stories is given by Anthony Buttitta.[6]

In his introduction to the Modern Library Edition of *Sanctuary,* Mr. Faulkner has indicated that his adoption of horror as a medium was deliberate. As "the right answer to current trends," he says that he "invented the most horrific tales I could imagine." This seems to give some basis for the theory that his preoccupation with brutality and degeneracy has come from a very violent reaction to the romantic tradition

[6] *Saturday Review of Literature,* May 21, 1938.

of the South. To make perfectly sure that he got away from the magnolias and rose gardens, he went in the other direction until he found sanctuary in the insane asylum and county jail. This over-compensation for the hated moonlight and mocking-bird tradition in Southern fiction makes him, in the opinion of Ellen Glasgow, as much of an "escapist" from the real South as the most loyal devotee of the school of Thomas Nelson Page, the only difference being that Faulkner "escapes" in the direction of horror rather than romance.

He has literally waded through rivers of blood in six novels in the nineteen thirties, coming in rapid succession, like the spread of a crime wave, from the gruesome *As I Lay Dying*, in 1930, through *Sanctuary, Light in August, Pylon, Absalom, Absalom*, to the *Wild Palms*, in 1939. In addition to these, there were four volumes of short stories published in the ten years. The themes look unbelievable stated in bald summary: *As I Lay Dying* tells the story of hauling a corpse for nine days in midsummer heat; *Sanctuary* chronicles a journey of a young girl and her escort searching for liquor, with the rape of the girl by a pervert named Popeye as the central feature, and the addition of a lynching and execution, and a devil's chorus of prostitutes and imbeciles. *Light in August* features a murder and lynching. *Pylon* is a little lighter, its high spot being a group of aviators with a common wife and a child of uncertain parentage. The *Unvanquished* has some variety by way of nailing up the corpse of a murderer on a door, and setting up his amputated hand on the victim's grave.

There is wide division over the meaning of this welter of carnage and brutality. Does it indicate a twist in the author's mind, or is it a genuine recording of a profound sense of the evil in life, such as is expressed by John Chamberlain: "He leaves you with a far better sense of the horrible depths that lurk beneath the surfaces of life than you could ever get from the scholarly realistic studies of writers who are concerned with what they fancy the cold truth"? Very possibly the answer to that question is both. To the degree to which the second answer is true, Faulkner's work acquires value and significance as evidence of a genuine mood of the times, in which the writer turns to violence as a protest against a false romanticism and superficial optimism. This, as we have maintained, has been paralleled by a movement in theology which has expressed a sense of the malignant evil in life, which a less thoroughgoing and more squeamish theology had shoved away out of sight. The Continental theology, so called, has had much to say of demonic forces, and Faulkner writes of demonic forces, indeed, like a man possessed of demons. The fact that Faulkner wrote and published in 1926 one of the first novels portraying the violent reaction of disillusion over the war, *Soldier's Pay*, a bitter ironic novel of the return of a maimed soldier after the war, may have a real light to throw on his subsequent preoccupation with the meaningless ugliness of life, its pointless suffering, its bestiality. He has furnished real data for a spiritual and moral estimate of war, and its effects, and for the spiritual history of a decade. Another aspect of moral significance is in the pictures which Faulkner gives incidentally of an aristocracy and economic system in decay.

Moral and spiritual decay is one central theme of the trilogy of Thomas S. Stribling, located in Alabama, *The Forge, The Store,* and *Unfinished Cathedral.* These could be regarded as elaborate demonstrations of the text, "The love of money is the root of all sorts of evil." They portray a society from which dignity and a stable sense of moral values have gone, leaving only acquisitiveness, with the injustices which that lust brings in its train. These novels begin with the time of the 1890's, and come down to later days. A decayed aristocracy tries to regain its old position of power, but without the old aristocratic character. In *The Store* and *Unfinished Cathedral* the central character, Col. Miltiades Vaiden, represents the moral decay of an exploiting group. Practically all the ills of the region and the time come into view; injustice to the Negro, the squeezing of the sharecropper, and the failure of religion to retain any prophetic quality or power, when churchmen themselves are the leading exploiters. When *Unfinished Cathedral* was published, the author was asked, "What will the people of Florence, Alabama, say about you now?" He replied, "They can't say anything. They said everything when they read the first two books." The contrast is drawn between the wonderful engineering triumph of Muscle Shoals Dam, in the midst of a terrifying social lag as represented in the neighboring city.

No glance at the literature of the South, however brief, could omit the dramatic work of Paul Green, now collected in one volume, *Out of the South*. A strong case could be made for him as the best balanced and understandingly sympathetic interpreter of the South, both of the white and black, both in fiction and drama. His Pulitzer prize play, *The House of Connelly*, deals with an aristocracy in decay, intellectual and moral, as well as economic, but still possessed of an unyielding will. His shorter plays dealing with the relations between whites and Negroes, *The Field God, Hymn to the Rising Sun*, as well as the longer play, *In Abraham's Bosom*, while presenting violence, are without bitterness or ranting, and display sympathy for all groups in the population, a real tenderness which never descends into banality or mawkishness. Yet there is continuous evidence of perception of the tragic quality of life.

Towns and cities are regions as well as farm country, and candid cameras have been turned on city life in great num-

bers. Some of these novels are centered so strongly on industrial life that they are considered under the later chapter devoted to literature dealing primarily with labor. Here a short
glimpse is taken at a class of fiction aiming to portray city life
with realism and accuracy. Of the samples taken, none would
be called "great"; all have documentary value.

Meyer Levin's *The Old Bunch* is a physical and spiritual
anatomy of Chicago, the collective story of two dozen Jewish
boys and girls from Chicago's West Side, who broke away
from the orthodoxy of their fathers, who were mostly tailors,
pawnbrokers, and small manufacturers. Again and again the
basic theme of the crumbling of religion comes into view.
These careers follow the current of American life during the
Jazz Age, the Coolidge prosperity and the depression. There
is a vivid expression of experience: parading school teachers
protesting non-payment of salaries, Al Capone and Insull,
union organizers beaten by Red Squads, evicted tenants, Big
Bill Thompson, the whole ribald chorus of the law courts
with their tricky lawyers and political machine judges.

Joseph Gollomb's *Unquiet* ought to be on required lists on
education, both religious and secular. It is an autobiographical
novel, a portrayal of youth in the streets of New York's
Ghetto, giving a glimpse into what happens to youth in the
city streets. Kandel's *City for Conquest* has New York for its
theme, East Side, West Side, and all around the town. New
York City is too big to be the theme of a novel, and the attempt to make its varied life a unifying thread inevitably gives
the impression of a kaleidoscope turning swiftly. Yet it is not
so "dizzy" as Dos Passos' *Manhattan Transfer,* and still
covers far more territory in presenting different groups and
localities, showing them as members one of another. The
synagogues of the slums, where a traditional piety confronts
a strange alien world, the greed and lust in Bronx apartments,

the ideological ferment in Battery Park, all appear in a literary semblance to motion pictures in technicolor.

James T. Farrell in his trilogy of novels, *Studs Lonigan*, has painted on an immense canvas, with a result something like a gigantic Diego de Rivera mural, or like the diplodoci of modern fiction, the French chronological novels of Romains or Gard. In size and sincerity and detail, at least, it ranks with Dos Passos' trilogy, *U.S.A.*, as an outstanding achievement of the decade. In the three volumes included, *Young Lonigan, The Young Manhood of Studs Lonigan* and *Judgment Day,* the hero grows from childhood to manhood in the South Side of Chicago. But Chicago is the real theme, the pressures exerted by the city in the moulding, and the mangling of life. Certainly, never has the American city been studied and portrayed with such multitudinous detail, or with clearer sight levelled at the effects of its influences on the life and character of its people. Whatever may be the defects of the trilogy as fiction, it has and will retain great sociological value. It will rightly demand the serious attention of all interested in education and character training. It is both a description and an indictment.

Farrell writes of a world he knows well, of the Irish gradually creeping up into the Middle Class, in a Chicago still booming and expanding, in a tenement neighborhood, where street gangs were the leading and only effective educational institution, and where the Negroes and Jews were pouring in, with all the attendant conflicts. Farrell strictly refrains from loading his story either with melodramatic plot or a proletarian 'message,' but it is truly a terrifying story in its calm piling on of detail. "Here," it says, "is the product of the school of the streets, the cupidity, the corruption of a city." Studs Lonigan's history is paralleled by that of his class and group, the Irish gangs. There is a struggling rise to power, defeat and death. The Middle Class Irish, when the bubble burst, when the Insull Empire of pyramided holding companies crashed, were forced back into the working class. Symbolically, at the end, Studs' drunken father stands looking at a parade of the unemployed, perhaps new patterns of conflict for the future. There is a strong implicit indictment of the church, not only for neglect but for betrayal as a social and religious institution.

The wonder persists whether the people in the book are worth the prolonged attention and mountainous detail. The interest wanes with repetition. A greater selectivity would have made a more artistic treatment possible. In his new cycle, chronicling another hero at the same inordinate length, *A World I Never Made* and *No Star is Lost*, Farrell is repeating the pattern in what is obviously a fictionalized biography.

Close-up, clear, lensed views of the forces at work in cities, as well as of the flow of life, have been made of many of the cities of the country, many of them being cut to the same pattern with local variations. Joseph F. Dineen in *Ward Eight* has delineated the political structure and motive power of Boston in the story of the rise of a boy from a tenement boyhood to the District Attorneyship, showing political corruption, but also a genuine moral code of loyalty to his crowd. Sinclair Lewis' *Ann Vickers* is only partly located in cities, but it contains accounts of social work and political life in New York City. A valuable part is its criticism of prisons and the questioning of the whole system of penology.

Mari Sandoz, in *Capitol City*, has told a contemporary story of a Middle Western state capital, to be identified as Lincoln, Nebraska, with its divisions, its shantytown and its "Gold Coast" on Blue Ridge, its corruption, labor conflicts and fascist-minded Gold Shirts. Benjamin Appel in a supertough story, *The Power House*, explores the gangster life of

New York, including the whole curriculum by which a corner hoodlum is graduated into a criminal leader. The labor spy racket is given its strongest portrayal in fiction. A vastly different story of New York is *Once Around the Block* by John Kempner, a careful and loving description of a family that must represent millions of other families. It centers around a chocolate factory in Brooklyn.

One of Josephine Lawrence's novels, *If I Had Four Apples*, brings on the stage a city family struggling with the great American ogre, the installment plan, by which they are defeated and devoured. It pictures the conditioning of the mind and soul of millions by the powerful forces of sales pressure. The hope springing eternally in the breast of the Hoe family that it might be possible to substract two apples from four and have four left is followed with harrowing detail. Incidentally, there is a concealed overtone of appraisal of an economic system which has to use such means to keep going, possibly more apparent to the reader than to the author.

In the field of non-fiction the amount of competent reporting and interpretation is very great. Literary scrutiny of America is nothing new. Ever since Captain John Smith recorded his impressions of Virginia, there has been no lack of note-takers. America has been a self-conscious nation, always betraying a nervous interest in its own portrait, particularly when drawn by foreigners. The great bulk of this reporting and exposition of American life and conditions lies entirely beyond the limits of our present concern. But one type of book is closely related to the theme of the present chapter. That is the report of travelers who have gone out to see and to listen, to gain by personal experience an understanding of what was happening to people, what they were thinking, what they were saying, how the burden of the days was affecting them. It was an enterprise not wholly removed from that of the prophet Ezekiel's achievement in imaginative projection of himself into other lives, as recorded in his statement, "I sat down where they sat." It is the rarest form of travel, adventures in other people's lives. One of the first of these recordings in the decade was Edmund Wilson's *American Jitters,* a sort of fever chart of the behavior of the patient during the crisis of the disease, the depression in 1933. There is vivid presentation of the human balance sheet, reporting done with imagination and feeling and economic understanding. The book has permanent historical value in capturing the mood and atmosphere of the time, which has already passed into history.

Similar in general purpose and effect is James Rorty's *Where Life is Better,* accurately sub-titled, "An Unsentimental American Journey." It is the record of an automobile trip from New York to the Pacific Coast with the purpose of attempting "to evoke and make understandable the tensions, the confusions, the feel of the country as a whole; to exhibit not so much the statistics as the people whose current dilemmas the statistics fail adequately to express." Mr. Rorty turns a clear seeing eye, a radical mind and an ironical spirit on large and varied sections of America,—Detroit, Chicago, the iron and steel front, the agricultural Mid-West, the Northwest and Southern California. The chapter on the Century of Progress Exposition is memorable in its irony and scorn. Its point of view is indicated in the quotation from Margaret Ayer Barnes, "Chicago is a child that would rather give a party like the Century of Progress than wash its own hands and brush its own teeth."

Two years later came Rollo Walter Brown's *I Travel by Train,* covering the same territory and with much the same spirit. Mr. Brown's chapter on the difficulties met with on coming back from a close look at America to the hatreds of

Cambridge, Massachusetts, with its obsession against Roosevelt and the aims of the New Deal, is a valuable record of the emotional aspects of the latter part of the decade.

Jonathan Daniels' two books, *A Southerner Discovers the South* and *A Southerner Discovers New England,* are more in the traditional travel book type, lighter in tone than the three just mentioned. Yet they are frank, with a primary interest in the effect of conditions on people, and written from a liberal standpoint. In an entirely different field, but having the quality of a relentlessly candid camera turned on the earth itself are such books as Sears' *Deserts on the March* and Carleton Beal's *American Earth.*

One wide area of American life, the life and problems of the Negro, came much more clearly into the focus of the literary lens than ever before. This is evidenced not only in a growing number of novels with the Negro as the primary theme but with many others, some of which have been noted above, which have as their interest the picture of a region, and into which the Negro inevitably enters. This is particularly true of literature dealing with the South, such as that of Paul Green, Robert Rylee, Erskine Caldwell, Faulkner, and T. S. Stribling, even when the central characters are whites.

Aside from such books, the novels dealing primarily with Negro life and problems fall into two classes. One is the more traditional type, more interested in "quaintness" and humor than the social situation. Among these authors is Julia Peterkin, represented in the decade by the novel, *Bright Skin,* in 1932, and the sketches, *Roll, Jordan, Roll,* in 1933, illustrated by photographs of the life described in her previous successes, *Scarlet Sister Mary* and *Black April.* The Gullah Negroes whom these works present are an almost exotic group in the South, and their psychology and ways are explored without reference to contemporary social implications. These people are far removed from the new type of Negro, conscious both of worth and injustice, and disposed to struggle for his rights. DuBose Heyward's work has had much the same prevailing interest, although his characters in *Porgy* and *Mamba's Daughters*, being located in the tenements of Charleston, are brought into closer contact with economic forces. Roark Bradford, in *Old Man Adam and his Children*, the stories from which was made Marc Connelly's very successful play, *The Green Pastures*, in 1930, presents the Negro religious world, with far less insight than Connelly shows in the play, and far more traditional patronage of "the darkey" as a comedy figure.

The most significant literature dealing with the Negro is of the second type, that setting forth the Negro in the stress of economic and social conditions, reflecting "sullen, straight, bitter realism," in the work of three Negro authors, Langston Hughes, Walter E. Turpin and Richard Wright. Hughes' novel, *Not Without Laughter* (1930) is far more than a stock protest against exploitation and racial injustice. It has great value as data for an understanding of characteristic issues of religion and morals. It shows vividly the clash between an older and younger generation, as the young people of a religious, self-respecting stable group, not in the South, but in Kansas, with the older submission attitude, break away not only from the "good Negro" and "white man's Negro" psychology, but from the church and traditional moral anchorages as well. Jazz becomes a substitute for religion, as among large white groups.

All these novels report in one way or another that Uncle Tom is dead and a new Negro has taken his place. This Negro has a great deal of disillusionment, and frequently some bitter despair. His cap is not in his hand; he has learned other words than "Yes, Sir." He resents all the exclusions of his race, from the Jim Crow cars to closed jobs and peonage. The climax of *Not Without Laughter* lies in the vicious revenge of the whites over evidences of what is regarded as the "uppity nigger," over painted cottages and one Negro buying a car. The whole village is burned. Hughes' *The Ways of White Folks* is a collection of short stories in which art is not subordinated to propaganda. One story is the delineation of a truly great character, *Cora Unashamed*, in which a Negro servant towers above the stupidity and blind callousness of her "betters" who employ her. Cora gives to a child in the household the only understanding and defense she receives.

That tension spot, Chicago's Southside, is the scene of two novels. One is Walter E. Turpin's *O Canaan!* It is an honest study, not so much of clash between Negro and white, as of the economic struggle in the city, as the Negro is encompassed with the same forces which affect the whites. It portrays the flow of life around a successful Negro business man, who had come north in the migration of 1916. He is "successful" in two senses, one financial, thanks to opportune bootlegging and real estate, and second, in leaving behind, as his ambition was to do, the old southern farm hand world and mentality. The hero, Joe Benson, meets financial ruin in the crash but has developed character enough to stand it.

O Canaan! has little of the atmosphere of tension and tragedy which marks the other Chicago Southside novel, that of Richard Wright's *Native Son*. This novel created something of a sensation on its appearance, and was hailed by many critics not only as the strongest novel ever written by an American Negro, but also as an outstanding achievement of the decade. It might be called a study in the economic determination of character and personality. But such a description would suggest a sociological tract, and it is primarily a novel, sustaining a gripping interest in its narrative and portrayal of a tortured and inarticulate mentality. A bald outline of the plot sounds as unpromising as a run-of-the-mill crime story or a particularly revolting police court item. Mr. Wright has had the courage to make the character about whom the story centers with the intensity of a burning glass, a particularly loathsome person, cowardly, deceptive, cruel, what is known in police language as a "rat." That the author is able to elicit sympathy for such a hero measures the extent of his achievement. For by his skillful delineation of the complex of forces which have helped to shape Bigger Thomas he does win sympathy and understanding. Bigger is a product of a tenement environment, in which high rents play a part, unemployment and blocked avenues for expression play a part. He gets a job as a chauffeur for a rich man, Mr. Dalton (who is the owner of the high rent tenement into which Bigger's family are crowded), a man interested in charities for Negroes. Dalton's daughter, Mary, makes Bigger take her and her communist friend out on an evening of drinking. On his return to the house he takes the girl, overcome by drunkenness, up to her room. The blind mother comes in and Bigger in fear smothers the girl to avoid discovery. The rest of the story is devoted to a vivid description of Bigger's flight, another murder to avoid discovery, the capture and trial. The trap in which he is caught, both before and after the crime, is powerfully presented. Thus, the murderer tries to describe his feelings to his communist lawyer:

"Mr. Max, a guy gets tired of being told what he can do and can't do. You get a little job here and a little job there. You shine shoes, sweep streets, anything. . . . You don't make enough to live on, you don't know when you're going to get fired. Pretty soon you get so you can't hope for nothing. You just keep movin' all the time doin' what other folks say. You ain't a man no more, you just work day in and day out so other folks can live." [7]

During his trial Bigger repeats what is in reality a central theme in the book, "They was crowding me too close." Earlier in the story before the crime, this conversation among the gang of pool room loafers and petty thieves, expresses the same sense of crowding and blocking:

> "They won't let us do nothing."
> "Who?"
> "The white folks."
> "You talk like you was just finding that out," Gus said.
> "Naw, but I can't get used to it. I swear to God I can't. I know I oughtn't to think about it, but I can't help it. Every time I think about it I feel that some lady's poking a red hot iron down my throat. God damit, look! We live here and they live here. We black and they white. They got things and we ain't. They do things and we can't. It's just like living in jail. Half of the time I feel like I'm outside of the world peeping in through a knot hole in the fence." [8]

The lawyer emphasizes this when he tells Bigger, after his capture, when a hatred was running in the city:

> "Listen, Bigger, you're facing a sea of hate now that's no different from what you've faced all your life. . . . Almost every white face you've met in your life had it in for you even when the white face didn't know it. Every white man considers it his duty to make a black man keep his distance. He doesn't know why he acts that way most of the time, but he acts that way." [9]

The long speeches of the communist lawyer have been objected to as moralizing and indoctrination. Yet they do legitimately bring the sense of social guilt, of communal responsi-

[7] *Native Son,* by Richard Wright. Harper and Brothers.
[8] *Ibid.*
[9] *Ibid.*

bility for conditions and forces which have produced such results.

Wright's earlier book of stories, *Uncle Tom's Children*, deals movingly with exploitation of the Negro in the South. He writes out of a wide experience as house boy, farm hand, dish washer, porter, everything open on the lowest rung of the labor ladder. He has stated his own aims:

"I wanted to show exactly what Negro life in the South means to say, the total effect, a kind of common denominator. I've used what I lived and observed and felt and I've used my imagination to whip it into shape to appeal to the emotions and imagination of other people, for I believe that only the writing that has to do with the basic issues of human living, moral, political or whatever you call it, has any meaning. I think the importance of any writing lies in how much felt life is in it: It gets its value from that." [10]

A varied group of books has been glimpsed here in this chapter, having the common factor of an aim of honest and realistic presentation of life in various regions. They have no didactic element or conscious ethical purpose. Their concern has not been to point morals. Indeed, one feature of a large amount of current literature is the complete disavowal of conscious ethical purpose. Yet, unintendingly and without explicit design at all, there are great and real moral values expressed in this group of novels.

For one thing there is the very real moral value of clear, honest eyesight. The promotion of "The diligent capacity of the eye" is a basic moral quality. It furnishes the data without which the most idealistic intentions are easily lost in a fog. Honest eyesight must precede any valuable insight. It is a mark of a central integrity of character. It follows the New Testament injunction, "Whatsoever things are true . . . think on these things." Any careful perusal of even the few books

[10] *New York Evening Post.*

mentioned in this chapter will not fail to detect an overtone of feeling that "things ought to be different," that they might be different. In that sense, even the novelist whose purpose is faithful description serves as a conscience,

> o'er which creep
> The else unfelt oppressions of the earth.

Rarely is even a vague or general solution offered for the problems explored. It does not appear in Wright's *Native Son*, or in Stribling, or Caldwell. Yet the very lifting of the questions has an element of moral judgment. That is to be felt even in the bawdy humor of *Tobacco Road*, as it is in the tragic seriousness of Paul Green. It is as though the author says between the lines often (as indeed he does), "Here is the thing that is. There's something wrong about it. It could be better. You find the answer." There is also apparent a sense of responsibility, of shared social guilt. This is never self-conscious or hortatory, but it is there. "This is the house that Jack built—" so runs the undertone of many fictional pictures—and not only Jack built the house, but Tom, Dick and Harry, until all of us, as a society, are arraigned at the bar.

There is genuine ethical value, finally, in the celebration of basic virtues. A great many little candles throw the gleam of a good deed in a bad world. Even in the defeat of a character, in frustration, the feeling, which has the aspect often of a religious conviction, with cosmic roots, the judgment is conveyed that integrity of spirit, as in *Court House Square*, courage as displayed by the heroine of *Deep Dark River*, struggle against wrong as in a score of novels, are inherently and everlastingly right.

CHAPTER 4

EXPLORING THE INNER WORLD

THE SUGGESTION has already been made that one prominent
literary trend of the nineteen thirties could be described as
the movement from the inner world to the outer. The evidence for that is voluminous. The outward world has broken
in over the stiffest barricades. Measles and mumps become of
minor importance during an earthquake. The irritations, the
carefully cherished complexes, the mad dashes for personal
liberty and self-expression, which seemed such cosmic issues
during the preceding decade, shrank in proportion, beside the
stalled and jammed economic machine.

Yet that interpretation is very misleading and distorted if
it be made to cover too much territory and leave too small a
place for the large body of work concerned with the eternal
theme of literature, character and personality. That theme is
called here, "The Inner World," a term deplorably vague and
inexact, but yet, it is hoped, one that may serve to indicate
roughly literature in which the primary interest is not the
action of environmental forces, economic, political or social,
but the inner world of the personality set against whatever environment. This delimitation is, and can never be sharply
defined. We cannot abstract the mind and spirit from environment. Character does not develop in a vacuum.

Assignment of a particular novel or play or poem to this
group of works dealing primarily with the inner life and

growth or decay of character, is purely arbitrary, often a matter of convenience. For instance, Ellen Glasgow's *Vein of
Iron* could well be regarded as a novel concerned with economic forces. They play a large part in it. Yet it seems to
have its chief significance in the portrayal of the persistence
of traditional virtues and values under harsh circumstances,
of personal integrity taking arms against a sea of troubles and
winning what is primarily a moral victory.

Margaret Ayer Barnes, who has written strong novels
centering on the development of character with a changing
native scene as the backdrop, has put this perennial interest
of the novelist into clear words. She says:

"A man, a woman and a baby are more important than anything else, but an over-wrought world has tossed such human
values out of the window.

"The world has been heading for some time," she said, "into a
period in which mass movements have become more important
than anything that can happen to the individual.

"This trend has made the books of many writers, including my
own, seem relatively unimportant; people apparently haven't the
time to read three or four hundred pages of what a man and a
woman think of each other. What they think is, of course, the
root and background of life, but it is overshadowed by this period.

"It explains why people prefer now to read about real things.
Nothing the fiction writers can concoct could be more exciting
than the day-to-day happenings of these times.

"Nevertheless, a brilliant character study of an individual actually is the most vital thing in literature, and when the world
calms down it will again become supremely important." [1]

Mrs. Barnes is too pessimistic. We need not wait until the
world "calms down" for a recognition that character study is
the "most vital thing in literature." For one thing it promises
to be a long, long wait. But, more importantly, character study

[1] *New York Times*, July 12, 1938.

is being done effectively in the midst of turmoil and mass movements. *Grapes of Wrath* would have been much less of a book without the superb character of Ma Joad. *The Yearling* would have been a slight story about a boy and a pet farm without Mr. Penny, the father. The same is true of the mother in Michael Gold's *Jews without Money*.

It is obvious that this whole field is one of very great importance for our present interest in the social, ethical and religious significance of current literature. This is equally true whether the work contains a positive celebration of great character such as the school teacher in *Seasoned Timber,* or the negative portrayal of character in decay, as in the world of John O'Hara in *Appointment in Samara.* In either case there is ethical valuation.

It is worth noting, moreover, that this exploration of the inner world deals with a whole spiritual dimension which is left out of so much tailored fiction, cut to a standard pattern, frequently a proletarian pattern, where the figures are often two dimensioned, without depth of soul. Nothing makes for thinner fiction and drama than the too simple explanation of blaming everything on "the system." That has been the weakness of a score of novels dealing with strikes, particularly such examples of marionette performances as *Strike* by Mary Heaton Vorse and the one hundred percent proletarian *Marching, Marching* by Clare Weatherwax.

The most valid works are those which include the inner drama of character, even when economic influences are realistically portrayed. That is seen in Clifford Odets' *Awake and Sing.* There is the omnipresent struggle with poverty, from the first line the boy speaks, "All I want's a chance to get to first base," to the very end. But there is more. There is the tremendous moral difference between the grandfather, a Hebrew prophet moved into the Bronx, with Karl Marx as Jehovah, but an authentic prophet, nevertheless, and the loathsome Moe Axelrod, whose outward success covers inward bankruptcy. No outward forces can explain that difference. It lies deeper in the mysteries of the soul.

Writing in this general field is not something to be lightly disdained by anyone with a good memory or historical sense. For much of the most widely read American literature has been devoted to what might be roughly called "the good life," depicting it against varying backgrounds. Hawthorne, Thoreau, Melville in *Moby Dick,* at least, Mark Twain, are all in the tradition.

One type of book in this loosely grouped class dealing with the inner life is that which presents, in John Drinkwater's phrase, "greatness passing by." It has been a continual theme of literature since Homer. It has not been a predominant type of literature in America in recent years, for many reasons. Perhaps one reason is that the celebration of virtue is a more formidable task for the writer than the portrayal of evil. Mr. Hyde is a far easier job than Dr. Jekyll. It is inevitable that, in a time of dislocation and disaster, themes dealing with them and their human results seem more timely and gripping than the tradition of delineating noble character. Yet notable work in that line has been produced without being didactic, or hortatory or damned by the limitations of the genteel tradition.

Willa Cather's most important work came before 1930. But one of her books of the thirties, *Obscure Destinies,* a group of three stories, does celebrate personalities of integrity and moral force. They are all of unpromising material and their greatness is only to be discovered by that sort of spiritual x-ray of sympathy and recognition which is part of the genius of Willa Cather. "*Neighbor Rosicky,*" the figure of one of the stories, is a man in whom it would surely take a keen eye to see anything great. He is an ex-tailor's boy, now a farmer, a "Bohunk," happy to be on the land again—to the outward eye a dumb peasant. But hard work and a good deal of failure do not sour or crush him. It is as though the author were proclaiming, as indeed she is, "Here is great human stuff, one of the wonders of the world." In the picture of Grandma Harris, in a small town in Colorado, the author has a person much more difficult to accuse of being "great." She is a drudge, hidebound in her ideas, a slave to conventional respectability. Yet there is a great person walking by. The same is true of the Irishman and the American in *Two Friends*, great in a friendship which not only ennobled them, but which is a positive spiritual force in the town.

Dorothy Canfield may be fairly regarded, and is frequently classified, as a regional novelist. Yet that limiting adjective is unfair. Her primary region is the human spirit, the geography of that partially discovered continent of personality, which is truly "the last home of mystery." She sets forth traditional virtues; they are often called "provincial virtues." Her themes have been, for the most part, all those included in a notable list made up long ago, "Whatsoever things are true, just, pure, lovely, of good report." She has treated marriage with abundant life-like detail, as a test of character and school for the growth of character; she has majored in parental relations, in unselfish devotion to causes. All this sounds faintly Sunday-Schoolish. It is interesting evidence on the change in spiritual climate since the 1920's, however, that Dorothy Canfield is far more "in date" today and for the past few years than in the days of boom and of conscious sophisticated revolt. Dorothy Canfield might well have repeated, in the nineteen twenties, John Burroughs' lines,

> Serene I fold my hands and wait
> And know my own will come to me.

For time has moved in a circle. Many qualities which seemed outmoded have come back and have a fresh valuation as indispensable elements of any endurable life. So Mrs. Fisher by the simple process of continuing to be herself has become something different, as far as the timeliness and relevance of her themes to current life are concerned. She is no longer "out of season," but in season, for the season itself has changed. The virtues which were popularly regarded as "quaint survivals" of a bygone day, have come to be more like the stone, rejected by the builders, which is made the head of the corner. Kingsley's lines come to mind in this connection,

> Be good, sweet maid,
> And let who will be clever.

These are undoubtedly very silly lines of verse in as far as they imply a vicious and disastrous separation of intelligence and goodness! Yet there is this to be said for them, that life and its happiness and usefulness depend very little on cleverness in the sense of "smartness"; they depend absolutely on goodness. This is a field in which Dorothy Canfield has chiefly moved. She has had, in the words of one critic, "a faith in self control as an antidote to adversity, persistence in the dignity of work, the beauty of primitive human relationship, the desirability of a simple life and only a small quid pro quo as a fair reward for effort." [2] If this merits the terrible word "wholesome," so be it. It is to be damned only as clean air, pure water, bread, peaches and cream are to be damned for being "wholesome."

The Deepening Stream, in 1930, continues the novels dealing with married life, its demand for personal discipline and understanding. Bonfire, in 1933, is more sociological in theme than most of her work, portraying rural slums in Vermont,

[2] Elizabeth Nyckoff, The Bookman, September 1931.

which can be as bad as city slums. The "shelf" is the back country of the central mountain range. Its somewhat melodramatic plot unfolds the ravages that can be wrought in life by an aggressive, unprincipled woman. But its real strength is in character drawing, in the rector of the church and a social worker in the mountain country, both unsentimentalized figures with insight and a sense of social responsibility. The social worker on one occasion is asked why she bothers with the personal problems of people which are technically none of her business. She gave a notable answer, "Because I know." Possession of knowledge brings a compulsion of responsibility and duty.

Seasoned Timber, in 1939, has as its central figure a school teacher, one of the most moving pictures of the great soul as teacher in American fiction. This teacher, Timothy Hulme, is not a stock heroic figure. There is more than a suspicion that he is something of a prig. But that makes him more real and less like a glorified statue. It is his loyalty to his educational standards, his growing devotion to a genuine democracy and an indomitable courage which make him a great creation. The school in Clifford, Vermont, becomes the center of a battle when a Wall Street operator endows it with a million dollars, on condition that it be closed to Jewish scholars. The fact that Jews in Clifford were about as rare as elephants only made harder the fight for the American tradition of democracy which Timothy Hulme and other embattled Americans made and won.

Vein of Iron, by Ellen Glasgow, is well named, for the heroine has the iron of integrity and character. The novel deals directly with the Christian religion and the sanctions of conduct and qualities of character historically associated with it. The novel is a demonstration of the author's own words: "I am persuaded that nothing could convey more happiness in a liberated world than the miraculous resurrection of the sense of duty. In a sultry age when we need the tonic of a bracing literature, character has become a lost quality in fiction, and we miss the full commanding note of the disciplined mind."

Alice Tisdale Hobart's *Yang and Yin* is the most adequate portrayal of a missionary to be found anywhere in American fiction. The story of a young missionary physician, Peter Fraser, head of a hospital in interior China, serves to illustrate the theme of the meeting of western and eastern thought. The book pictures in a moving way the heroism and social importance of foreign missions. Dr. Fraser, when he finds that the only way by which he can bring the germs causing an Oriental disease into the United States for study and experiment, is to innoculate himself with the germs, deliberately takes that grim method. That incident comes from actual history.

China also furnished the scene and theme of Pearl Buck's *The Good Earth*. That great book won its wide acclaim from many causes. Its style, simple and rhythmic, in a manner so often called Biblical, which has turned out to be rather good Chinese, the author's knowledge of China, like Sam Weller's knowledge of London being "extensive and peculiar," its dealing with the basic elements of life, its timeliness in being a story of a struggle against poverty and hunger when such a struggle was a major issue in America, all contributed to the success of the novel. But unquestionably one of the greatest values of the novel is the character of Wang's wife, O-Lan, for there was greatness indeed, almost majestic in its simplicity and fidelity to fundamental human virtues that know no geography.

Marjorie Kinnan Rawlings' *The Yearling* leaped into fame with very little that would seem to give promise of best-seller qualities. For it was a story almost without plot, no spice or sex or love story, depending on the creation of beauty and character in a father and his boy and a rare gift for picturing animal life and the unusual surroundings of Florida swamps. But the most notable portrait in the book is that of a man, Penny Baxter, great enough to understand a boy, a personality who conveys a sense of something inherently worthful in the processes of life itself and in its relationships. His was a life stripped down to its elements of minimum subsistence, a man without benefit of formal education, yet undeniably a great person. It is to that quality of moral greatness to which multitudes of readers have responded. It is as though the author had said, "Come unto me all ye that are weary and heavy laden with Jeeter Lester and Studs Lonigan and Hemingway's tough guys and I will give you Penny Baxter." They came.

Yet even with such a gallery before our eyes, and we have glimpsed only a part of the pictures of positive great character available, a question stays in the mind, Why is not such assertion of the possibilities of life more frequent? Why does it occupy a relatively minor part of the decade's literature? One answer is that the major part of the writers did not have the spiritual experience out of which a convincing affirmation of the good life could come. The words of Peter at the Beautiful Gate of the Temple in Jerusalem are applicable to literature as to other things, "Such as I have I give unto thee." There has been a lack of spiritual resources and experience of the inner life, using these terms not in the sense of a lack of orthodox religious faith, but meaning a lack of participation in the life of the spirit, of a sense of undebatable realized values in living. Dr. Henry Seidel Canby lists this spiritual vacuum as one of the obvious marks of much current literature, calling it a "shrinking and aridity of the inner life." "Certainly," he writes, "that inner life so manifest in the

leaders of the last age of intellectual revolt in America—
Thoreau, Emerson, Melville, Whitman—is woefully absent
in the new American literature. . . . It is hard to depict truly
and sympathetically and prophetically the life of others without a rich, vivid and confident inner life of your own." [3]
Words spoken a long time ago and a long distance away are
applicable to the lack, "The well is deep and I have nothing
with which to draw."

Negative testimony concerning the inner life is just as
pertinent as positive evidence. Novels depicting life without
moral standards, in an atmosphere from which the oxygen of
all sustaining faiths and restraining codes has been with-
drawn, offer as convincing data on the place of moral and
religious values in life as novels marked by the affirmation
of such values. Indeed, often the most impressive data on
the question whether traditional virtues and ideals and faiths
add much to the dignity and satisfaction of life are an honest
portrayal of life lived without them. Such fictional presentation says in effect, most persuasively when there is no conscious intention on the part of the author, "So? . . . moral
standards are mere obsolete hangovers from a bygone day,
crippling inhibitions to freedom? All right, here is life without any such encumbrances! How do you like it? How does
it smell?"

One of the most skilled guides through this American
waste land is John O'Hara, particularly in the novel, *Appointment in Samara*. The symbolism of the title suggests
that the sort of life lived by the chief characters is an "appointment" with death. The group put under the microscope
is a country-club group, a café society in a manufacturing
town. It might be anywhere, though located in a region near
Pottstown, Pennsylvania. The banality and vulgarity of a

[3] *Seven Years' Harvest*, by Henry Seidel Canby. Farrar and Rinehart, 1936.

crowd devoted to getting on and taking their fun (though even the participants find it pretty sickly fun) where they find it. Bed, booze, fistfights, bootlegging, divorces, suicide make up the plot. The novel is one long bar room, almost as continuous as that which stretches through Hemingway's *The Sun Also Rises.* O'Hara is not a moralist intentionally. He is a deft reporter, with an accurate ear for the speech of the class he presents, and a skill in the creation of character. But the novel might well be taken as a study in the punishment of sin, a sermon in fact on the text, "Whatsoever a man soweth, that shall he also reap," or "The wages of sin is death." Here are people who let themselves go; they are also people in a state of moral decay, from lack of any inward spiritual experience or values, from any central reverences, or moral compulsions. Their all inclusive attitude to life seems to be expressed in four words, "To hell with it." Yet there is a sense of fine capacities frustrated, a blight on something that might have been a fine bloom. The novel well illustrates the moral judgment of a theologian, Walter Horton, "Our merriment is that of one who plunges into revelry to forget his mental misery."

On a much lower level of writing ability and sincerity of purpose are the novels of James M. Cain. *The Postman Always Rings Twice* is so "tough" that it could easily be read as a burlesque on the "tough guy" school of literature. Its adolescent delight in bad words, its belated feeling that sex is still big news, betray its meretricious character.

Of a different sort is the novel, *Harry Pickering,* by Robert E. McClure. This is a serious study of a moneyed society in decay, a picture of what the environment of wealth as the end of existence can do to flatten out what might have been a real person. "The love of money is the root of all sorts of evil" might have been the text and it is given a thorough exegesis. The weakness of the novel seems to be that the dice are too strongly loaded against Harry. The stars in their courses were fighting against him in the malign conjunction of adverse planets—the money of his father and the social ambition of his stupid mother. Yet the story does indicate with restraint rather than exaggeration the conditioning of character by environment. Harry limps through life under the burden of an automobile fortune; schooled early in what psychologists call "infantile hallucinatory omnipotence" and in snobbishness, he "flunks out" of Yale, makes a mess of two marriages, "downs" rivers of alcohol. The theme is stated sharply by Mr. McClure, "He remained quite unaware of the deeper implications which have shown to what shattering proportions life's disappointments may obtain when they are magnified by an ego dwelling in a spiritual vacuum." The author seeks, and needs, no illicit aid from melodrama in working out the destiny of the hero. He rather demonstrates by credible processes that the wages of sin is boredom.

Step down several flights lower into "spiritual vacuum," into the work of a "slick" purveyor of life without benefit of principle, or even minimum decency, Jerome Weidman. His work does not rate attention as literature but as evidence of a part of the times, a notorious product of the writers consecrated to the cult of the hard-boiled. His principal hero (rat or "heel" is a more accurate name), in the two novels, *"I Can Get It for You Wholesale"* and *"What's in It for Me?"* is a smart Jewish crook in the garment trade in New York. He outsmarts everyone, betrays everyone, until he finally comes to a crash himself, at the end of the second novel. It is naturalism in a period costume on Seventh Avenue and Broadway, a hero and supporting cast, most of whom have no values, just a form of behavior. When one finishes these novels it comes to mind that here is that same distorted world of the Nazi mentality. The writing is hard, like the characters, made tiresome by an unending succession of wisecracks, set up with the sputtering persistence of a boy's Fourth of July pinwheel. The effect of such microscopic study of the unspiritual anatomy of an alley rat is very well expressed by Ralph Thompson, critic of the *New York Times*, "During the last few years I have never once felt the urge to go back and read about Pollyanna, the Glad Girl, but after a few more Weidmans I may."

Tess Slessinger's case histories of an ultra-sophisticated New York crowd, whose Holy Trinity is Sex, Gin and Marx, offer data on the inner life of a group which has been rather stridently vocal, if small. Her novel, *The Unpossessed*, gives a choice collection of posturing exhibitionists, tired radicals, the disillusioned, and the damned. Social protest, "fellow-traveling," is for most of this neurotic group not a genuine conviction, but an escape from a personal conflict, a fad. One young character, Elizabeth, a belated relic of the Jazz Age of the twenties, has three continuing reliances in life, "chain smoking, chain drinking, chain loving." The author does not turn moralist, but her ridicule of many of the characters reflects a real scorn for the thin and empty attitudinizing which has become a substitute for any integrity of personality, a veritable mess of pottage for which a real heritage of potential character has been traded. Here is one little cameo piece of Logan Pearsall Smith which has a direct pertinence to this whole body of writing, the atrophy of moral sense and compulsion:

"The anecdote which had caused the laughter of those young people was not a thing to joke about. I expressed my conviction briefly; but the time honored word I had made use of seemed unfamiliar to them—they looked at each other and began whispering together. Then one of them asked in a hushed voice, 'It's what did you say?'

"I repeated the monosyllable loudly.

"Again they whispered together, and again their spokesman came forward?

" 'Do you mind telling us how you spell it?'

" 'I spell it with a W, I shouted. W-R-O-N-G—Wrong!' " [4]

Ernest Hemingway will not go into a few paragraphs; his work cannot be evaluated under the particular heading of this chapter. His two most notable novels and the bulk of his stories were written before the nineteen thirties. The one book considered here is a collection of short stories, *Winner Takes Nothing* (1933). Set in the low point of the depression, they have a curiously remote and irrelevant quality. Indeed, the urgent problems of the depression have made clearer the highly specialized world of Hemingway's hard, tough characters. They seem as much an "escape" from the major issues of the time as the most romantic historical novel, or woman's magazine serial. They are noticed here for the inner emptiness of the characters, the absence of normal human values of the characters. They fit, as fiction, perfectly into behavioristic psychology; they have action, but no moral absolutes or even moral values that are at all transcendent to immediate conduct. Hemingway's much imitated style is an admirable medium for the content. It is a cliché to call it clipped and stripped of verbiage. It represents a world clipped and stripped also,—stripped of standard human spiritual equipment. In this sense, they are "grotesques" to the same degree that many of Caldwell's misshapen characters are. That famous style has been described as a combination of "a grunt and a hiatus." There is a notable hiatus where the soul is frequently found. He is an amazingly skilled observer; one has the feeling that

4 *More Trivia* by Logan Pearsall Smith. Harcourt Brace and Co., 1921.

if he ever looked at anything really worth describing the result would be great literature. But the game of continually observing and reporting the behavior and speech of a static world of characters much alike, hard, stupid, cruel, greedy and lustful, is not worth the candle of the skill. The title, *Winner Takes Nothing*, strikes the note of futility felt through the stories. The central characters do take nothing from life. They are for the most part his favorite primitives, or "simples," hardly distinguishable from morons, some of them inarticulate prizefighters. The opening story, "Fathers and Sons," revolves about a theme of not remarkable freshness, fornication; the hero of "The Mother of a Queen" is a prizefighter touched with megalomania. The humane qualities have been so depleted that a blood transfusion is necessary.

Yet one cannot overlook the fact that in a world in which the reversion to the primitive looms as the most disturbing feature, in which a dehumanized mentality with sadistic gifts runs amuck, the people whom Hemingway records are of real importance. For our present interest, however, the stories give evidence of a fact of first importance about literature and its relation to morals and religion. That relationship has been expressed forcibly, not by a professional moralist or a preacher, but by a practicing novelist and short story writer, Margaret Culkin Banning.

"Books without any moral standards or any hope of them, especially the ones which pride themselves on such lacks, are beginning to approach the end of a blind street. They have nowhere to go. It is hard to keep on making interesting stories out of people who are only game and unafraid and headed for the rocks. The fiction readers have found this out. The writers are finding it out. Alcoholism is all right as a fictional setting for a while; but anyone, even a reader, gets tired of being with people who are tight all the time. He gets tired of being with people who keep on going to bed with each other. It stops being interesting and credible.

If realistic fiction is to hold its readers today, it must have as much of a moral pattern as has sound contemporary biography. This implies an adherence to no single rule of conduct, nor to a definite set of morals. Fiction is not propaganda. But it does mean that in so far as there is effort in the world toward creation of a better society and the preservation of the spiritual quality in life, fiction must take cognizance of these things or lose its public.

All this is a long way around Robin Hood's barn to say that fiction is no more devoid of moral standards than is life. And at the moment it needs heroes and heroines in the literal sense quite as much as the world does. Perhaps a few more are on the way." [5]

Dorothy Parker should not be left out of any roll of those who explore the inner life of character rather than rely on dramatic situation. She is a humorist and satirist, but she is also a moralist. She knows much of "the long littleness of life." She knows the "stuffed shirt" and the "cat" well, and has drawn some savage pictures of them. She does not suffer fools gladly; she is angered at stupidity. Yet it is clear that the ugliest personalities she impales with her mockery are more than stupid. They are, to use an old-fashioned word, "wicked," and she despises them for the pain which their ridiculous qualities cause. Her indignation is the anger of a moralist, a quality which has led the English novelist, H. E. Bates, to call her "the softest hard-boiled egg in American Literature." Most of her new short stories of the ten years were those in *After Such Pleasures*. In such a story as "Dusk before Fireworks," she draws a conceited cad who has a flock of girls yearning for him, an amusing picture. But the suffering of the girl, Kit, who really loves him, is not a matter of amusement. Mrs. Parker lets her anger at callous cruelty make itself felt in her contempt for the empty inanity of the boastful pose of the woman in "A Young Woman in Green Lace," and the actress portrayed in "Glory in the Day Time."

[5] *The Saturday Review*, July 1, 1939.

The moral judgment is all the stronger in that it is expressed
not through solemn denunciation but through mockery, sarcasm and irony.

The Late George Apley, by John P. Marquand, ran as a
serial in the *Saturday Evening Post.* That fact ought to rate it
as one of the seven wonders of present-day America, and is
the highest compliment which the *Post* has paid itself in
many years. For this novel stands in violent contrast not only
to the type of high-powered but innocuous romance which is
the staple of that magazine's fiction, but also to the previous
work of Mr. Marquand. It is a delicately done, sustained
satirical picture of the Brahmin castes of Boston in the person
of George Apley, a consummate representative. The framework of the story is amazingly well constructed. It purports
to be a biography of the scion of an upper-crust Boston
family, done by an admiring friend. The biographer never
gives any indication that what he sets forth in loving and
painstaking tribute will convey any other impression to the
reader. He does convey a strong feeling for the high qualities of the late Mr. Apley, who functioned in the traditional
manner of his caste from his youth in the 1880's down
through the war and the chaotic years following. We see his
rectitude, his high sense of obligation to the family character,
his civic responsibility.

We also see what the biographer pretends never to see, the
pathetically frustrated life, the soul that trembles on the verge
of birth and never quite comes into being, eternally crushed
by caste and tradition. The novel might be an expansion of
the remark of one of the Forsytes in Galsworthy's saga: "I
have lived through everything but life." Apley's life is that
of one completely strangled by etiquette, a doomed Laocoön,
hopelessly and pathetically struggling against fears, codes,
conventions. Not least of the values of the book is the deadly

revelation of the impotence of a prostituted religion, stripped of all its reality, led along by a chain at the tail of the chariot of a dominant economic and social caste. Marquand's *Wickford Point* is a very different novel than *The Late George Apley*, and a much more important one, in its social and ethical interpretation and judgment. It is an outstanding fictional achievement in its picture of a class in decay, the cultural and financial aristocracy of New England gone to seed, in moral decay and social and economic futility, unable to escape from a tradition, and equally unable to make it a force in the present world or to build any structure on it. To emphasize this is to do injustice to a fine novel of social comedy. *Wickford Point* is not a moral tract, but a novel in the tradition of Galsworthy, worthy of that tradition. Yet in addition to its artistic excellence as a novel, it has the element of a moral analysis, a whole caste whose inner life is rotting at the center. It is like a medical diagnosis of a fatal blood clot, an occlusion which prevents any flow of life-giving blood going either to the heart or the head.

The novel might well have the title, "Ichabod"—the glory has departed. The old tradition hangs on when life has departed. The main concern is not a plot, but character, the degeneration of the Brill family of Wickford Point, a house and estate which were bought by a domineering forceful New England trader, Great-grandfather Seabrook, for his family. We see the elder generations and their descendents. Indeed, William Watson's oft-quoted lines about the survival of a tradition in the church after all life has passed from it, express rather accurately the theme of the story:

> Outwardly splendid, as of old,
> Inwardly sparkless, void and cold—
> Her force and fire all spent and gone,
> Like the dead moon, she still shines on.

In a real way, the place itself, Wickford Point, is a symbol. It is no longer economically solvent, but it is kept going on, sustained by inertia and nostalgia. And the aristocratic tradition is socially insolvent, but it still goes on. The inner bankruptcy of various members of the clan is sharply evident in Cousin Clothilde, whose children go to the dogs while she chants the secular equivalent of "Peace, perfect peace, in all this world of sin"; in Harry Brill whose graduation from Harvard was the high spot in his life, after which he did nothing but pulverize into dry rot; in Bella, a case ripe for the psychopathic ward. The "deep tangled wildwood" around the place was full of poison ivy. Mr. Marquand writes: "The others, when they faced New England, saw only white houses, church spires, lilacs and picket hedges, gingham hypocrisy and psychosis and intolerance. . . . There was something which they did not see, an inexorable sort of gentleness, a vanity of effort, a sadness of predestined failure." The motto on the wall of Belshazzar's palace, "weighed in the balance and found wanting," is spelled out in the vernacular of New England.

The theme of inner moral decay appears in many dramas of the period. Two in particular center on it—"Merrily We Roll Along" by George Kaufman and Moss Hart, and "Dinner at Eight" by George Kaufman and Edna Ferber. "Merrily We Roll Along" is not an important play; it was not a great success on the stage. The outstanding feature was the experimental technique of having the drama appear backward. The story begins at the end and goes back to the start. It presents the progressive artistic and moral degeneration of Richard Niles, a playwright, who starts out as an idealist with an artistic conscience, and ends up as a commercially successful purveyor of smooth, meretricious comedies. The opening scene shows him at a moment of glamorous "success," when another theatrical "hit" is made, the scene being his Long Island home, at which his second wife, an actress for whom he had deserted his first wife, throws iodine into the eyes of his newest love and featured actress. This second wife thus characterises his personal bankruptcy. "You'd sell your soul to get a hit. Fashionable playwright! Fashionable prostitute,—That's what you are." [6] The verdict of his discarded friend is quoted: "a money loving, social climbing, second rate hack!" The play does present a picturesque illustration of an old question, "What shall it profit a man to gain the whole world and lose his own life?" In reverse order, the history of the damnation of a soul is presented scene by scene, winding up with the author giving a valedictory at his college commencement ending with the words:

"Lastly, this I have learned. I have learned to value ideals above all else. As we go out in the world, as we take up our dozen professions, we are clad, as it were, in shining armor. Let nothing sully that. With you goes a new hope, a new idealism. Carry your banners high. Compromise them never. I give you the words of Polonius:

> This above all; to thine own self be true
> And it must follow, as the night the day,
> Thou canst not then be false to any man."

From the standpoint of religion one wholly unintended lesson of the play, but a valid one, is that Polonius is not enough. The platitudes of an ancient Babbitt are not enough as a fortification of life against compromise and collapse.

Dinner at Eight is a well tailored, sophisticated melodrama. It is done in the breadth-wise cutting made popular by *Grand Hotel*, an episodic succession of scenes in the lives of a group of people who have no connection except the theatrical one

[6] *Merrily We Roll Along* by George S. Kaufman and Moss Hart. Random House, 1934.

of being expected guests at a dinner at eight. They are shown before the dinner hour, skeletons in many closets are unveiled, comedy and tragedy crowd closely on each other. It would be unjustifiable to read much serious purpose other than good "theatre" into the play. Yet the fact does stand out clearly that at the center of many of the characters is a spiritual vacuum. Lives are tangled in a mess because of moral failures, collapses of integrity.

Thomas Wolfe was such an individual and unique personality, both in himself and in his writing, that it is hard to place him in any topical arrangement. Indeed, that very difficulty testifies to the inadequacy of a topical classification of authors. He is included in this group of writers dealing primarily with the inner life, not because a preoccupation with his own emotions and desires and frustrations is the whole of Wolfe, but because it is central in him. Not since James Joyce's *Ulysses* has there been such a prodigious performance of celebration of the inner life. If Joyce's novel was, as it has been called, the greatest "intellectual strip tease act in history," Wolfe is a formidable rival. He wrote millions of words, leaving behind him at his death over a million words of unpublished manuscript. He once took two hundred pages to describe a comparatively short train ride. The most accurate description of his writing is Southey's poem, *The Cataract of Ladore:*

> The cataract strong
> Then plunges along
> Striking and raging
> As if a war waging
> Its caverns and rocks among
> Rising and leaping
> Sinking and creeping
> Swelling and sweeping
> Showering and springing

Flying and flinging
Writhing and wringing
Eddying and whisking
Spouting and frisking
Turning and twisting
Around and around.

Wolfe wrote three massive novels: *Look Homeward, Angel,
Of Time and the River* and *The Web and the Rock*. Yet they
are all practically versions of one story, the life and times of
Thomas Wolfe. In his later years he strongly resented the
common accusation that he wrote nothing but autobiography.
He did give his characters, often, a universal quality, recognizable as more than regional characters. Yet he always returned to the one theme of commanding allurement—himself.
His gigantic output represented Whitman's:[7]

I celebrate myself.

.   .   .

The smoke of my own hearth,
Echoes, ripples, buzzed whiskers, love-root,
    Silk-thread, crotch and vine.
My respiration and my inspiration, the beating of my heart, the
    passing of blood and air through my lungs,

.   .   .

I dote on myself—there is a lot of me, and all so luscious
Each moment, and whatever happens, thrills me with joy!

The channel through which the full stream is poured is the
life of Eugene Gant, a thinly disguised Wolfe. His boyhood
home and experiences in Asheville, North Carolina, college
years at the University of North Carolina, his going to
Harvard, wanderings over Europe, life in Boston and New
York, make up the Pilgrim's Progress. In the course of the

[7] *Leaves of Grass* by Walt Whitman.

stories, *Look Homeward, Angel, Of Time and the River,* and large parts of *The Web and the Rock,* there is much magnificent rhetoric and much interpretation of significant emotional and spiritual experience of youth in the 1920's.

Two aspects of this vast body of work are relevant to our present interest. The first is the significant preoccupation with himself, with his own inner life of emotion and desire. It is the outstanding example of a trend which has had many exemplifications in the thirties. It would be too pretentious to call it a Narcissus Complex, but that formidable term does indicate something of its value and direction. The ego has become the supreme object of interest, almost an object of worship. This preoccupation becomes a sort of alternative to the traditional outlook in which the personality was a created thing, responsible primarily to its maker. This has not been a new thing in literature, but it has flowered luxuriantly in Wolfe. One of the best analyses of this celebration of the self, as found in literature, is that of the British critic, R. Ellis Roberts. Writing in 1933 on *"The Confusion in Literature,"* he traces this absorption in the ego back to Lawrence Sterne.

"Briefly, one might say the idea is this. The soul is supplanted by the ego: that which is made by that which makes: that which is dependent by that which is independent: that which is by that which dreams, the social in the solitary. * * * Sterne is the first considerable author who deliberately trusts to his own interest in his own character and his own idiosyncrasies to awaken and sustain interest in his readers."

Mr. Roberts points out in connection with Rousseau, that the old Greek apothegm has "been disastrously remodeled. The measure of all things is no longer man—It is I. We pass from the judgment of the created, social, worshipping individual to the rule of the dreaming, rebellious defiant solitary, which may mean a passage from sanity to madness." [8]

This has a real relevance to Wolfe, and to a literary emphasis and concern which his work represents. Roberts' phrase, "the substitution of the ego for the soul," describes the emergence of a modern psychological substitute for a traditional theological religion. A good deal of the bombast in Wolfe, and the tiresome glorification of triviality, come from this eclipse of God and the responsible soul, by the ego.

The other aspect of Wolfe, in close relation to religion and ethics, is that he does represent and portray a search for salvation. The characterization of his novels as a modern *Pilgrim's Progress* is not limited in its application to the form of an autobiography. It is a definite search for salvation. The questions, "Who will show us any good?" and "What must I do to be saved?" are continuous. The search does not lead to any orthodox altar of repentance. The word "lost" in its evangelical theological sense has dropped from our common speech. But the search for "salvation" goes on. The world is full of the inadequate and frustrated, eagerly seeking life, looking in many directions for wholeness and fullness of life. This search for completion, fulfillment, finds a notable expression in Wolfe. It is a witness to a continuing quest of the good life. The conclusion of Wolfe's celebrated passage on *"The Names of a Nation"* voices the aspiration and desire to find some pearl of great price.

"For what are we, my brother? We are a phantom flare of grieved desire, the ghostling and phosphoric flickers of immortal time, a brevity of days haunted by the eternity of the earth. We are an unspeakable utterance, an insatiable hunger, an unquenchable thirst; a lust that bursts our sinews, explodes our brains,

[8] *Christianity and the Crisis.* Edited by Percy Dearmer. Victor Gollancz Ltd., London, 1933.

sickens and rots our guts, and rips our hearts asunder. We are a twist of passion, a moment's flame of love and ecstasy, a sinew of bright blood and agony, a lost cry, a music of pain and joy, a haunting of brief sharp hours, an almost captured beauty, a demon's whisper of unbodied memory. We are the dupes of time.

For, brother, what are we?

We are the sons of our father, whose face we have never seen, we are the sons of our father, whose voice we have never heard, we are the sons of our father, to whom we have cried for strength and comfort in our agony, we are the sons of our father, whose life like ours was loved, we are the sons of our father, to whom only can we speak out the strange, dark burden of our heart and spirit, we are the sons of our father, and we shall follow the print of his foot forever." [9]

No large amount of fiction has dealt with mental life in exploration of the abnormal. This may seem strange in view of the great interest in psychology and the enormous amount of writing in that field. No doubt the psychiatric clinic is a difficult field for fiction. There has been no lack of psychopathic characters, as we have seen, such as crowd the pages of Faulkner, Eugene O'Neill, Caldwell, and Jeffers' poetry. But they are not treated from the standpoint of mental hygiene. The outstanding achievement in this realm was Millen Brand's *The Outward Room,* which tells movingly and with plausible detail and insight the story of the recovery of a mind. A young woman escapes from a mental hospital, finds refuge with a workman in New York, and comes back to mental balance and control through finding a place for herself in the world of labor and human relationship. The part played in the mental and spiritual recovery by development of the sense of responsibility, and the restoration of the withered sense of personal validity and significance, is convincingly shown. In the dramatic version, particularly, it

[9] *Of Time and the River* by Thomas Wolfe. Charles Scribner's Sons, 1935.

documents the affirmation that "he that loseth himself shall find himself."

A large amount of poetry had as its theme the emptiness of the inner life of many people, its banality, its barrenness of individuality and any significant spiritual resources. This is often savage, sometimes motivated by class hatred, often displaying the satirical contempt which so marked Ring Lardner in the preceding decade, a positive hatred of empty-headed fools.

In sharp contrast to this, is a great deal of the spirit and emphasis of Robert Frost. He, too, revolts against the regimentation of life, against people with mechanized "insides," against empty deserts where the soul ought to be. But his feeling is expressed in positive rather than negative or satirical terms. He celebrates a Puritan individualism. Without running at all into didactic generalities, his poetry affirms the dignity of the life of the individual, expressed in vivid concrete detail in a score of portraits. Frost's individualism cannot be taken as a defense of any economic or social status quo. It is rather an affirmation of love for and faith in a world of fixed personal and moral values.

The negative, satirical portraits of the absence of character and inner resources pay an inverted tribute to moral and spiritual values. They express the judgment that when the mind and spirit become a mere cave of echoes, something monstrous has happened. This is artistically done in a poem entitled *The Mask* by Helen Haiman Joseph:[10]

> Always a mask
> Held in a slim hand, whitely,
> Always she had a mask before her face
> Smiling and sprightly,
> The mask.

[10] *Saturday Review of Literature*, August 13, 1932.

Truly the wrist
Holding it lightly
Fitted the task:
Sometimes however
Was there a shiver,
Fingertip quiver,—
Holding the mask?

For years and years and years I've wondered
But dared not ask

And then—
I blundered,
I looked behind,
Behind the mask,
To find nothing—
She had no face

She had become
Merely a hand
Holding a mask
With grace.

Edna St. Vincent Millay has many attacks on the inner
Sahara desert. Her *Conversation at Midnight* has many passages reflecting her feeling of the habit of conformity and
the pressures of a mechanized mass production world tending
to depersonalization.

One sample poem, by Kenneth Fearing, may stand for
many with the same general spirit and idea. It might be
called the picture of a synthetic soul, outwardly groomed in
the latest mode, the mind stuffed with approved clichés, in-
wardly a spiritual vacuum.

The clear brown eyes, kindly and alert, with 20-20 vision, give
confident regard to the passing world through R. K. Lampert
& Company lenses framed in gold
    his soul, however, is all his own
        Arndt Brothers necktie and hat (with feather) supply
        a touch of youth.

With his soul his own, he drives, drives, chats and drives the
     second and third bicuspids, lower right, replaced by bridge-
     work, while two incisors have porcelain crowns

(Render unto federal, state, and city Caesar, but not unto time
     render nothing unto time until Amalgamated Death serves
     final notice, in proper form

The vault is ready
     the will has been drawn by Clagget, Clagget, Clagget and
     Brown
          the policies are adequate, Confidential's best, reimbursing
          for disability, partial or complete, with double indemnity
          should the end be a pure and simple accident)

Nothing unto time
     nothing unto change
          nothing unto fate
               nothing unto you, and nothing unto me, or to any
               other known or unknown party or parties, living or
               deceased

But Mercury shoes, with special arch supports, take much of the
wear and tear
     on the course, a custombuilt driver corrects a tendency to
     slice
          love's ravages have been repaired (it was a textbook
          case) by Drs. Schultz, Lighter, Mannheim, and Goode
               while all of it is enclosed in excellent tweed, with Mr.
               Baumer's personal attention to the shoulders and the
               waist

And all of it now roving, chatting amiably through space in a
Plymouth 6
     with his soul (his own) at peace, soothed by Walter Lipp-
     mann, and sustained by Haig & Haig.[11]

[11] *Dead Reckoning* by Kenneth Fearing. Random House, 1938.

CHAPTER 5

THE IMPACT OF THE DEPRESSION

"SIR," SAID SAMUEL JOHNSON, in one of his booming pronouncements from Sinai, "a book should either help us to enjoy life or endure it." If this magisterial verdict had been widely accepted it would have shut out a large library of authentic literature. Dr. Johnson left out two of the great services of literature, that of helping us to understand life and to feel it. That has been the part played by writing which records the impact of the depression of the thirties on millions of people. Such writing does not help anyone in the enjoyment of life; it is not designed particularly to add to the resources for enduring it. But it does help to understand and to feel. For that reason it should have a permanent historical importance.

Of course, it is an arbitrary and unreal proceeding to fence off a group of books, novels, stories, poems and plays and label it specifically "depression literature." That label could be attached, with real pertinence, to most of the writing of the decade. The lean years were the very atmosphere in which literature was created. All literature that was an authentic product of the time was influenced by the depression. The writing dealing with labor, to be considered later, was emphatically depression literature, in that the issues and problems of labor and industry became acute to a new degree. It is reserved for treatment under the head of labor, because it deals, in such characteristic books as *The Grapes of Wrath* and *Citizens* by Meyer Levin, with conditions bigger and more permanent than an economic collapse.

Beyond that, much other literature might fairly be classed as a product or impact of the depression. A large part of what is roughly called "escape" literature reflects the economic conditions. The breakdown itself created a demand for something that did not deal with the immediate omnipresent woe and fear. In 1931, a cartoon in the *New Yorker* expressed with the characteristic timeliness of that periodical a prevailing mood. A perplexed dowager is shown in a bookstore asking earnestly of the clerk, "Have you a book that isn't about poor people?" The sigh of the psalmist has been echoed often, "O that I had the wings of a dove, then would I fly away and be at rest." The longed-for wings were provided in the pages of romantic literature, on which many tired minds and souls flew away, a little distance, at least, and were at rest, for an interval.

The great flood of historical novels, particularly the large number located in America, could also with truth be called a variety of depression literature. The vogue was increased, if not created, by the experience of the depression. It was not only that historical fiction provided a magic carpet on which to voyage to other times, but that it also met a newly awakened interest in America, a new interest in its traditional values, a new wonder about how the present developed out of the past. In another way the depression has been an influence on many books, both fiction and non-fiction, books which do not have the depression as a theme at all. There can be no doubt that what has been called the savage and melancholy note of the 1930's voices the moods and feelings induced by insecurity and collapse. Joseph Wood Krutch calls it "spleen": "It is clear enough," he writes, "I think that in few if any other epochs has spleen in its various manifestations unmistakably set the dominant tone of literature as it sets it in the twentieth century." The majority of the books which he mentions as illustrating this thesis are books of the 1930's.

Yet there has been an important group of works which in a much more specific sense may be regarded as recording the impact of the depression on millions of Americans, writing which promises to be historically valuable. It has acted as a sensitive film on which has been imprinted some of the effects of the black plague of unemployment during the thirties. They are not books concerned primarily, in most cases, with seeking the cause of the conditions, or a remedy for them. They carry no load of ideological content, arrive at no conclusions. They describe. They give the data for sympathetic understanding and feeling, when they present individual lives, as is done in Martha Gellhorn's *The Trouble I've Seen*, caught in the jamming of a complicated economic machine, which the engineers can no longer control or run.

But there is more than descriptive value in such literature, great as that is in itself. There is a genuine ethical judgment on a system which so conspicuously fails to conserve human values. This judgment is all the stronger in that it appears not in didactic form but is implicit in the character and narrative. That judgment is evident also in the valuation of man, the high valuation found in studies of people under the harrow. It is found in indignation over the ruthless waste of human worth. A common slang phrase of the period has a real moral connotation: "It shouldn't happen to a dog." Under scores of pictures in fiction, poetry and drama, could be written the words of moral condemnation, "It shouldn't happen to a man."

Going a step farther, there is in the sincere records of what happened to people an element of religious thinking, the raising of basic questions about the spiritual order of the universe, if any. A sharp expression of clearly religious and theological questions forced upon the mind by the events of the years with their human devastation is found in a poem by Ogden Nash, in ironic parody of William Blake:

> Beggar, beggar, burning low
> In the city's trodden snow,
> What immortal hand or eye
> Could frame thy dread asymmetry?
>
> In what distant deep of lies
> Did the fire of thine eyes?
> What the mind that planned the shame?
> What the hand dare quench the flame?
>
> And what shoulder and what art
> Could rend the sinews of thy heart?
> And when thy heart began to fail,
> What soft excuse, what easy tale?
>
> What the hammer? What the chain?
> What the furnace dulled thy brain?
> What the anvil? What the blow
> Dare to forge this deadly woe?
> 　　When the business cycle ends,
> 　　In flaming extra dividends
> 　　Will He smile his work to see?
> 　　Did He who made the Ford make thee? [1]

"Did He who made the Ford make thee?"—A question as old as Job—but with a mass production background.

Reporting of the breakdown in terms of turmoil and anguish in individual lives, did in print what was done for the physical eye in the dramatization of the lot of the share crop-

[1] From *The Face Is Familiar* by Ogden Nash. Reprinted by permission of Little, Brown & Company.

per on Routes 60 and 61 in New Madrid County, Missouri. There, as a grim laboratory exhibit of the sickness of a nation, hungry, shivering homeless families exhibited themselves, to the consternation of passing motorists, and the rage of the "hush hush" fraternity of politicians and business. A poetical audit of America in mid-depression, which might be taken as a summary of many records in fiction and poetry, is found in Stephen Vincent Benét's ode to Walt Whitman:

IT IS WELL WITH THESE STATES?

"We have made many, fine new toys.
We—
There is a rust on the land.
A rust and a creeping blight and a scaled evil,
For six years eating, yet deeper than those six years,
Men labor to master it but it is not mastered.
There is the soft, grey, foul tent of the hatching worm
Shrouding the elm, the chestnut, the Southern cypress.
There is shadow in the bright sun, there is shadow upon the
    streets.
They burn the grain in the furnace while men go hungry.
They pile the cloth of the looms while men go ragged.
We walk naked in our plenty."
"My tan-faced children?"
"These are your tan-faced children.
These skilled men, idle, with the holes in their shoes.
These drifters from State to State, these wolfish, bewildered boys
Who ride the blinds and the box-cars from jail to jail,
Burnt in their youth like cinders of hot smokestacks,
Learning the thief's crouch and the cadger's whine,
Dishonored, abandoned, disinherited.
These, dying, in the bright sunlight they cannot eat,
Or the strong men, sitting at home, their hands clasping nothing,
Looking at their lost hands.
These are your tan-faced children, the parched young,
The old man rooting in waste-heaps, the family rotting
In the flat, before eviction,

With the toys of plenty about them,
The shiny toys making ice and music and light,
But no price for the shiny toys and the last can empty.
The sleepers in blind corners of the night.
The women with dry breasts and phantom eyes.
The walkers upon nothing, the four million.
These are your tan-faced children." [2]

It may be granted freely that none of the novels to be briefly noted here are, from the critical standpoint, great novels. If one asks why such major social experience did not call forth fiction of major rank, there is a ready answer in the words of Lincoln Steffens,[3] "You can't put the facts of experience in order while you are getting them, especially if you are getting them in the neck." But whatever the critical rating, there is great value as truthful recording and interpretation of experience.

A bit of description in George R. Leighton's *Five Cities* gives theme for a whole library of depression literature. On one page there is

". . . a photograph of a stoutly framed, neatly latticed billboard, foursheeted with a plump, fashionably-clad family smiling through the windshield of their shiny sedan, emblazoned with boxcar legends: 'World's Highest Standard of Living—There's No Way Like the American Way.' But beyond the billboard lies a rank weedpatch, a rubbish heap, a rotting shanty with a patched roof, and a brick backwall which bears a sodawater advertisement."

Come behind the billboard!

Novelists, in treating the depression, in selecting their cast of characters, have followed the command in the gospel parable, "When thou makest a feast, call the lame, the halt, the blind." Here they are.

[2] *Burning City* by Stephen Vincent Benét. Farrar and Rinehart, 1936.
[3] *The Letters of Lincoln Steffens.* Edited by Ella Winter and Granville Hicks. Harcourt, Brace & Co., New York.

Martha Gellhorn's *The Trouble I've Seen* is a collection of four long stories based on the writer's experience working for the Federal Relief Administration, each dealing with the effects of the depression on a person or family located in a different part of the country, South, West and East. Reporting is lifted to art and case work walks into literature. In each story, there is the bewilderment of people who have been competent and self sustaining, when everything they have believed in collapses. One insight is notable, that during unemployment men degenerate more quickly than women, for the woman still has a job even though it is only caring for children and trying to make one potato do the work of four. The story, *A Pair of Roller Skates,* is memorable for a little girl's prayer—'O God, if you've got time, get me a roller skate'—and the tragedy when she learns how a girl can get roller skates—and other things.

A depression novel with both pain and art in it is Dorothy Thomas' *Home Place.* How does it feel to become so "down and out" that one man has to take his family back to the home place to live on the charity of his parents in an overcrowded house, with the zero temperature outside matched by the cold welcome from other members of the family inside? Doubtless, thousands of people in the United States could answer that question from their own experience. Their answer becomes vocal to some extent in Miss Thomas' short but vivid book. There is effective character drawing which makes up for the lack of any notable plot.

In these stories and in others to be noted we get a clear picture of what the sociologist calls "downward mobility," which breaks up the unity of the personal organism as security gives way, and status and support for one's sense of personal importance are lost. We also get a vivid commentary on the word of Mrs. Alice Meynell, "The Lady Poverty was fair, but she has lost her looks of late."

A depression story of a very different type is Robert Nathan's beautiful and moving fantasy, *One More Spring*. This is a modern fairy tale recounting the adventures of a banker, cleaned out by the crash, a park employee, and a girl of the streets, who find a strange common abode and a stranger companionship in a Central Park tool house.

The life of the derelict vagrant during the leanest of the lean years is vividly portrayed in two stories, both of which read like autobiography, and probably do include a great deal of personal experience, *Hungry Men* by Edward Anderson, and *Waiting for Nothing* by Tom Kromer. Both record the story of a tramp. But that word "tramp" has become entirely obsolete. There have been so many involuntary additions to the ranks of the homeless wanderers on the road to nowhere, that the old connotation of "tramp" and "bum" as a lazy, somewhat comic figure who prefers panhandling to work, has lost its meaning. The central figures in these stories are no "weary willies," knights of the tomato can. They are casualties of an economic disaster. Both of these stories are reports from the ultimate bottom of a diseased society. They are not humorous characters, any more than a corpse in a morgue is humorous. Mr. Kromer, for instance, still only 28 years of age when his book was published in 1935, was, five years previously, a teacher in West Virginia. Losing his job, he went to Kansas to look for work in the wheat fields. There was no work there or anywhere, so he did the only thing possible: obeyed the policeman's order to "move on and keep moving." He rode the freight train to California. His experiences are set down in *Waiting for Nothing*. The book does more than relate the story of that odyssey, with its squalor, its tentative excursions into crime, its revolting scenes in a bunk house and the spiritual squalor of pretended conversions in a mission under the lure of a bowl of soup. It also pictures the social bankruptcy of a society which had, at that time, no treatment of a symptom of maladjustment other than the policeman's club, and the calloused indifference of the well-fed. *Hungry Men* is the same type of record, the principal character being an unemployed musician who tumbled down the ladder to dish washer, then to hobo. Here is clearly expressed in terms of narrative the sense of exploitation that those men feel when faced with local welfare agencies. They feel it better to "keep going" than to work for six hours a day for ninety cents a week. Both books give documentation to the speech of a young man in Elliott Arnold's novel on the burden of the depression as it rested heavily and cut cruelly on the shoulders of the young: "You associate hopelessness with old people . . . but there's something horrible about a boy of twenty-two being hopeless."

What does it feel like to be on relief? Twenty million people can give a first hand answer. Joseph Vogel in his novel of 1938, *Man's Courage*, has made one of the most convincing answers to that question. It is not only one of the first novels exploring a new and far-extended area of experience, that of public relief as it is undergone by people who never dreamed of such a plight. It is a singularly gripping record of life, novel and frightening. The story shows steps going down—from a confident, indeed proud, self-reliance and competence of Adam Wolak, a Polish-born American and his family. The Holy Grail which led him on was that which has been the quest for numberless others, the hope of a bit of land. Instead of that, the way down went from odd jobs, in which there is a pathetic trade of his farm tools for a snow shovel in the deluded hope of making some money, accepting help from friends, then hunger for the family, and the final laceration of spirit in accepting public relief, with eviction as the last step down. But it is not a sob story; it is a story of courage which rises with each new adversity.

Stories of life on relief are just beginning to come through. The whole experience was so new, so bewildering to millions, that a space of time has been necessary for artistic treatment of the experience. As is inevitably the case, the most permanently valuable fictional records of the thirties will appear during the succeeding decade. Another record of courage of a very different sort, but high courage, nevertheless, in meeting the blows of outrageous fortune is found in a novel of the spring of 1940, *The Triumph of Willie Pond* by Caroline Slade. Miss Slade unites the imagination of a novelist with the experience and sincerity of a social worker in an extremely original novel of a family of "down and outers" on relief. She reveals what a complex world that of relief is, with its own social gradations and caste. Here we get first hand authentic portrayal not only of the physical and material costs of ten million unemployed, but also the moral and psychological consequences. Here we are shown how people exist, how the children take it, how the inner breakdown of personal stamina goes on. The Pond family who are the beneficiaries of relief, ("victims" is often a more suitable word) are not Jukes; they are not abnormal, but a normal family, the kind of stuff that makes America. In a world stacked against them, the inner as well as the outer fortifications give way. Even the very processes of awarding relief in the hands of well intentioned social workers become a means of depersonalization. Willie Pond, the father, after years of hopelessness, becomes more a number on a roll of relief cases than he is a man. He is a W.P.A. worker earning ten to twelve dollars a week to support a family of nine. He is injured in an accident, and the examination at the hospital reveals that he has tuberculosis. By a technicality, he is worth more money a week to his family as a charity patient in a public sanitarium than he is as a healthy worker. For then his family is transferred to another relief agency, which gives the mother a pension. That is an important step up, the family is better off than it has been for years. Then Willie's impending recovery from tuberculosis threatens financial disaster to the family. Willie's triumph consists in suicide, thus assuring the continuance of his widow's pension. The novel carries by its plot and characters a strong indictment of a socially imbecilic society in which a dead man or a T.B. patient supported at great cost is more valuable to his family than a strong workman.

A very different sort of novel than any yet mentioned is W. L. White's *What People Said* (1938).

A town itself is the chief character. It is the story of a Kansas town through the boom years preceding the depression and then through the valley of the shadow of unemployment and the economic collapse. It comes close to being a condensed, novelized version of the Lynds' great social studies of mid-America, *Middletown* and *Middletown in Transition*. We get the atmosphere, the social and economic codes and pressures, the very feel and flavor of life in a town suspiciously like the author's own Emporia, Kansas. It is simple in plan, unostentatious in writing and colloquial in speech. It probes deep into the underlying forces in the country, with much ethical and psychological insight and grasp of economic realities.

Mr. White's theme is not only the economic depression as it struck a typical town, but also the moral degeneration which follows in its train. He tells the story of the Norssexes, father and son, bankers in the city. The progress of the Norssex family against the social barriers set up by the older established society is convincingly portrayed. Their greatest asset is the friendship of the progressive leader, Charles A. Carrough (a figure almost drawn from the life of Mr. White's father, William Allen White). The figure through whom the story filters at third hand (a decided defect in the narrative) is Junior Carrough, the friend of the younger Norssex, Lee. One great contribution of the novel to social history is the description of the way in which the Norssexes, first the son, then the father, cross the line from pushing, shrewd business into fraud and forgery. This degeneration is told with such convincing detail and atmosphere that it is made quite understandable. Lee, the younger, goes from one game of wits to another, ending finally in the forgery of bonds, dragging his father and the father's bank down with him, the son ending up with a long penitentiary sentence and the father with suicide.

The novel suggests relationships to two notable American stories, Edward Howe's *The Story of a Country Town* and Sinclair Lewis' *Main Street*. Howe's novel, published fifty-seven years ago in 1883, was the pioneer of American realism in dealing with the small town. In a time when fiction was overwhelmingly of the "wisteria and honeysuckle" school, it turned a sharp camera on the actual towns with the first hope of pioneer days gone. It was as though Howe had said to his readers: "You have heard what a lovely place the country town is—full of hope, optimism and trust and love. Well, all right, take a look at the real thing." And he showed the people of the town defeated, sullen, rough, small-minded. Now almost two generations later comes W. L. White with a more penetrating story in the same tradition, showing the action of economic forces at the close of another period of false optimism, at the close of the 1920's.

What People Said has many relationships with *Main Street*. White does not approach the narrative skill of Lewis, nor

match his powers of mimicry and literary ventriloquism. On
the other hand he does not stoop to caricature and comic strip
effects, as Lewis often does, and his economic penetration far
surpasses that of Lewis. Mr. White is very explicit in tracing
the events and moral degeneration to some of their root causes
in concentration of economic power. He might be said to have
a text paralleling Edith Cavell's "Patriotism is not enough."
He says, "Progressivism is not enough." He makes very clear
the pressure which our materialistic civilization and profit-
driven economy puts upon every man, how they determine
the political institutions and practices of a community. The
book is a great picture of American life in the present and
recent past, worthy of a place on the same shelf with Lincoln
Steffens' *Autobiography*, John Chamberlain's *Farewell to Reform*, the Lynds' *Middletown* and Dos Passos' three novels
comprising *U. S. A.*, for light for the interpretation of an era.

Thomas Boyd in his novel *In Time of Peace* gives a picture of the roller coaster of the post-war years, with its swift
breath-taking ups and downs. He had already written one of
the best descriptive novels of the war, *Through the Wheat*,
and the underlying theme of the second novel was that the
1930 years were a continuation of war on another front.
Hence, the title is ironical. Just as in the international arena
in the late 1930's it was agreed that there was little difference
between peace and war in that the technical peace covered an
active war on the economic front, it was still a form of war.
At the end of the story, after Bill Hicks, the central character,
is shot in a demonstration of unemployed, he concludes that
it is not very different from being shot in France, as he was
fifteen years earlier. The author writes, "If this was war, he
was glad to know it. He at least had something to fight for
now."

It is a credible story of multitudes of normal Americans

from the "little" depression of the early twenties, through the
boom, the top of the roller coaster, down with the big dip.
Hicks has a brief moment as a returning hero, then the only
employment he can find, twelve hours a day in a giant machine shop in Chicago, is physically too great a strain. His
newly married wife gets him into the white collar class on a
newspaper. The cynicism prevailing around him leads him to
drop his radical ideas and sail along in the feverish twenties in
a "hard-boiled" mood. Then with the crash, when he is
ashamed to live on his wife's earnings, he drops out of the
white collar heaven into a search for a job in an automobile
factory only to get shot at the gates, (evidently a thinly disguised version of the Dearborn shooting at the Ford works).
The real theme is explicitly stated at the end. He sees that his
blunder was "in thinking that peace and war were two different animals."

"Pain rushed with the air into his wound—hot, exquisite stabs
of violence. His chin dropped, waggling from self-pity. But no, by
God! Back of the guards stood the police, back of the police the
politicians, back of the politicians the Libbys, and behind them
all the sacred name of Property. In the name of property men
could be starved to death, and if they even so much as raised their
heads, there was war." [4]

Josephine Lawrence has worked steadily through the years,
producing successive treatments of problems of the time. She
has written more specifically what used to be called "problem
novels" than any other contemporary novelist. It is not surprising if the problems stand out more notably than the characters who illustrate them. Miss Lawrence does not push
through in her analysis to any clear or effective indication of
the economic roots of the various problems she deals with.
Yet the situations are so detailed and true to life that the nov-

[4] *In Time of Peace* by Thomas Boyd. Minton Balch & Company, 1935.

els do have great value for the understanding of the period. Three of her novels deal specifically with the impact of the depression on middle class people. *Years Are So Long* deals with one of the biggest themes of the decade, the tragedy of insecurity in old age. It enables the reader to enter painfully into the experience of being an unwanted guest in the homes of the children. It shows what happens to old people in a highly individualistic society, when they have not been able to save, or their savings have been swept away, and when the children themselves with their families are hanging on by their finger nails in a collapsing order. We can better understand the deep reasons behind the Townsend movement if we have lived through this novel. It is easy to ridicule the "Ham and Eggs" crusade in California and other places; easy to demonstrate that "twenty dollars every Thursday" is fantastic economic nonsense, as a means of solving our economic puzzle. But such a movement is not to be dealt with by ridicule. An economic order which throws people on the industrial and business scrap heap in middle years is one that is painfully sick. A contemptuous laugh is no substitute for facing the economic maladjustment, which calls forth a fairy tale remedy. It is not unnatural for the middle aged and elderly to refuse to starve quietly in the backyard and not cause any trouble about it.

In *The Sound of Running Feet*, Josephine Lawrence again presents her favorite type of hero, an idea. It deals with insufficient income, a variation of the text, "The lack of money is the root of all evil." The laboratory selected for observation is the office of the real estate firm of River, Mead and Luth, in a middle-sized city. She cuts crosswise into the lives of a dozen employees and the families of two of the firm. All are hunted by the hounds of debt and the need of more money and the fear of insecurity. The title comes from a dream of one of the characters, a dream in which the sound of running feet behind continually strikes the ear. It is the endless footfall on the pavements, the feet of those crowding from the rear, ready to pounce on one's job, the next generation eager to step into one's place, the feet of the debt collector—endlessly hurrying feet. The younger group in the office want to organize a union; they wish the older ones to take a pay cut. The office workers regard the firm as "bloated capitalists." Miss Lawrence takes us into the lives of the two brothers of the firm and shows that they too are harassed and crowded by running feet.

Back of the persons are family groups, which afford the author opportunity to bring to bear her remarkable skill in portraying character and in analyzing emotion. She "stacks the cards" by assembling a group of mental and spiritual cripples in these family connections, so that the whole gallery is an abnormal collection of warped and frustrated personalities. But they are done with deftness and insight. A sample is her description of the moronic wife of one of the employees, Johnny Palmet: "artificial, over-dressed, without tenderness or sympathy, she was fated to desire the wrong things, to shop for poor values." Miss Lawrence has much to say of the shoddiness of people's ideals, lack of education and mental maturity. The main thing is the way she catches the panting fear of the loss of a job. The running feet we hear are not those of a hound of heaven but of a hound of hell. The bitterness and fear of the middle aged is well expressed in this angry tirade of an old employee, Jim Andrews:

"Youth is a big smoke-screen to hide the mistakes the half-baked, poorly trained mollycoddles of today make on their jobs. When you ball up the works you shriek that you're young and inexperienced, but when you're after the jobs at the top your cry is that Youth must take the helm. Yes, and you prolong this youth business till you're in your middle thirties, yet according to you a man in the forties is tottering to the grave." [5]

A characteristic depression situation, multiplied literally by the million, is that in which the one wage earner in a large family is one of the young children. This is what Miss Lawrence deals with in *But You Are Young*. Kelsie Wright, a young girl working in a beauty parlor at sixteen dollars a week, is the heavy laden Atlas who carries a world on her shoulders. There is Grandma Wright, to whose home all the refugees from the depression, including the whole Wright family, come, her son, jobless for years, his wife and four children. Kelsie is the only one with a job. The theme of the novel is that of the frustration of the young girl's life, whose natural aspirations for a life of her own are met with the objection, "But you are so young." There are vivid etchings of the psychological effects of unemployment on the two men in the family, resentful at having to exist on the earnings of a young girl, the father who has had his last job and the young brother who has never had his first. The portrayal of the home, of the inner feelings of all the family, is a reading experience something like having an operation without an anaesthetic. It hurts. When finally Kelsie, after two abortive reachings after romance, finally walks out with a third love, the reader feels that whatever happens to the Wrights, Kelsie has won a right to live.

Upton Sinclair's *Co-Op* is emphatically a depression novel, with a strong element of real history. The obvious thing to say about Upton Sinclair is that he is a poor novelist, and with what tiresome and thoughtless repetition it has been said! That has been said for thirty years. It was untrue when it was first said about *The Jungle* in 1906, and it is still un-

[5] *The Sound of Running Feet* by Josephine Lawrence. Frederick A. Stokes Company, New York, 1937.

true when it is said about *Co-op* in 1936. Sinclair is not Charles Dickens or Willa Cather. But he can tell a story which has continuous interest and make it carry a load of ideas and propaganda without breaking its back. The present story is frankly the presentation of the Epic idea, cooperatives of the unemployed. The hero is not a man but a group of the unemployed, who emerge from Hobo City in which the houses are a row of sewer pipes in a vacant lot, to take hold of the idea of the exchange of labor for commodities. The detailed working out of the idea is not merely imaginary. It has been done. And as it becomes evident that unemployment on a large scale is permanent in the United States, to the number of four or five million, the whole idea embodied in the story has far more than a temporary importance.

One novel produced under the Federal Writers' Project is in a class by itself in that it deals with the new strange complicated and bitter world of the writer driven to Federal relief. Norman MacLeod in *You Get What You Ask For* brings a report on the country of the hungry and discouraged and disillusioned world of the so called "intelligentsia" which has struck the empty space below the bottom rung of the economic ladder. The adventures in relief, stretched all the way from New York to New Mexico, are told with emotional power, if, in places, with a feverish bitterness, especially when dealing with experiences in the ranks of the writer's project. He becomes so vitriolic there that the reader's suspicions that he is "airing a grudge" rather than doing objective reporting, are aroused.

Sterling North in his *Seven Against the Years* gives another panoramic view of the "years of the locust." He has used a suggestive framework, that of following the careers of seven men who graduated from the University of Chicago in the year 1929. He has chosen his men to illustrate different fields of life and different types of character. Some learned nothing and the years are passed in a long drawn snarl. One turns to fascism to cover up his own failure and resentment. Another, a frustrated geologist, becomes a labor organizer. The third goes into cooperatives. Mr. North shows insight in that not all his failures are due to the times or "the system." There are failures of personal character. His moral judgment is indicated in the fact that the real failures are commercial successes.

The attention called in an earlier chapter to the books of factual reporting of the effects of the depression will bear repetition here. These are not works of imaginative creation; they are "keyhole" reporting, the catching of the actual speech and thought of real people, caught in economic fire, flood and hurricane. One of the finest tributes ever paid to literature was in the words of Humpty Dumpty's explanation of Alice's uncanny knowledge in *Alice in Wonderland*. He exclaims, "You've been listening at doors—and behind trees and down chimneys—or you couldn't have known it." Alice meekly protests, "It's in a book."

There has been much successful "listening at doors." We hear the results in *These Are Our Lives,* stories told by the people themselves and written down by members of the Federal Writers' Project in North Carolina. It is the very stuff of life and deserves permanent historical importance as data on a bewildering era. It is reporting which rises to the stature and richness of fiction and drama. Millhands, farm laborers, gas station attendants, negro shoe blacks, the quick lunch proprietor, the whole varied *dramatis personae* speak their piece, trippingly on the tongue and not mouthed. Other valuable books of accurate reporting are Mrs. Armstrong's *We Too Are The People,* dealing with people on relief in northern Michigan, where the lumber industry has collapsed, and

Youth Tell Their Story, a study of young people in Maryland between the ages of sixteen and twenty-four, published by the American Council of Education, and Benjamin Appel's *The People Talk*, the transcontinental journey of a listener at all sorts of keyholes.

One theme of great importance and far reaching moral and religious consequences is touched on in many plays and novels, that of the impossibility of young people to marry, due to the lack of a job and income, and the hopelessness of getting either. The resulting frustration and repression with its many sided social consequences has been a major evil of the economic debacle. It is a problem which has been passed by with far too much blind complacency, not only by the public at large, but by those professing a deep concern for sexual moral standards and religion. One of the most poignant pictures of this trap in which young lovers are caught is in the story of Jim and Lou in Martha Gellhorn's *The Trouble I've Seen*. They are deeply in love, unable to marry, yet clinging to their romance, hating a cheap substitute for marriage. "It's not our fault," young Lou cries heatedly. "We *can't* be ashamed. We may as well go ahead and die if we're ashamed." Jim finally steals the clothes he needs for the wedding ceremony.

This theme runs as a thread through Albert Halper's *The Chute*. Rae Sussman puts off her own marriage in order to help her younger brother, Paul, who has promise as an architect, to go to school. It is a moving act of unselfish devotion to help one of the family climb out of the pit of poverty, but it is achieved at a terrible personal cost. Rae and her lover, unable to marry, enter into an extra marital liaison from which both revolt, and from the sordidness and furtiveness of which they both suffer. In Irene Baird's story of depression years in Canada, *Waste Heritage*, the same prison bars appear, sketched at length in the love story of Matt, a union organizer, and Hazel, a department store worker, giving a forceful portrayal of the defeat and hopelessness of youth.

"I want a home of my own, a place where you don't get chased around and spied on, where you don't have to punch a time clock every morning to prove to yourself it's another day. I could do with a slew of kids, too. . . . Crazy, isn't it?"

"I don't know that it's crazy," Matt answers, "but you've got expensive tastes. Those things cost money." [6]

The relationship of this blocking of youth to moral and religious questions has been put into stinging words by Harry Emerson Fosdick, words that challenge the complacency and hypocrisy of many religious people, in their indifference to economic change:

"Nothing much more arouses one's indignation than elderly sentimentalists who, softly cushioned themselves, shake their heads over the informal liaisons into which young people enter on every side, and ask me whether I do not think it lamentable. Of course I think it lamentable and would do anything in my power to keep my young friends from getting into these alleys that lead only into misery. But the more important fact is that the young people themselves think it lamentable. They too want homes. They too want children. Do we elderly head-shakers think the young people like this situation? But if we of the older generation are going on with war and with an economic order which gives to youth no opportunity or security, we cannot expect high standards of personal morality except in a selected group. That is the realistic fact." [6a]

A great deal of printed matter has been a consequence of the depression, matter of which little or none at all has attained to the rank of even third rate literature. That is the new propaganda of intolerance, of race hatred and religious bigotry. It grew like a poisonous weed in the late thirties.

[6] *Waste Heritage* by Irene Baird. Random House, New York.
[6a] *The Church Monthly*, New York, October, 1935.

Such a development seems to indicate that tolerance is a function of prosperity, showing its benign face when fear and distress are absent, going under a dark cloud when they appear. The use of the Nazi hatreds and intolerance in Germany furnish evidence to this gloomy conclusion, and a similar trend is disturbingly evident in the United States. The one literary treatment of this growth of the storm trooper mind in this country is James T. Farrell's short story in book form, *Tommy Gallagher's Crusade*. The movement which found expression in the voice of Father Coughlin appears in the transparent disguise of "Father Maylan," radio priest and publisher of "Social Justice," with a crusade to drive the Jews out of America. Farrell describes with insight and great psychological acumen the effect of this emotional hatred on young Tommy, out of a job, with a badly deflated ego. It is an alarming analysis of the possibility of the development of an American fascism. The roots of a new barbarism in America are clearly shown in the absence of jobs, in the resultant self pity and the desire to find both a scapegoat for frustration and an assertion of personal significance.

Sinclair Lewis' *It Can't Happen Here* is much more than a depression story. However, his picture of the coming of fascism in America would be meaningless without the foundation for such a cancerous growth in economic blight and unemployment. When Lewis is describing present conditions which make for the fascist solution of economic difficulties, he is on sure ground and does a job comparable to the best in *Main Street*. Events which have happened since the publication of that novel in 1935 have increased rather than decreased its importance. Chapter and verse from the daily papers could be assembled as documentations even for some of the incidents which seem most fantastic and improbable. What is unconvincing in the story of a future fascism in America, under

the leadership of "Buzz" Windrip, is that he has had it all
happen in too short a time frame, and without the necessary
preliminary weakening of government. The book, however,
taken in connection with the trend of events, particularly the
weakening of democratic safeguards under the war hysteria
of the summer of 1940, does raise the speculation that the
most important literature of the depression will be that written in later years, depicting the history of the growth of fascist mentality and action in America.

It is not surprising to find that the years of unemployment
registered much sooner in the short story, and even in the
drama, than in the full length novel. That medium can respond more quickly and the mood can be more easily sustained for short story length. There have been many sharp
scathing stories. One of the most notable is Albert Maltz's
story, *The Happiest Man On Earth*, which won first prize in
the O. Henry memorial award. It tells the tale of a man so
long unemployed that even life itself shrinks in value in comparison to the prospect of a job. Thoroughly desperate, he applies for and receives a job as the driver of a wagon loaded
with explosives, despite the warning he is given that the job
means eventual death. But something in him is stronger than
the love of life, the need for personal valuation, as a man with
a place in the life of society, a need for the reinstatement of
manhood. When he gets the job he is, ironically, "the happiest man on earth." [7] In the same volume is a powerful story,
one of the earliest publications of Richard Wright, *Fire And
Cloud*, describing the way in which a negro community in
the South is made to bear the brunt of the depression by the
whites. Fred Miller's story, *New Year's Eve*, is a typical one,
describing a few hours in the life of a family, up against hun-

[7] *O. Henry Memorial Award Prize Stories of 1938.* Edited by Harry
Hansen. New York: Doubleday, Doran & Co.

ger and cold, with three potatoes and a window smashed in by jolly revellers. Albert Maltz is represented with another story, with too much piled-on horror, *Season of Celebration,* recording Christmas in a flop house among the derelicts washed in by the tide of unemployment.[8]

The Federal Theatre contributed notably to the dramatic representation of the depression and related problems, and by the small charge for admission, reached a much larger audience than that of the commercial theatre.

In the series of four plays produced under the head of *The Living Newspaper* was worked out a new technique for dramatic presentation of contemporary social issues, which were successful "theatre." Among the necessary conditions with which the experiment had to deal were that of employing as many unemployed actors as possible and also avoiding competition in theme and type of play with the commercial theatre (a compelled homage to the sacred cow of private profit). Two plays on major themes of the period were *Triple A Plowed Under,* by the Living Newspaper staff and *Power* by Arthur Arent. Some of the motion picture technique was adapted to the stage, with the employment of many scenes and the radio to furnish continuity. The most notable of the Federal Theatre plays was that dealing with the primary question of human shelter, with particular application to the contemporary housing problem, *One Third of a Nation,* using President Roosevelt's famous phrase. This was also written by Arthur Arent. It combined both sociological research and dramatic skill. The blindness by which a congressional attack, under reactionary hysteria, in 1939, wiped out the Federal Theatre, marked a new low in American social intelligence.

Clifford Odets, in two of the most important plays of the

[8] *The Way Things Are And Other Stories* by Albert Maltz. With an Introduction by Michael Gold. New York: International Publishers, 1938.

decade, considered from the subject matter in relation to contemporary life, dramatized the life and plight of the middle class under the depression. In *Awake and Sing* he unrolls the life of a Jewish family in the Bronx, the Bergers, as they are pushed around by outward forces, which they do not even understand. Odets not only catches in a remarkable way the idiomatic speech of the people, but also skillfully reveals their inner feelings. The frustrations and handicaps of a whole family group are depicted by action and speech in a manner to impart understanding and awaken sympathy. The characters are typical of economic conditions and yet achieve life in themselves; they are not marionettes of propaganda. Myron, the father, is a prototype of millions, sober, hard working, considerate, who has never in thirty years' struggle as a clerk made enough wages to support the family. He is oppressed by his failure, carries a sense of shame and yet is unable to understand what has blocked him. The wife, Bessie, is a combination, natural as a result of the necessity of stretching every dollar to impossible lengths, of sacrifice for her children and a rather savage acquisitiveness. Her love for her son thus struggles with a fierce opposition to his marrying a girl whom he loves, but who has no money at all. Bessie sees this as another weight dragging the family down. This same conflict leads her to condone tricking a suitor of her daughter into marriage, when she was pregnant by another man. The mother seems to be indifferent to the natural longings of her children, but she makes her case in a vigorous defense, which carries conviction:

"Ralphie, I worked too hard all my years to be treated like dirt. . . . Summer shoes you didn't have, skates you never had, but I bought a new dress every week. A lover I kept—Mr. Gigolo! Did I ever play a game of cards like Mrs. Marcus? Or was Bessie Berger's children always the cleanest on the block? Here I'm not only the mother, but also the father. The first two years I worked in a stocking factory for six dollars while Myron Berger went to law school. If I didn't worry about the family who would? On the calendar it's a different place, but here without a dollar you don't look the world in the eye. Talk from now to next year—this is life in America." [9]

The son Ralph replies to this outburst in words that carry the moral judgment implicit in the whole play:

Then it's wrong. It don't make sense. If life made you this way, then it's wrong! [9]

The most memorable character in the play is the grand-father, Jacob, an Isaiah of the Bronx, a veritable Hebrew prophet, even though his deity is Karl Marx rather than Jehovah. The social idealism and passion of the great Hebrew prophets speak in the words of Isaiah which give the title to the play, "Awake and sing, ye that dwell in the dust," and in this exhortation to his grandson, Ralph:

"Boychick, wake up! Be something! Make your life something good. For the love of an old man who sees in your young days his new life, for such love take the world in your two hands and make it like new. Go out and fight, so life shouldn't be printed on dollar bills." [10]

That last line well expresses the moral and spiritual judgment and protest against the flattening out of personal values by property values—"so life shouldn't be printed on dollar bills." The grandfather takes a heroic way of liberating young Ralph from his economic prison by committing suicide so that the boy may have his insurance.

In *Paradise Lost* Odets presents the coming of the depression to a family in New York, the Gordons, higher up in the

[9] *Awake And Sing* by Clifford Odets. Random House, New York, 1935.
[10] *Ibid.*

middle class. The giving way of the economic security of the family is an event which they never faced. The play deals not only with the financial decay but also with the moral decay of the children, showing clearly the lack of any moral or spiritual resources which might have held character stable even against disintegrating forces. The spoiled son, Ben, sooner than face the deflation of his personal importance by unemployment, participates in a hold-up. Two other children react in various ways to the ruin that impends: a son stricken by sickness turns to dreams of a strike in the Wall Street gamble, the daughter becomes embittered because her musical career is impossible. The final note is not despair, however. It is spiritual awakening and dedication to social struggle. This is expressed in the final speech of the husband, Leo Gordon, who turns from the ruin of his own hopes, to the larger social struggle of which his is a part. Hence the "Lost Paradise" of a comfortable middle class prosperity may give way to a new and larger sort of paradise.

"For the first time in our lives—for the first time our house has a real foundation. Clara, those people outside are afraid. Those people at the block party whisper and point. They're afraid. Let them look in our house. We're not ashamed. Let them look in. Clara, my darling, *listen to me.* Everywhere now men are rising from their sleep. Men, men are understanding the bitter black total of their lives. Their whispers are growing to shouts! They become an ocean of understanding! *No man fights alone.* Oh, if you could only see with me the greatness of men. I tremble like a bride to see the time when they'll use it. My darling, we must have only one regret—that life is so short! That we must die so soon. (*Clara slowly has turned from Julie and is listening now to her husband.*) Yes, I want to see that new world. I want to kiss all those future men and women. What is this talk of bankrupts, failures, hatred . . . they won't know what that means. Oh, yes, I tell you the whole world is for men to possess. Heartbreak and terror is not the heritage of mankind! The world is beautiful. No fruit tree wears a lock and key. Men will sing at their work, men will love. Ohhh, darling, the world is in its morning . . . and *no man fights alone! (Clara slowly comes down to her husband and kisses him. With real feeling. Everyone in the room, Leo included, is deeply moved by this vision of the future. Leo says:)* Let us have air . . . Open the windows. (*As he crosses to the windows a short fanfare is heard without.)*" [11]

The depression found constant expression in contemporary poetry and in that verse which need not be dignified by the august term of poetry. The reflection of the social world in poetry is considered in a later chapter. Here can be included only a few of the many poems dealing specifically with some consequences of unemployment on the lives of people. Of all those with this particular theme one of the most emotionally powerful and artistically skillful is Muriel Rukeyser's *Boy with his Hair Cut Short,* already become something of a classic. It has no chamber of horrors to reveal. But its restraint gives a moving picture of love and hopelessness, a sister giving her young brother a haircut so that he shall look "spruce" and get a job tomorrow, a prospect which each of them knows is utterly hopeless, but which neither will confess.

Sunday shuts down on this twentieth-century evening.
The L passes. Twilight and bulb define
the brown room, the overstuffed plum sofa,
the boy, and the girl's thin hands above his head.
A neighbor's radio sings stocks, news, serenade.

He sits at the table, head down, the young clear neck exposed,
watching the drugstore sign from the tail of his eye;
tattoo, neon, until the eye blears, while his
solicitous tall sister, simple in blue, bending
behind him, cuts his hair with her cheap shears.

[11] *Paradise Lost* by Clifford Odets. Random House, New York, 1936.

The arrow's electric red always reaches its mark,
successful neon! He coughs, impressed by that precision.
His child's forehead, forever protected by his cap,
is bleached against the lamplight as he turns head
and steadies to let the snippets drop.

Erasing the failure of weeks with level fingers,
she sleeks the fine hair, combing: 'You'll look fine tomorrow!
You'll surely find something, they can't keep turning you down;
the finest gentleman's not so trim as you!' Smiling, he raises
the adolescent forehead wrinkling ironic now.

He sees his decent suit laid out, new-pressed,
his carfare on the shelf. He lets his head fall, meeting
her earnest hopeless look, seeing the sharp blades splitting,
the darkened room, the impersonal sign, her motion,
the blue vein, bright on her temple, pitifully beating.[12]

Typical of many poems is that of Robert Friend entitled
Unemployed.

Under the roofs of houses a sullen force is sleeping,
resting its weight on motionless rocking chairs,
on papers fallen to floor, tables littered with dishes,
hairpins dangling in hair.

And if the clock is the one thing still in motion,
it is because something must go on
in a world gone dead, and people
with their wish for living gone.

Their despair is quiet, the miserable marble
expressing an infinity of pain:
the man sitting there on the sofa brooding
will he ever lift a hand again?

[12] *U.S. 1* by Muriel Rukeyser. The Viking Press, New York, 1938.

Will the hand reach out for a comforting cigarette,
caress the woman in the cheap gingham dress,
will she put up the coffee, arrange her hair,
give back the touch of love in happiness?

There were a thousand thousand homes that evening
as the moon slid across the sky,
where the clock tick was the only sound
to measure their history by.

But the moon said: It is going to happen,
that room is going to explode and there'll be nothing to lose.
The stars knew that small flames everywhere
were eating themselves to the fuse.[13]

Helene Margaret has made a survey of the blight on America in terms of an answer to the hopefulness and optimistic faith of Walt Whitman, patterned after his *I Celebrate America.* Her poem is entitled *Song of the Answerer,* (a reply to Walt Whitman). Here are the first two stanzas:

I celebrate America,
For every atom belonging to America belongs to you and me,
And is part of us.
Walt Whitman, come down!
And I will sing your message back to you.
Now, in the fourth month, shoulder to shoulder let us talk.

I celebrate the shanties of river-rats no less than the skyscrapers
eighty stories high,
The widow reading, 'We regret we must waive dividends again,'
The Chairman of the Board still drawing his hundred thousand
twice a year.
I am satisfied with what I see:
Sharecroppers starving in the South, mobs milling in Detroit,
The machine guns down the alleys of Chicago,

[13] *The New Republic.*

Thieves, murderers, men who traffic in women,
I give all the same, I receive all the same.
And there will never be any more perfection than there is now." [14]

This whole body of literature embodies a big, stark question mark. It is a moral and spiritual question mark as well as a material one. It is not merely the observation that an economic system hasn't worked. It is the judgment that there is something desperately wrong in a way of life that has issued in so great a catastrophe. The old political and economic faiths have been suspected as being fairy tales in which people did *not* live happily ever after. There is also a feeling of fear, resentment, revolt over the vast dark power of money over life. The decade witnessed a rising sense of fear of political totalitarianism. The histories of lives under the depression give evidence of an awareness of another totalitarianism, equally real, powerful and frightening, the totalitarianism of money.

[14] *The Saturday Review*, December 17, 1938.

CHAPTER 6

THE VOICE OF LABOR

In A. A. MILNE's *Autobiography* he describes a tandem bicycle on which, in his childhood, he used to ride with his brother. He writes, "We had a tandem bicycle. Ken sat behind and had the steering, the bell, and the brakes under his control. I sat in front and had the accidents."

That tandem bicycle pictures rather clearly the theme of labor during the 1930's. Owner and managers sat behind with the economic steering wheel and bell under control. Labor sat in front and got the bumps.

The record which American fiction, poetry and drama set forth of what happened to the great bulk of the people in an economic convulsion, to labor, using this word in largest sense of those whose sole or chief capital is the labor of body and brain, is the most extensive and detailed portrait which any literature of any time can show. It is the most significant and important body of literature of the decade, and may have the most permanent historical value. Certainly it is most important for anyone interested in religion and ethics in the contemporary world.

In a newspaper account of an automobile accident, there was an inspired misprint which throws light on this whole sum of literature dealing with labor. The last line of the report read, "The victim suffered consciousness." That has happened on an enormous scale. The millions of victims of industrial blowout have "suffered consciousness." America has suffered acute consciousness of the human side of the industrial ledger when it goes into the red. A vast service of this class of literature has been to increase that consciousness. For any social progress must come out of a heightened awareness.

Here are considered those portrayals of labor, not merely or primarily descriptive or photographic, but which to some degree embody protest, look in the direction of structural economic change, whether strictly Marxian in character or not. This literature deserves attention for help which it gives in diagnosis of the ills of society and individuals, for its pathway to understanding, and for its challenge to action. Here is what our economic system is doing to people—so what? Where do we go from here?

This is not easy or pleasant reading. Indeed, let it be frankly said, one cannot concentrate on it. Man cannot live on bread alone. He cannot live on realistic social fiction alone. But we must find a place for it in our mental and spiritual outlook, or we become refugees from reality. As we have said, a great liability of life is that of living behind barricades, barricades against ugliness, pain, and against disturbance.

Not all, by any means, of the value of labor literature is to be found in those novels, short stories and plays which deal with conflict situations, with strikes, or which are written from a standpoint urging structural change in the economic basis of society. There is immense value for understanding and for moral and spiritual awareness in the literature which depicts men and women at work, which presents in detail industrial processes. For that furnishes the data for a sharpened sensibility and a vicarious extension of experience.

The increase of knowledge of exactly what multitudes of men, women and children do to earn a living makes for a more genuine appreciation of human worth. There have been a score of novels, only two or three can be glanced at here, which carry the reader into the varied worlds where people supply the primary physical needs of society.

Such an extension of living can be a deeply ethical and religious experience. We can learn what complex machine production means in terms of people; how things are made; what our economic jungle is like to those caught in the lower depths; how it feels to be jobless; what is the terror of losing a job. In *Sun on Their Shoulders* by Elizabeth Eastman, we stoop with the Finns and Portuguese in the mud and muck of a cranberry bog on Cape Cod; in John Klempner's *Once Around the Block,* we work in a Brooklyn chocolate factory with people who are as real as your next door neighbor; in Edward Seaver's *The Company,* we work in an office; in *Christ in Concrete* by Pietro di Donato, we crawl under the skin of an Italian bricklayer and learn what the collapse of an ancient gutted building means.

One sample of the moral value of understanding the process of labor is Wessel Smitter's *F.O.B. Detroit.* In this novel is told a story of workers which avoids both patronizing sentimentality and sensational exaggeration. There is no bugle blown at dawn calling the comrades to the barricades. There are no barricades; not even a strike. There is, however, a portrayal of the inside of Mr. Ford's big machine shop at River Rouge, vivid and full in detail, with an impressive clarity in dealing with technical processes and a fine skill in conveying the feel of life in the shop, its noise, and speed, the tensity of nerves under pressure. There is also the highest achievement of any novelist, the creation of real character. Russ, the hero of the story, is a memorable character, a big human in every sense, made for the life of a pioneer but strayed into the wrong generation, a man who loved 'machines he could run' but who hated 'machines that ran him.' Large parts of it might stand as a true portrait of the adventures of the soul among Mr. Ford's machines. Two men, Russ and Bennie, meet casually in the long line waiting before the gates of the Holt factory, while seeking a job. (The name Holt is substituted for that of Ford, but the eye reads 'Ford' continually.) The two men are skillfully contrasted: Russ, an outdoor man who had never seen a factory till he starts to work in the auto plant, innocent of formal education but keen in mind, a master of big machines, who found a real fulfillment of himself in handling a giant manipulator in the drop forge and whose marvelous capacity was finally wasted on the assembly line; Bennie, his partner, who had worked in a factory all his life, docile, kindly, dumb.

Russ learns to run the great machine which throws around ten-ton lumps of metal as though they were pieces of sugar in genteel tongs. Then with ruthlesness the job, the machine and the man become obsolete through technological change. Russ and Bennie go on the line. The description of the work on the line is the high spot of the book, as strong a piece of writing on the effect of mass production on men as I have ever read. Then comes the layoff, the dwindling cash, the breaking of morale, all the features of the life of thousands in "dynamic" Detroit.

Into the mouth of Russ is put incisive criticism of the process, with irony and sarcasm. Let one quotation suffice as a sample of the flavor. Russ is talking of two kinds of machines:

"Some machines build us up—help us to make the most of ourselves. Some tear us apart—grind us down. A machine geared to a man—is one thing. A man geared to a machine—is something else. One's human, gives you a chance to be your best self. The other works on you, like a gear-cutter—whittling you down, chiseling at you, cutting grooves in you, making you like all the other small gears that work on the line.

But in the motor assembly, Bennie, it's different. There the machine is the boss. The machine does the nice work—the hard work—the part that takes skill. The machine's everything and gets credit for the work done. You're nothing until you've learned to be a gear—a small part of the big machine—until there's nothing left of you but a very small cog without any will. You start and stop when the machine's ready—go slow or fast as the machine tells you. The machine counts—you don't. Any why should you? You don't furnish the brains. You don't furnish the skill. All you do is fasten a nut, put on a washer, stamp on a number. The machine does the real job. It's the big boss standing over your head—grinding you down—wasting your strength—whittling away at your brain. Making you a small part of its dead, mechanical self." [1]

In great contrast to this, another sort of labor is drawn in John Herrmann's *The Salesman*, a picture of the life of a salesman in depression days; the story of a dull little man leading a dull life, but the very lifelikeness of its detail and the pathos of its character make it an authentic and moving tale. The man on the road, trying to pump up sufficient enthusiasm over selling picture frames, is a familiar figure. Robert Cranford wanted to be an engineer. The depression caught him as it did thousands, at college. He became a salesman on commission for the Marvel Art Frame Company whose owner kept the best accounts for himself and allowed the salesman the privilege of pegging away at hopeless prospects. It says, convincingly, "This, too, was the life of labor."

Some look, even though it must be a hurried one through a telescope, must be taken at one of the most bitterly contested literary battlefields of the decade, the subject of the "proletarian novel," its nature and destiny. Dealing with the phrase in its strictly ideological meaning, (terrifying word, that, ideological) the end of the long discussion seems to be that while

[1] *F.O.B. Detroit* by Wessel Smitter. Harper and Brothers, New York, 1938.

there was much heated argument about it, there were very
few samples of simon pure totalitarian literature produced.
That is, proletarian in the sense of V. F. Calverton's definition as "literature dominated by a dynamic revolutionary idea
and inspired by a collective purpose." Trying to discover such
literature in terms of particular novels and plays brings reminders of the familiar poem about the "man who wasn't
there" again and again on the stairway. But while the battle
was going on it was fast and furious. Left wing literary criticism hotly and dogmatically asserted that no literature was
significant that was not written from the proletarian standpoint, that is, that did not have as its basis the class struggle
and a belief in the working class as the dominant class of tomorrow and the maker of the future. But it is easy to see that
the end of that way is death to literature, for, again in Calverton's words, it "substitutes for the literary worth of a novel or
play, a judgment on its economic point of view." That would
mean the arrival of a new paralyzing orthodoxy, with Karl
Marx at the fords of the Jordan, with his uplifted sword, or
more appropriately, a hammer and sickle, demanding of the
author, "now say, Shibboleth."

Against the pretentious jargon of defining an orthodox literary party line, a large company of readers have had their
minds expressed in the deflating verse of Arthur Guiterman,
in his plea to the ideologists:

> There used to be conclusions, thoughts and notions
>   Unbound by crooked etymologies,
> But now we may not even have emotions
>   Except as parts of ideologies.
>
> Oh, writers, pedants, students of psychology,
>   Professors old, reporters fresh and green,
> Please let us hear no more of "ideology;"
>   The word "ideas" expresses all you mean.[2]

[2] *The Saturday Review of Literature*, January 22, 1939.

A few years ago, *The Saturday Review* published a rather terrifying cartoon showing a young woman with an uncompromisingly intellectual face and gleam in her eye, demanding of a baffled clerk in a book store, "Show me a class conscious Mother Goose."

That stern demand is not so many miles away from one much fought battlefield in the realm of fiction. Sentinels on the watch tower signal down that the demand for 'a class conscious Mother Goose' and other forms of creative literature is abating, even in 'class conscious' circles. This has been evidenced in many ways and from many sources, from the changing attitude toward literature shown in Russia, to the work of novelists who carry no burden of 'party line' or propaganda purpose. One strong impression which is made by the fiction parade is that novelists dealing with contemporary life, economic and social, are not only increasing in quantity, but, in notable examples, are far better in quality than their predecessors dealing with the same material. This one fact, if it be a fact, and not merely a personal judgment, is of first importance and interest to all concerned with the ethical and social and, in a broad sense, the religious, issues of our time. For it means that novels, which are the only windows through which a large percentage of the population look out on the contemporary social scene, are clearer and more revealing. We have seen many impressive instances of the paradox of fiction, that just in proportion that a novel is a work of sincere art and less of a propaganda tract, does it become an effective opinion-making force.

Of course the theological debates in the sanhedrins of 'literary leftism' still go on. There is still much reverential hailing of third rate literary hacks, as geniuses, and still the application of the one rule of Marxian orthodoxy to all fiction, poetry and drama. But, in general, the judgment of John

Chamberlain that 'the literary left is growing up' has much foundation.

The subsidence of the issue of strictly proletarian fiction may be more clearly understood if we take a historical recollection over the ten years. In the early years of the nineteen thirties, which were the years when the disturbance of the depression was deepest and most shocking, there was a distinct messianic mood abroad, not only among the left wing of labor but more widely extended, including authors. Such prophets had ribald skepticism for the hope that prosperity was just around the corner. They did believe that revolution was just around the corner. The latter proved to be an even more naive faith than the former. Yet in the early years of the depression, large numbers stood on tip toe and strained their eyes, convinced that the day of the Lord was at hand, coming, naturally, from the general direction of Moscow. The hope of the Magnificat was to be brought about in economic terms, "He hath put down the mighty from their seats and exalted them of low degree." This revolution, which never came, was responsible for the confidence which looked for a revolutionary literature, embodying the class struggle and all the thirty-nine articles of the Marxian creed. With the hope long deferred as the thirties turned into the forties, as reaction got up from a sick bed and stretched its muscles again, as the Russian-German agreement completed the process of disillusion, the revolutionary hope died or retired to obscure cellars. There have been a few "proletarian" writers in the sense of the strict definition, such as Dahlberg, Edward Newhouse, Albert Maltz, Grace Lumpkin. But the great majority of books dealing with labor, and by far the best part, has been done by writers not concerned to toe a party line but showing emphatically an awareness to the major issues of their generation. It has been marked by something far more valuable than any radical orthodoxy, that is by "direct honest writing about workers, not in the mass, but as individuals." This body of work does disagree entirely with the arbitrary pronouncement of Willa Cather, "Economics and art are strangers," a typical apology from one who has conducted one of the most conspicuous retreats from contemporary life of any first-class artist in her time. Economics, covering as that word does, so much of the vital interests of humanity, furnishes themes to stir the artist, as every human situation does. Robert Herrick, one of the pioneers of realistic fiction in America, has expressed a legitimate theme of the sincere artist, "the horror, the squalor, the physical and spiritual degradations of the mass who are the hopeless, and often sordid victims of an incoherently motivated society."

An underlying reality in most of the literature broadly dealing with labor and industry, is the familiar "social lag." Collectivism is an already achieved reality in the economic, social and political framework of our society. But the type of social thinking which is necessary to direct those collectivist realities is still individualistic. So are the mass of the people. A clear picture of that lag is found in a symbolic form in Anne Morrow Lindbergh's *North to the Orient*. She describes the first airplane trip she took from her home in New Jersey to her summer home in Maine. It was a journey which she remembered well having taken fourteen hours by train. The airplane trip took two hours. Mrs. Lindbergh observes quaintly that her body got there twelve hours before her mind did. That is a fair picture of the industrial world. Its body has arrived at collectivism. Its mind is sadly belated. The literature of labor deals with the results on the lives and personalities of people while this tragic lag is going on.

Very possibly one natural reason for the appearance of a number of novels of genuine power dealing with economic and social questions is that the depression has gone on long enough to allow for artistic interpretations to be made of its impact on life. It was ten years after the war that the best of the novels dealing with the war began to appear. We cannot say that these recent novels are the depression "remembered in tranquillity," for no tranquillity has appeared. But there has been a long enough time to bring perspective and allow for artistic presentation.

It is evident that if literature is forced to wear the clothes of her loud sister, propaganda, she would soon lose her identity. There could be no art, only the mechanical assault and battery of beating a theme to death with a sledge hammer. It is so easy for novelists who are concerned with sociological problems to make their characters mere by-products of these problems or pegs on which to hang their ready-made solutions. Now there is general recognition that it is not the function of the artist to teach economics, but to open men's eyes and to warm their understanding. That is the great value in labor literature, in the broad sense of that dealing with industrial and rural life from the point of view of the factory worker and the poor farmer under conditions which are destroying him and forcing him to fight. It renders great service to real understanding in showing the condition of life by the environment. In the words of Dr. Henry Seidel Canby—

"It is folly to suppose that a society which reads a daily paper, sees a news reel weekly, and hears the radio every other hour, is going to be novelized successfully by the old-time story teller who assumed that a 'character' was an independent personality instead of a consciousness, floating on a stream of impressions." [3]

That is a sort of vacuum literature which shows diminishing returns. The big thing is that interest moved from surface problems to deeper ones—from an itch to cancer. Through it

[3] *Seven Years' Harvest* by Henry Seidel Canby. Farrar and Rinehart, 1936.

is heard the rumble of Lowell's line, "The time is ripe, and rotten ripe, for change." Our effort to sense some of the feeling of the literature of labor must be by brief and few selections from a great number. Note two points of great value first. The appearance of this new labor literature, following a period when the neurasthenic school of post-war decadents concerned with gin, sex and Freud received wide homage, is very significant. It would be hard to overestimate its immense social, ethical and religious importance.

Second, much of this literature was lived before it was written. Most of the writers are young. They write what they know intimately and painfully. It is more than clever reporting. Authors can say with Ulysses, "I am a part of all I saw."

The world reported by John Dos Passos is far more than a labor world. He has taken as his theme nothing less than the U. S. A., which, most appropriately, is the inclusive title given to the one volume edition of his trilogy of novels, *The Forty-Second Parallel, 1919* and *The Big Money*. It is probably the biggest canvass ever worked on in American literature. Thomas Wolfe wrote more words, but his themes are far smaller in range and significance. Yet so much of Dos Passos' work deals with labor in one form and another, reveals so continuously the consequences of a profit-motivated order, that the general field of labor seems the most fitting place to include him. Much might be said of Dos Passos as an inventor of techniques, the "breadthwise cutting," the camera eye, the biographies inserted between chapters of narrative. But that is not our present interest in his work. Our concern is the ethical implications of his picture of American life. This is to be found in his weaving of a highly colored and complex fabric out of the threads of individual lives from many sections of the population. In spite of his desire to present a representative portrait, whole areas of life are left out entirely and so give a badly distorted picture. Accepting Dos Passos' gallery of characters as a fair presentation of America would be as great a mistake as making up our mind about the health of Chicago on the basis of data gathered exclusively from medical clinics. To many people, reading a Dos Passos novel is a new form of torture. But he has caught realistically the swirl of life, particularly the downward pulling current. There is realism, sympathy, poetry and hot moral indignation over waste of valuable human material.

Here is the *U. S. A.* in a typical etching, incidentally, it is a characterization of his trilogy:

"U. S. A. is the slice of a continent. U. S. A. is a group of holding companies, some aggregations of trade unions, a set of laws bound in calf, a radio network, a chain of moving-picture theaters, a column of stock quotations rubbed out and written in by a Western Union boy on a blackboard, a public library full of old newspapers and dog-eared history books with protests scrawled on the margins in pencil. U. S. A. is the world's greatest river-valley fringed with mountains and hills. U. S. A. is a set of big-mouthed officials with too many bank accounts. U. S. A. is a lot of men buried in their uniforms in Arlington Cemetery. U. S. A. is the letters at the end of an address when you are away from home. But mostly U. S. A. is the speech of the people." [4]

In his first novel, *Manhattan Transfer,* there is the movement of a whole city; in the trilogy, that of a whole country. It is done by type characters, by devices to catch the fleeting and chaotic life of the country, by the newsreels, headlines, songs, conversation, the mixed blur any time gives, the camera eye. He gives biographies of representative figures. His best work appears in these. He gives life stories, showing for the most part that interlaced individual destiny is controlled by the drift of society as a whole. He has a strong sense of the waste

[4] *U. S. A.* by John Dos Passos. Modern Library Edition. Random House, 1938.

of human material, and indignation over vulgar and materialistic standards. It is a varied gallery, a printer who joins the
I.W.W., an advertising man, a Harvard poet, a Chicago
minister's daughter, a Swedish boy, drifting from job to job,
a bespectacled Jew from Brooklyn, who becomes a radical
and pacifist. His social feeling shows strongly in the last novel
—*The Big Money*. It is well named, for Big Money is its
theme. It follows both *The Forty-Second Parallel* and *1919*
in theme and technique. The author's real hero is America;
he has aimed to give a cross section of American life at three
periods. *The Forty-Second Parallel* has as its theme the expansion of business before the war, the reckless, bumptious optimism of those lusty years, seen through its impact on a
group of widely different lives. *1919* pictured the effect of the
war on the America which stayed at home. *The Big Money*
catches the mood and tempo of the 1920's, with its big booms,
with multitudes rushing after money under one impulse, like
Gadarene swine towards a steep place. The reader should
begin with the biography of Thorstein Veblen, for the mind
of Veblen is central to the whole interpretation of the money
domination of American life and its effects. Indeed, Mr. Dos
Passos has furnished a dramatization of Veblen's *Theory of
the Leisure Class*, and *The Theory of Business Enterprise*.
The narrative shows people in a mad rush to the points where
money is flowing. Here are the tragedies of people warped and
distorted in an age of shoddy culture and vulgarity. On the
structure of four lives, Mr. Dos Passos hangs a massive pan-
orama of the 1920's: New York, Hollywood, inflated Miami
before the boom burst, 'dynamic' Detroit, Minnesota farms
and Colorado mines, with a wide ranging dramatis personae
from big bankers to communist organizers and movie queens.

In the main, there is a truly Elizabethan quality about him,
the capacity, that is, which the great Elizabethan dramatists

had so markedly, of visualization, of making abstractions and symbols come to life as concrete things. To a strong degree, *The Big Money* has the aspect of being a highly moral tract, a tragic homily on the text 'the love of money is the root of all kinds of evil' with its Q.E.D. of wasted lives and a whole culture debauched by a lust for material wealth. It is an American success story, with a savage satire on the 'success'— Horatio Alger in reverse. It has also the unintended but striking value of showing the futility of lives not far above the level of the animal, the emptiness of life in which God and all absolute values and standards have been abandoned. The novel might well be a footnote to the picture of our time given by Berdyaev, in *The End of Our Time,* "When man broke away from the spiritual moorings of his life, he tore himself from the depths and went to the surface, and he has become more and more superficial. When man lost the spiritual center of being, he lost his own at the same time." The conclusion of *The Big Money* gives a memorable picture of Youth in the United States—a hitch-hiker hailing for a ride:

"The young man waits at the edge of the concrete, with one hand he grips a rubbed suitcase of phony leather, the other hand almost making a fist, thumb up

that moves in ever so slight an arc when a car slithers past, a truck roars clatters; the wind of cars passing ruffles his hair, slaps grit in his face.

Head swims, hunger has twisted the belly tight,

he has skinned a heel through the torn sock, feet ache in the broken shoes, under the threadbare suit carefully brushed off with the hand, the torn drawers have a crummer feel, the feel of having slept in your clothes; in the nostrils lingers the staleness of discouraged carcasses crowded into a transient camp, the carbolic stench of the jail, on the taut cheeks the shamed flush from the boring eyes of cops and deputies, railroad-bulls (they eat three squares a day, they are buttoned into well-made clothes, they have

wives to sleep with, kids to play with after supper, they work for
the big men who buy their way, they stick their chests out with
the sureness of power behind their backs). Git the hell out,
scram. Know what's good for you, you'll make yourself scarce. Git-
tin' tough, eh? Think you kin take it, eh?

The punch in the jaw, the slam on the head with the night-
stick, the wrist grabbed and twisted behind the back, the big
knee brought up sharp into the crotch,

the walk out of town with sore feet to stand and wait at the
edge of the hissing speeding string of cars where the reek of
ether and lead and gas melts into the silent grassy smell of the
earth.

Eyes black with want seek out the eyes of the drivers, a hitch,
a hundred miles down the road." [5]

It is to be hoped that some day the biographies of prominent American figures which are found in profusion in the
trilogy will be assembled and printed in a separate volume.
There are insight into the real forces of American life, tributes
to truly great people, these being often people who carried on
the battle for a genuine democracy against a dominant money
empire. His biography of the unknown soldier is a piece of
withering irony and sarcasm. Here is an illustration from the
biography of Wesley Everest, the labor leader so brutally
lynched and tortured in the red hysteria in the Northwest in
1919. Dos Passos' passionate anger is strongly felt:

"Wesley Everest was a logger like Paul Bunyan.

The lumberjacks, loggers, shingleweavers, sawmill workers were
the helots of the timber empire; the I.W.W. put the idea of industrial democracy in Paul Bunyan's head; wobbly organizers said
the forests ought to belong to the whole people, said Paul Bunyan
ought to be paid in real money instead of in company script,
ought to have a decent place to dry his clothes, wet from the
sweat of a day's work in zero weather and snow, an eight hour
day, clean bunkhouses, wholesome grub; when Paul Bunyan came

[5] *The Big Money* by John Dos Passos. Harcourt, Brace & Co., 1937.

back from making Europe safe for the democracy of the Big Four, he joined the lumberjack's local to help make the Pacific slope safe for the workingstiffs. The wobblies were reds. Not a thing in this world Paul Bunyan's ascared of.

(To be a red in the summer of 1919 was worse than being a hun or a pacifist in the summer of 1917.)

The timber owners, the sawmill and shinglekings were patriots; they'd won the war (in the course of which the price of lumber had gone up from $16 a thousand feet to $116; there are even cases where the government paid as high as $1200 a thousand for spruce); they set out to clean the reds out of the logging camps; free American institutions must be preserved at any cost;

so they formed the Employers Association and the Legion of Loyal Loggers, they made it worth their while for bunches of ex-soldiers to raid I.W.W. halls, lynch and beat up organizers, burn subversive literature." [6]

Dos Passos does not write from a literary soap box. His 1939 novel, *The Adventures of a Young Man,* shows clearly how far he is from any communist "party line." Indeed a main reason for writing that story seems to have been to give him opportunity to criticize and "show up" the communist party, its leadership and methods, by showing the disillusioning experience of Glenn Spotswood, a labor organizer who tries to work for the party, is betrayed and killed in Spain. Yet the force and the point of Don Passos' indictment of society are clear. Strangely enough, an accurate description of Dos Passos is to be found in Judge Learned Hand's description of an ideal Supreme Court bench: "They must be aware of changing tensions in every society which make it an organism; which demand new schemata of adaptation; which will disrupt it if rigidly confined." Of all this Dos Passos is continuously aware. He sees that under the present technology life is collective; he knows the social forces which are conditioning it. He sees America as a fighting arena, with "two nations," after the

[6] *Ibid.*

pattern of Disraeli's analysis of mid-victorian England, the exploited and the exploiters.

Albert Halper has been one of the most skillful portrayers of labor, writing from a varied experience in all sorts of labor. *Union Square* was a kaleidoscopic glimpse of the churning life centering about Union Square, when that breathing spot in New York in the twenties was far more of a municipal soap box and radical center than it is now. All varieties of life cross its pages as they crossed the square. He is no solemn propagandist. Indeed, the most vigorous scene in the book is that in which he deflates the pretentiousness of literary, "arty," sentimental communists. When a demonstration was being arranged, all that these precious fellow travelers could do was talk and drink gin; the only craftsman who could actually do anything of value was the carpenter who made the signs. *The Foundry* is a breadthwise cutting of a Chicago electrotyping factory, one of the most human and balanced pictures of a group of men at work which has ever been drawn in the United States. Like a bass chord in the symphony, the foundry roars, pounds, hammers and rattles. That roar affects everyone in the book. There is enough photographic detail to satisfy Zola. "Here," the novel says to the reader, "is life conditioned by the job." We can feel the raw Chicago streets on zero mornings in winter; we perspire with the heat of August. The conflict of labor with the machine has a central place. The proprietor buys a plate flattening machine. The men, when they realize the threat of the new machine to their jobs, revert in fear to the old smash-the-machine methods of the Luddites in England. Max'l complains of the wrecking to the business agent of the union. When the agent gets the promise that no workers will be discharged, the machine works perfectly. This gives the workers a feeling of a great victory over the machine. But an old fashioned radical soon brings

out the realities of modern industry: "Now don't get cocky.
This little victory of ours is only temporary. Don't think we
can go on beating the machine forever."

The Chute is the exploration of a microcosm in Chicago,
the inside of a mail order house. It is just as though the author,
in the manner of Tennyson's "Flower in the Crannied Wall,"
had taken a seventy-nine cent pair of Sears Roebuck overalls
in his hands, saying: "If I could know all about you, all the
human life that has gone into your making and distributing,
all the labor, turmoil, the killing speed, the sweat, the tears,
the blood, the vigor, the courage, the heartbreak, I would
know a lot about American society." Halper comes close to
fulfilling that promise, as far as the physical and emotional
details are concerned. It is high tribute to the book to say
that it is a long headache. His conveying of the noise, the
speed of the work of assembling the orders, the fear of insecurity, is so real that it hurts. Halper has been an 'order
picker' in a mail order house.

In one sense, the hero of the novel is the merchandise and
the mail order business. Customers down in Arkansas, Missouri, Texas, Alabama, were clamoring for the Ironsides Whip
and Work Pants, Big Four Star Quality Never Rip Husky
Shirts, and Grizzly Bear Champion Overalls. In the cotton
patches of the south, and the corn lands of the mid-west,
farmers and their sons, sitting down by light, wrote in their
painful scrawls, asking the Golden Rule Company to 'please
hurry up their orders as Luke and me are spring plowin' and
need the new overalls quick, as the old ones are 'bout gone.'

That is the receiving end. At the firing end, we see the
chute, a symbol of the whole process, comparable to William
Vaughn Moody's 'The Brute'—a machine devouring human
sacrifices. It is a round black monster in the center of the building into whose open mouth must be poured every half-hour

the offering of merchandise collected at exhausting speed. The thread running through the book is the story of the Sussman family. The boy, Paul, is forced to give up a dream of an architectural career, modeled after that of Louis Sullivan, to work in the mail order house.

No aspect of the frantic bustle is left out, the boys zooming down the aisles on roller skates, the ruthless lay off and unpaid overtime, the toll of tuberculosis, the difficulties of labor organization in such a group, the crafty paternalistic policy of the company, the higher-ups themselves being the pawns of high finance, which finally grasps the company and closes it out. And all through can be heard the harsh accompaniment, "Feed the chute, feed her, your ten-thirty orders are ten minutes late!"

During the ten years, the strike as a labor weapon has had its most complete and effective portrayal. Part, at least, of that library ought to be required reading for every person who wishes to understand the tensions and major issues of his time.

We can get the feel of the background from a description by James Rorty in his travel book of America during the depression, *Where Life Is Better*. Here is his picture of steel towns about Pittsburgh:

"The dreary sodden steel towns; the vast sprawling weight of collapsed industry choking the valleys of the Monongahela, the Allegheny, the Ohio; the blind bitter clutch of the steel masters on this clutter of inert machinery; the aimless drift of harassed half starved men through the streets; the dogged struggle of the union against a terror that speaks sharply in Court, but barks out of muzzles of automatics in the walled towns where steel is made, and where, under cover of pious phrases, the Amalgamated is being whittled and starved and blacklisted to death."

Not all are as bitter as Mr. Rorty, but are marked by competent factual reporting and sometimes by creative imagination. They give authentic data for a front trench history of labor's war.

Only a few of the novels portraying strikes can even be named here as samples, much less dealt with in any adequate way. No one will need to read a large part of the novels to get some, at least, of the contribution they have to make to social awareness, understanding and sympathy. Many have suffered from following a formula which becomes trite, mechanical and tiresome. They follow a pattern as rigid as the lived-happily-ever-after romance, for which their authors have lordly contempt. We have the grinding down of the workers, the strike, its defeat, and as a climax, a sort of Hollywood "came the dawn" ending in which the hero (and heroine, usually) see coming over the hills the messianic vision of worker's solidarity. Sinclair Lewis has summed up this pattern as "moving from back-ache to belly-ache."

But a growing number of labor novels have a far more adequate content than this. There is accurate recording of strike procedures, real human characters, and insight into motivation. Among the novels of permanent worth are Robert Cantwell's *Land of Plenty* dealing with life and labor in an Oregon lumber mill; John Steinbeck's *In Dubious Battle* located among the fruit pickers of California, and William Rollins, Jr.'s *The Shadow Before*, portraying a strike, using as his models a combination of actual history of textile strikes in New Bedford and Gastonia, North Carolina. *In Dubious Battle* is both proletarian in its sympathies and artistic in its execution. It deals with the west coast, communist-led strike of apple pickers. There is no direct propaganda; no editorial writing. The book is not a tract. The agricultural and economic background is clearly spread out. The focus of the action is strike headquarters, the two communist leaders, and the doctor who gave his services and sympathy, but remains aloof from the fury and the fervor. All the community alignments are pictured in realistic fashion—the holy denunciation of the "reds," which is so constant a feature of labor clashes, the patriotic spasms of the Hearsts, the struggle within the strikers' ranks. Mr. Steinbeck also makes sharp comments on "the infantile disease of leftism," to use Lenin's words. The book has the rare advantage among labor novels that it can be read as an exciting story and psychological study of mass action by one who has small or no sympathy for the radical labor movement.

Rollins' *The Shadow Before* suffers from too much stylistic homage to Dos Passos and, apparently, to James Joyce. At times he seems to tire of labor as a theme and turns eagerly to sex. Yet it is one of the most carefully documented studies of a strike that has ever been done. In particular, his narratives of strike strategy and the life-like recording of what actually happens on a picket line are superb. The clashes between police and strikers, the barrages of insults and, at times, good natured, if rough, repartee, the "framing" of the leaders and the crushing of the strike give a strong sense of the discipline achieved by labor in an unequal fight.

The textile strikes at Gastonia and Marion, North Carolina, have had the most elaborate fictional treatment of any. They appear in four novels of the ten years, two by Fielding Burke (Mrs. Olive Tilford Dargan), *Call Home the Heart* and *A Stone Came Rolling*; and two by Grace Lumpkin, *To Make My Bread* and *A Sign for Cain*. They deal with an important historical development, a shift of population due to economic forces, one of the significant "treks" of the twentieth century, not nearly as large as that from the "dust bowl" westward a few years later, but one exemplifying the way in which modern industrialism has caused a reversion to the old nomadic tribe migrations of early history. The people of the mountains of western North Carolina and Tennessee came down from the hills, drawn by the powerful magnet of the newly located mills, which had been coming south all through the twenties. Often the moving of the highlanders was made even more compulsory by selling their land out from under them to lumber companies, in somewhat the same manner that English farm laborers were driven into the factories by the enclosures of the common land in the early stages of the industrial revolution. These people from the hill country were in no position to bargain for wages. They took what was offered them; they were the "cheap and docile" labor which was the attraction drawing the mills to the South. The theme of these four novels has been crowded into a few words of concise description:

"To be given a company house with a bathroom, to live in a town, to work for a money income, to be offered employment for all the members of the family: the golden age so long promised by Republican orators had arrived. Potential workers swarmed into the mill towns. But there, alas, new-found miseries proved worse than the old. There were not enough houses. Several families were herded together. The bathrooms had no water. They were used as sleeping quarters, the tubs as beds. The wages did not meet minimum expenses. Mothers saw their babies sicken for lack of milk. The company doctor recommended orange juice! The babies died. The machines, the stretch-out, the increased quotas forced many from their jobs. Pellagra smote them. They brooded in hopelessness. Their incomprehending desperation was the opportunity for the labor organizers. The way out was a strike. The workers strike. They are answered by the state militia and the hired and deputized thugs imported to beat down the workers. They are denied the elementary rights of free citizens. They are clubbed, gassed, shot, imprisoned, starved and evicted. They are caught in the trap of ignorance and of poverty, and what can they do? They can suffer and then they can die. For nothing is cheaper in American industry than human workers."

The novels of both Fielding Burke and Grace Lumpkin

follow the same general scheme, showing the exploitation of the new labor supply, the results of the stretch out system, the goading to resistance, strike, and defeat, with the strong implication of the futility of anything less than a reshaping of the economic order, with labor organization as a primary tool. The novels of Fielding Burke are unusual in their style and skill in human portraiture. She is a poet, with a poet's sensitiveness to nature, and deep and genuine human feeling. Beyond that, there is the clearest appreciation of the relation of religion to the class struggle, both as a hindrance and potential power, that has ever been shown in a labor novel. This will be noticed more closely in a later chapter.

Less distinguished for style, but realistic in detail and grasp of the economic and social issues of textile towns in the South, are Grace Lumpkin's *To Make My Bread* and *A Sign for Cain*. She deals with the same region as does Fielding Burke, and through the aristocratic and political feuds, the race antagonisms and the labor conflicts, the rising tide of social unrest is seen and felt. There are both melodrama and a frankly "proletarian" viewpoint. There are also vivid drama and an economic realism which enable readers to look out on a too unfamiliar scene. The implication in both novels is that expressed in the last words of Joe Hill, the I.W.W. hero and martyr, "Don't weep for me, organizer." The heroine of *To Make My Bread*, Bonnie McClure, is shot during the strike, and John Stevens, the leader, as indigenous a product of the neighborhood as the red earth, even though the company designated him as an "outside organizer," thus puts the case for action by the workers. He is referring to the restraint of the conventional clergy, acting as a drag on the workers:

"And, so we won't do anything about our misery, they keep us in the darkness of ignorance and talk about death, to keep our eyes on death and heaven, so we won't think too much about life. We are taught that to struggle is a sin.

But it ain't a sin, John . . . We must join with all others like us and take what is ours. For it is our hands that have built, and our hands that run the machines and ours that dig the coal and keep the furnaces going, and our hands that bring in the wheat for flour. And because we have worked and suffered, we will understand that all should work and all should enjoy the good things of life. It is for us who know to make a world in which there will not be masters, and no slaves except the machines." [7]

Citizens by Meyer Levin, published in the spring of 1940, seems by far the strongest novel dealing with labor which an American author has produced. It is a massive and effective social case study of the so-called "Memorial Day massacre" in South Chicago during the Little Steel Strike in 1937, when ten strikers were cruelly shot down and killed, and many others wounded, by the Chicago police. In this novel, the voluminous records compiled by the Senate Committee on Education and Labor, popularly known as the La Follette Committee, come to life in human character and drama. Let it be granted that *Citizens* is more notable as an impressive project in education in the realities of the labor conflict than as a strictly literary achievement in the realization and creation of memorable characters. That does not detract from its importance and interest. No book of the decade carries a greater amount of accurate material, based on well documented sources necessary to understanding an area of life, of first importance today; destined to be still more important, in view of the present temper of the country, with all sorts of reaction coming out of convalescence with new-found strength, red hunts conducted under every bed and in every pulpit and school room, with a war hysteria providing the perfect climatic conditions for

[7] *To Make My Bread* by Grace Lumpkin. The Macaulay Co., New York, 1933.

an American fascism, decked out in the trimmings of a "defense of democracy." Mr. Levin takes as the central figure a man entirely outside the ranks of labor, a citizen, Dr. Mitch Wilner. This indicates the significance of the title, *Citizens*. It is the record of the education of a normal citizen, by his contacts with the "massacre," begun accidentally. Thus the book becomes a means for the education of the conscience of the reader, as the history it records gave an education in responsible citizenship to Dr. Wilner. He and his family happened to be driving by picnic grounds from which started the peaceful and unarmed mass picketing parade to the steel mill, where the police, for reasons never clearly discovered, opened fire. Dr. Wilner is carried along with the advancing group of workers, sees the shootings, becomes the physician of many of the wounded, some of whom died. Gradually he is drawn into the protest activity, getting, against his intention, deeper and deeper into the struggle, and learns at first hand the tortuous windings of the whole labor world—the activities of the police, and the political powers behind them in preventing the truth about the shootings coming out, the distortion by the newspapers, the activities of the communistic factions in the union. All this raises new and disturbing questions in Dr. Wilner, leading to an alarming discovery of an America he never knew. At the outset we find him, standing in the place of an average middle class American, just aware of his ignorance of the industrial processes.

"Beyond the tracks, on a lip curving into the lake, was the steel plant. The mass of buildings with long high windowless walls and peaked roofs, the batches of smokestacks, stood cut out against lake and sky. There came to him, momentarily, the same sense of inexcusable ignorance he had often felt on driving past such plants, or past oil refineries: how could a man remain so ignorant of these processes that were fundamental to his civilization? He had passed his life within a few miles of all these things, but did not know what the shapes of the buildings held." [8]

The main body of the story is interspersed with biographical studies of the men who were killed. This makes a sort of labor *The Ring And The Book;* various histories leading up to the same event are told, giving a close-up picture of the human units in the steel industry. There are nine stories in all, including that of a Polish crane man, "Wyzy"; Damon, an open hearth man; a young Swede on the rolling crew; a Mexican brick loader, originally imported as a strike breaker; and various others typical of racial and occupational groups. His shock at such discoveries in his own backyard is thus described:

"Then, as he stumbled into that dark chamber, Mitch Wilner experienced the ultimate sensation of helplessness; it went all through his being like the dying vibration of a shut-off current. The shock of the scene was like nothing he had ever known before, was far beyond that of the first time he had lost a patient, was altogether different from the prepared-for shock of a first entrance into a dissecting-room. During one long instant he wanted to flee; somehow he would convince himself he had never been here, never been confronted with this task; this scene had never existed." [9]

His conscience begins to awaken and disturb him:

"Yet he could not deny to himself that in a way a man's place in society did not end with his profession. If it was his duty to do all he could as a doctor, wasn't it likewise his duty to do a complete job as a citizen?" [10]

The personal problem of the danger to his economic and professional security, the price that might have to be paid by

[8] *Citizens* by Meyer Levin. The Viking Press, 1940.
[9] *Ibid.*
[10] *Ibid.*

his family if he gave the aid to the workers' cause which his conscience demanded, is strongly brought out in a conversation with his wife. (This is a crucial problem of every liberal stirred to indignation against gross injustice).

"Oh, Mitch," Sylvia said, "why waste anymore time on this whole affair? It's all right to be idealistic, and I still sympathize with the strikers of course, but it's all mixed up with things that we never bargained for, and when it comes to such things as supporting every plan that Frank Sobol might have had, I don't know why we should sacrifice ourselves."

"I don't feel that I'm sacrificing anything," he said.

"Oh, no. Only your practice and your clinic, and by the time you get through they'll even drop you from the staff. Don't you think I don't know what's happening even if you don't feel your family is important enough to be confided in about these things." Her voice was dry in her throat. He felt a warm, intimate pity for her, but he could not help her.[11]

Toward the end he discerns what before had been unbelievable, the outlines of an American fascist mentality, a vicious totalitarianism which springs from profit and speaks dogmatically with guns, blackmail, economic pressure and murder. He sees, as Dos Passos does, the "two nations" facing each other in battle, within the same political framework:

"And why should it be astonishing to him that the same people who broke strikes were the people who agitated against aliens and who printed anti-Semitic stuff and who distributed literature supplied through a German consulate? This should be no more astonishing than that the people who organized unions were the same people who agitated for unemployment relief and for racial tolerance and eventually for some kind of socialism."[12]

Notable in this novel is the absence of any party line dogmatism. The central feature of it is agony of wonder, bewilder-

[11] *Ibid.*
[12] *Ibid.*

ment and questioning in the mind of the "citizen" who can see
the competition for power among labor groups, with the
jealousy and "double crossing" as well as the ruthless violence
of the "Consolidated Steel Corporation," which forced the decision by the gun, rather than trust any democratic processes
of settlement. The novel has no solution; it does describe the
presence of a situation that must be solved, if anything resembling the United States as a democracy is to be preserved.

Among the large number of novels dealing primarily with
labor, only a few with varied locations can be named, as
samples of a dominant interest. Leane Zugsmith's *A Time To
Remember* carries the reader into a relatively fresh world, that
of the white collar worker in a department store. The world
of Diamond's department store comes to life from the King
down through shoe salesmen to stock boys and teamsters. The
intricacy of the caste system in the store, the frantic pressure
for jobs and the haunting fear of losing them, the conflict
of a strike, are convincingly handled. The growing sense of
solidarity in these hitherto aloof workers, painfully conscious
of their own "genteel" quality, with the proletarian workers,
is the climax, even the "message," of the book.

Jordanstown by Josephine Johnson deals with poverty and
the "lower downs" in a typical American middle western town
near the border between north and south. It has beauty, a gift
for arresting figures of speech, social protest. It is both timely
in its portrayal of relief problems in the years of the depression, and timeless in its overtones of the continuing struggle of man.

Jordanstown itself is the theme—it might be Everytown—
its divisions of class and race, its contrasts of comfort and suffering, smug content and despair. The central figure is Allen
Craig, whose father lost everything in the stock crash of '29, a
sensitive young man, dropped from the top class to the bottom.

Craig buys, on a shoestring and hope, the local newspaper and tries to give voice to the inarticulately disinherited. More than that, he organizes a protest of the people on relief, starts a movement to build a hall, which promises to turn into a co-operative movement. A Labor Day demonstration is smashed by the police, with the inevitable arrests which form an old, old story in hundreds of American towns. The leaders go to jail; Craig's friend, the radical David, dies as a result; but at the end we get the suggestion of the ongoing struggle.

A group of novelists could without great injustice be classed as proletarian in the more strictly ideological sense of that word, as writing from the Marxian and revolutionary standpoint. Though, in all of them, what makes the work of real value as literature is not the burden of didacticism, but such skill in observation and delineation of character as they have shown. Of the strictly proletarian novels from a definitely class conscious point of view, Jack Conroy's *Disinherited* is noteworthy. It depicts life and labor in a coal mining district. There is a familiar triteness of plot, the wandering of a boy whose parents want to keep him out of the mine, so he makes his odyssey into many fields of labor, working on a railroad, rubber factory, steel mill, automobile plant. He ended up, inevitably, as a radical and labor organizer. Yet, within this hackneyed pattern, there are real people who carry their lives on the printed page, there is a background of real experience, and a tenderness and humor. The lifelike observation present throughout the book is evidenced by this bit of experience:

"And what does it feel like to have been out of a job for months? Nothing impairs morale like the dissolution of a last pair of shoes. Maybe it starts with a little hole in the sole; and then the slush of pavements oozes in, gumming sox and balling between your toes. Concrete whets Woolworth sox like a file, and if you turn the heel on top and tear a pasteboard innersole, it won't help much—I worried about pants. Every icy blast off the lake found the thin spots unerringly. I brooded about the disastrous consequences of a sudden breaking asunder . . . You walk and stare in shop windows. A pink and white ham simmers in the Bandbox lunch. You suck up your guts as the sergeant used to tell you to do. . . . Ye Cozy Radio Shoppe flings harmony for five blocks and a thunderous optimist yammers . . . We are now in the dining-room of the Commodore Perry Hotel. Lights! Good food! Music! Youth! Is everybody happy! The orchestra enters into the spirit of the occasion with that tuneful selection: 'Happy Days Are Here Again.' " [13]

Josephine Herbst is a "proletarian" writer who deserves far more attention than she has received. The acclaim of critics has not been matched by sales. If the dangerous business of prophecy might be risked, the judgment is here ventured that the passage of time will make clear that in Miss Herbst's trilogy of novels there has been painted one of the largest canvasses of American life which has ever been attempted, filled with lifelikeness of detail and historical value. It is comparable to the *Forsyte Saga,* or one of the large French social histories which have been produced in such profusion. It is a saga of the working class covering three generations, done with honesty and skill, with the author's radical viewpoint held for the most part, in such effective leash, that it does not make the novels into political tracts. The first novel, *Pity Is Not Enough,* begins the story of the Trexler-Wendell family in the post-Civil War days, when the carpetbagging era offered great opportunities to a shrewd youngster stung with the itch for profit. A second novel, *The Executioner Waits,* carries on the fortunes of a widely ramifying family group, the Wendells, related by marriage to the Trexlers and gifted with a talent for failing in business. In this novel, there is a remarkable panoramic picture of the post-war days, with

[13] *The Disinherited* by Jack Conroy. Covici-Friede, 1933.

representative forces portrayed realistically, including the notorious Palmer red raid era, the growing restlessness of the
young, and the large theme of moral values in a shifting,
changing society. The third novel of the trilogy, *Rope of
Gold*, brings the stories of various people down through the
1930's. The narrative and characters are interesting; the reproduction of the colloquial speech testifies not only to the
accuracy and sensitiveness of the author's ear for actual speech,
but also to her intimate knowledge of the people she writes
about. The chief value of the work, as is appropriate in a
novelist faithful to a sincerely held economic radicalism, is as
a picture of society in decay, the portrayal of individual and
social failure. The effect is like that of a large mural, resembling the many produced by W. P. A. artists, now decorating
public schools and city halls and libraries all over the land.
Rope of Gold is something of a Grant Wood mural in prose,
though the congestion of population is far greater than in
Wood's paintings or those of Thomas Hart Benton. The middle west has here its history through the decade, the wind
and flying dust, grasshoppers, every aspect of the years, from
the revolt of mortgaged farmers to the sitdown strike.

Among other novels in this field are Edward Dahlberg's
Those Who Perish, Elliot Paul's *The Stars and Stripes For-
ever*, Pietro di Donato's *Christ in Concrete*, (written by a
workman resembling more nearly the much heralded actual
"proletarian" author than any other), Edward Newhouse's
This is Your Day, Robert Whitcomb's *Talk United States*,
Leslie Edgley's *No Birds Sing* (located in a typical steel town,
U. S. A.) and Willie Ethridge's *Mingled Yarn*, set in a
Georgia textile mill town.

Leave cannot be taken of this labor literature without some
note of the fact that in biography, letters and criticism has
appeared some of the most important record and interpreta-

tion of labor issues. One of the major books of the decade and
of a generation, Lincoln Steffens' *Autobiography*, Mary Heaton
Vorse's stirring personal history, *Footnote to Folly*, Louis
Adamic's *Dynamite*, John Chamberlain's *Farewell to Reform*,
all have the progress of labor as a central theme.

Here then, are some treatments of labor in the grimmest
decade of national history. There has been a great deal written
to the effect that the thirties were an arid period for literature,
compared with the twenties, that the writers of the depression
years missed an opportunity unparallelled in theme and feeling. Only time can tell about this judgment. But such a
comparative judgment seems to be an instance of too easy devaluation of the achievement of the present. Even so frag-
mentary an exhibit as that offered in this chapter makes an
impressive total of sincere and powerful interpretation of experience in fiction. The work represented here is not merely
descriptive. It is not dispassionate. Yet very little of it is shrill
or mechanical. It is full of moral judgment. Most of the novelists of labor are prophets in unorthodox clothes.

Sometimes the question is raised by people within the
churches asking why fiction dealing with labor is all done by
writers with little or no religious interest, and slight concern
for conventional morality, meaning by that phrase orthodox
sexual morality. The answer is easy to find. Writers within
the Christian tradition have shown neither the desire nor
knowledge necessary to deal with this primary issue of this
generation. It is no task for a Lloyd Douglass. The ostenta-
tiously Christian writers have been like the lawyers denounced
by Jesus who would not themselves lift a finger to ease human
burdens. In the writers who have dealt with labor, there has
been genuine ethical insight, and more, there has been a
battle for spiritual values. Dos Passos, for instance, is not a
Sunday School writer. His books would shock the Ladies Aid

Society, and almost as badly, most of the Monday morning Preachers meeting. Yet his sense of the spiritual tragedy of Charlie Anderson in *The Big Money* indicates a sensitive recognition of the personal waste when personality and potential character are mangled by financial wolves.

In many of the books mentioned here, there is a strong sense of the futility of reform which leaves the central idols of our money culture untouched. There is also reflected again and again an understanding greatly needed and usually absent in conventional thinking. That is the understanding that any real defense of democracy must include the creation and preservation of a democracy that actually works, one that goes on to industrial democracy, that goes on to the socialization of industry and of the human spirit.

CHAPTER 7

OF MORTGAGES AND MIGRANTS

"Dust to dust"—so run the solemn words of the ritual of the Burial Service. Longfellow assures us:

> "Dust thou art to dust returneth"
> Was not spoken of the soul.

But there has been a growing terrified realization that the words may be accurately spoken of the earth. One of the darkest clouds of ten years was that made of dust storms, the portent of the land in motion through the air. It has thrown a deep shadow over the continental landscape. In alarmed wonder the question is asked, Is it more than the end of an era in agriculture? Is it the death of the American earth?

The question is seriously put in ethical and even religious terms. Has man's sin, the sin of the land skinner, the timber hog, the exploiter without any conscience in dealing with the land, caught up with him? Morris Llewellyn Cooke, in writing of the degradation of the soil and the consequent degradation of man, has brought together in striking contrast two passages from the Old Testament, the first from Deuteronomy, picturing man's rich endowment in the good earth, the second from Job, revealing the catastrophe when that heritage is prodigally wasted:

. . . A good land; a land of brooks of water, of fountains and depths that spring out of the valleys and hills; a land of wheat and barley, of vines and fig trees and pomegranates; a land of olive oil and honey. . . . Here thou shalt eat bread without scarceness; thou shalt not lack anything. . . .[1]

The waters wear the stones; thou washest away the things that grow out of the dust of the earth; and thou destroyest the hope of man. . . . If my land cry against me, or that the furrows thereof likewise complain . . . let thistles grow instead of wheat, and cockle instead of barley. The words of Job are ended.[2]

That quotation from Job has a disturbing relevance to the United States in the 1930's. The land cried out against man and the furrows thereof complained. The crying out of the furrows has found strong expression in a body of literature here to be briefly surveyed.

> The orchard, the meadow,
> The deep tangled wildwood

have been a scene of physical and human desolation and tragedy. The sum of it all is nothing less than that, over wide sections of the country, farming as a typical American way of life has gone to smash. Nature, in drought and dust storms, and man, by depression and the tractor, have conspired. Mortgages, the failure of credit, debt and insecurity, have been the prelude to migrancy. Paul B. Sears, a prophet of agriculture, in the direct apostolic succession to Micah and Amos, thus draws the physical picture and the moral judgment:

"The sins of our fathers are being visited upon the heads of their children. The raging waters of today are the price of waving fields of grain, of forests destroyed, of roads and cities thrown together with no far-seeing plan. To an eye trained to read the landscape, this tragic disaster of flood has but one meaning. Our continent is sick.

The floods of today are boiling over a land stripped of its cover

[1] Deuteronomy viii: 7-9.
[2] The Book of Job.

and so robbed of its moisture that wells must sink from twelve to sixty feet deeper than ever before to strike water. This land is covered by a network of highways which defy natural drainage patterns.

How far must suffering and misery go before we see that even in the day of vast cities and powerful machines, the good earth is our mother and that if we destroy her, we destroy ourselves." [3]

The literature dealing with labor in agriculture deals in the main with three features of the situation, the degeneration of the land, the plight of the people on it and the incursion of big business into agriculture, with the resultant growth of an American peasantry.

The books and stories dealing with this area of American life are not nearly so great in number as those treating labor in industry. The agricultural problem has hardly been touched on in the drama at all. Yet this group of works which look at the face of the fields with a new clarity and honesty includes the most powerful American novel of the twentieth century so far, and one which through an amazingly faithful and gripping screen version reached a large audience, John Steinbeck's *The Grapes of Wrath*.

It is not a pleasant library in which to read, and it has met with violent condemnation. Naked light turned on any subject is always a criminal misdemeanor in the eyes of those who like, emotionally, and profit from, financially, the status quo. The portrayal of real character in the actual agricultural framework has been a bewildering spectacle to many whose eyes are conditioned to nostalgic views of the noble and happy farmer. It is the same kind of an upsetting experience as was caused in many minds by Thomas Hart Benton's paintings. Many Missourians, probably a majority of those who ever saw them, were exasperated at the lack of dignity and stateliness

[3] *Deserts on the March* by Paul B. Sears. Simon and Schuster and University of Oklahoma Press.

in the figures of these people as painted by Benton. As Clyde Brion Davis puts it:

"They want Missourians depicted as dreamy-faced, broad-shouldered young men and deep-bosomed women standing in quiet dignity before compositions of shocked golden wheat and cog wheels, with railroad trains, setting suns, and steamboats in the background. Benton gave them Huck Finn and Jim, Jesse James holding up a train, and—most shocking of all—the shooting of the fabled and faithless Johnny by the equally fabled and outraged Frankie." [4]

Another reason for the reluctance to revel in the new literature of the farm was expressed in the complaint of one reader, "These farm novels take away my appetite. I have no appetite for beets when I remember the children in the beet fields. Shrimps, prunes and cranberries are off my list too. Even oranges remind me of the Joads."

Let us begin with that epic, *The Grapes of Wrath*. It is the epic of the uncovered wagon, the "39ers" pushing west in ancient "jalopies." It presents in terms of life one of the great paradoxes of American history, that just at the time when there was "nowhere to go," there was more going than ever before.

The Joad family are blown and tractored out of Oklahoma, their land sold for mortgages to large scale farming companies. They become part of the migration of sharecroppers and small farmers driven off their fields, 300,000 of them leaving Oklahoma for the West. It was one of the largest migrations in American history, and by far the most tragic and hopeless. It is all seen through the history of a typical family, the Joads, lured by handbills proclaiming the seductive lie of steady work at fruit picking in California.

Tom Joad comes out of the state prison on parole (for killing in self defense) just in time to join his family, who had

[4] *The Saturday Review of Literature*, January 20, 1940.

been forced off the land, and were heading west. The characters are alive—Ma, a genuinely great woman—and Pa, practical, wise with a tenant farmer's knowledge of the under side of life, Grandpa, an obscene old goat, Casy the preacher who saw and thought beyond his backwoods evangelism. They are not like a family out of Caldwell's *Tobacco Road*; they are not degenerates or freaks, but human beings.

Their laughter subsides as they get farther west. The grandparents are left in unmarked graves on the roadside. On to California and to disillusion. In New Mexico they get rumors of what awaits them, and in this quotation from a returning pilgrim, is the core of the book:

"You never been called 'Okie' yet? 'Okie' use' to mean you was from Oklahoma. Now it means you're scum. Don't mean nothin' itself; it's the way they say it. But I can't tell you nothin'. You got to go there. I hear there's three hundred thousan' of our people there—an' livin' like hogs, 'cause ever'thing in California is owned. They ain't nothing left. And them people that owns it is gonna hang on to it if they got to kill ever'body in the worl' to do it. An' they're scairt, an' that makes 'em mad. You got to see it. You got to hear it. Purtiest goddamn country you ever seen, but they ain't nice to you, them folks. They're so scairt an' worried they ain't even nice to each other." [5]

It would be hard to pack more observation and psychological understanding of a social and economic situation in a few words.

Their money gave out when they arrived. They pursued rumors of work in this direction and that. They found the California Gestapo burning the Okie camps, arresting objectors as dangerous 'reds,' riding herd on those who did not get work in the orchards at starvation wages. (Here a 'red' is a person who asks for 30 cents an hour when the owners are

[5] *The Grapes of Wrath* by John Steinbeck. The Viking Press.

paying 20!) There is no happy ending. It is to the everlasting credit of the movies that there was no Hollywood "came the dawn" ending in the film version. For this they should be forgiven many sins. The meaning of the title is that their situation sets the stage for revolution—the promised grapes of California have become the grapes of wrath, full and heavy.

There is much impressive description, poetical, observant, vast, human, tragic. Here for instance is Route 66 as the unending procession of cars go by:

"Highway 66 is the main migrant road. 66—the long concrete path across the country, waving gently up and down on the map, from the Mississippi to Bakersfield—over the red lands and the gray lands, twisting up into the mountains, crossing the Divide and down into the bright and terrible desert, and across the desert to the mountains again, and into the rich California valleys.

66 is the path of a people in flight, refugees from dust and shrinking land, from the thunder of tractors and shrinking ownership, from the desert's slow northward invasion, from the twisting winds that howl up out of Texas, from the floods that bring no richness to the land and steal what little richness is there. From all of these the people are in flight, and they come into 66 from the tributary side roads, from the wagon tracks and the rutted country roads. 66 is the mother road, the road of flight." [6]

That is a glimpse of an American *Via Dolorosa*.

This novel is more than the description of an economic and social problem. It is a real novel, the celebration of great human stuff. It is a convincing record of comradeship, and last ditch courage. The human, moral and religious significance of the novel comes in large part from its depiction of the way in which comradeship creates and sustains courage in desperation. Here is a piece of prose, destined to become a classic, on the growth of solidarity, a journey from "I" to "we":

[6] *Ibid.*

"One man, one family driven from the land; this rusty car creaking along the highway to the west, I lost my land, a single tractor took my land. I am alone and I am bewildered. And in the night one family camps in a ditch and another family pulls in and the tents come out. The two men squat on their hams and the women and children listen. Here is the node, you who hate change and fear revolution. Keep these two squatting men apart; make them hate, fear, suspect each other. Here is the anlage of the thing you fear. This is the zygote. For here 'I lost my land' is changed; a cell is split and from its splitting grows the thing you hate—'We lost *our* land.' The danger is here, for two men are not as lonely and perplexed as one. And from this first 'we' there grows a still more dangerous thing: 'I have a little food' plus 'I have none.' If from this problem the sum is 'We have a little food,' the thing is on its way, the movement has direction. Only a little multiplication now, and this land, this tractor are ours. The two men squatting in a ditch, the little fire, the sidemeat stewing in a single pot, the silent, stone-eyed women; behind, the children listening with their souls to words their minds do not understand. The night draws down. The baby has a cold. Here, take this blanket. It's wool. It was my mother's blanket—take it for the baby. This is the thing to bomb. This is the beginning—from 'I' to 'we.' " [7]

There is traced the natural and psychologically credible growth of social feeling, the realization that their experience was part of a larger struggle which called for dedication to the larger group. This is shown in the evolution of Casy, the preacher, who finds his lost "religion" in the labor conflict, and in the final scene where Tom Joad, now again a fugitive from justice, takes leave of his mother with the words—

"I'll be ever'where—wherever you look. Wherever they's a fight so hungry people can eat, I'll be there. Wherever they's a cop beatin' up a guy, I'll be there. If Casy knowed, why, I'll be in the way guys yell when they're mad an'—I'll be in the way kids laugh when they're hungry an' they know supper's ready. An' when our folks eat the stuff they raise an' live in the houses they

[7] *Ibid.*

build—why, I'll be there. See? God, I'm talkin' like Casy. Comes of thinkin' about him so much. Seems like I can see him sometimes." [8]

Not often is a work of fiction given such a documentary footnote as *The Grapes of Wrath* received in the publication of the non-fiction, historical and descriptive account of this migration and the California labor problem, in Carey McWilliams' *Factories in the Fields*, published in July, 1939, three months later than the novel. It gives striking testimony to the accuracy of Steinbeck's picture. Mr. McWilliams is California State Commissioner of Immigration and Housing. His book is historical, showing the development of large land holdings and of absentee ownership. In 1919, the Southern Pacific Railroad owned over two and one-half million acres of land in Southern California alone. The Bank of America is said to control half the farm area in the Northern and Central parts of the State.

The significance as well as the theme of *Factories in the Fields* can be best conveyed in the condensed and eloquent panoramic view given by Ella Winter, which appeared under the appropriate title, *Hell's Orchards:*

"McWilliams is the Dante on a tour of what has always been supposed to be the Paradise of America. The sunkist mists dissolve and you see the real picture. You see the rich farmlands, divided up by fraudulent land grants that expropriated the actual settlers and gave million-acre ranches to a few great owners. You see these owners crying for cheap labor, and always too much of it: willing, docile, humble, 'amenable' labor; 'hands' that would harvest the crops, hoboes or blanket stiffs or fruit-tramps who would make no fuss over the dirt and disease, half-starvation and insecurity. Bodies, yellow, brown, black or white, that would stoop or squat over the rows of lettuce, melons, beans, asparagus; that would cut, chop, top, dry, pack, can, the brussels sprouts,

[8] *Ibid.*

cotton, beets, figs, peaches, apricots, prunes, berries; in the torrid
sun, all day, for a few hundred dollars a season (with exorbitant
prices charged for food at company stores. No overcharge seemed
too mean for the great California farm corporations). The owners brought in successively Chinese, Japanese, Hindus, Negroes,
Mexicans, Filipinos; worked them as coolie or peon labor, and,
when they asked for more wages or objected to the stench and
filth of their shantytowns and ditch-side squatters' camps, drove
them out of the fields at bayonet's point, herded them in corrals
and stockades, beat and jailed them, and even murdered—these
'patient little slant-eyed people,' 'quiet, unaggressive Mexicans,'
'easy-to-handle ragheads' (Hindus)." [9]

The La Follette Senate Committee which investigated The
Associated Farmers piled up an even larger mountain of documentation for the essential truth of *The Grapes of Wrath*. It directed attention, not only to California, the goal and end of
the migrations, but also to the agricultural conditions in other
parts of the country, for the willingness to undertake the painful and "long shot" chance of migration tells much of the
pressure for jobs farther East.

On the same shelf with *The Grapes of Wrath* should go two
remarkable books of photographs with texts. The first is Archibald MacLeish's *Land of the Free*, ironically titled, a poetical
accompaniment or "soundtrack" to a group of photographs.
These were largely taken from the work of various government bureaus, portraying the dead end perplexity of American
farmers, driven on to the roads as the last place to go, raising
from their experience, for the first time, fundamental questions about the validity of the American tradition of liberty
and democracy which they had always taken for granted. The
other book is *An American Exodus*, a record of Human Erosion, by Dorothea Lange and Paul S. Taylor. In photograph

[9] *The New Republic.*

and text they have caught both the human tragedy and the social portent of the great migration.

The share cropper of the Southeastern states presents a problem, of which the "Okies" were only a part, a problem of enormous dimensions and urgency, a descent into peasantry and peonage, which often makes the pre-civil war days seem like "good old times." The share cropper has furnished theme and characters to many novelists and short story writers. But he has never received the literary attention brought to the "Okies" by the genius of Steinbeck. It is hardly possible to exaggerate the importance or threat of the issues of sub-marginal people on sub-marginal land. There are about 9,000,-000 share croppers and tenant farmers in the United States. The average "income," to use a ridiculously pretentious word in such a connection, is often as low as ten cents a day. Malnutrition (another pretentiously euphemistic word which throws a camouflage over an uglier word, "starvation") and disease are common. As soon as the children can walk they take their place in the fields, so that little schooling is possible. To complete the picture of democracy, the Southern poll tax, which the share croppers are too poor to pay, prevents them from having any more voice in their government than the Poles have under Hitler. The picture covering millions is sharply etched by Sterling Brown in a poem entitled, *Master and Man*:

> The yellow ears are crammed in Mr. Cromartie's bin.
> The wheat is tight sacked in Mr. Cromartie's barn.
> The timothy is stuffed in Mr. Cromartie's loft.
> The ploughs are lined up in Mr. Cromartie's shed.
> The cotton has gone to Mr. Cromartie's factor.
> The money is in Mr. Cromartie's bank.
> Mr. Cromartie's son made his frat at the college.
> Mr. Cromartie's daughter has got her new car.
> The veranda is cold, but the fireplace is rosy.
> Well done, Mr. Cromartie. Time now for rest.

Blackened sticks line the furrows that Uncle Ned laid.
Bits of fluff are in the corners where Uncle Ned ginned.
The mules he ploughed are sleek in Mr. Cromartie's pastures.
The hoes grow dull in Mr. Cromartie's shed.
His winter rations wait on the commissary shelves;
Mr. Cromartie's ledger is there for his service.
Uncle Ned daubs some mortar between the old logs.
His children have traipsed off to God knows where.
His old lady sits patching the old, thin denims;
She's got a new dress, and his young one a doll,
He's got five dollars. The year has come round.
The harvest is over: Uncle Ned's harvesting,
Mr. Cromartie's harvest. Time now for rest.[10]

One of the best novels dealing primarily with the Southern
share croppers is *Land Without Moses*, by Charles Curtis
Munz. Gerald W. Johnson, who knows his South up and
down and criss-cross, says that it "makes *Tobacco Road* look
like a Glad Book." The hero, Kirby Moten, is first shown as
a young man perfectly normal in his mental and physical
equipment, who makes a futile fight against the share cropper
system, a battle as hopeless from the beginning as the in-
genious "bricks without straw" system under Pharaoh. There
is no piling on of physical horrors: the real emphasis of the
book is in the psychological and moral field, its persuasive
descriptions of personal disintegration under a hopeless battle
to wring even a subsistence living under the share cropper
system. Throughout the very readable and effective story
there runs the doomed dream which Kirby has of reaching
a "promised land flowing with milk and honey," (again
paralleling the Biblical history of Israel in Egypt), the goal
in this case being Halishaw County, "where every man owns
his own farm." But poor Kirby never crosses the Jordan into
his Canaan.

In his more recent stories, Erskine Caldwell, as has already

[10] *The New Republic*, November 18, 1936.

been noted, brings in much more direct dealing with the agricultural system than in his earlier stories and novels. The victims are not portrayed as ludicrous degenerates, to be treated with ribald humor. In the collection of stories entitled *Southways,* for instance, while some continue in the bawdy strain of *Jeeter Lester* and *God's Little Acre,* there are others which express bitter description of and protest against the tragedies of the submerged, of workers driven into actual slavery, of dispossessed mothers dying of childbirth, and of many other common experiences in the land of the free. There is passion and conscience in such stories as *A Knife to Cut Corn Bread With* and *Wild Flowers.* It must be added, however, as a very practical matter, concerning the possibility of the stories depicting social injustice being read by many who should be exposed to them, that there is so much lewd horseplay in many of the stories that many readers will be retched with nausea before they reach the "required" reading.

Leane Zugsmith treats the same general field from a fresh angle and purpose in her *The Summer Soldier.* This is more of an exploration of the mental and spiritual anatomy of the "fair weather liberal." She describes an investigating committee going into the South to make a report on a strike, a committee made up of typical figures, a radical preacher, a liberal professor, a professional writer, and a society woman, much soiled. Some run under fire, some stand up to continue the fight. Incidentally the savage, near-fascist climate of the region is strongly conveyed.

In non-fiction, the ramifications and human as well as agricultural results of the system have been set forth. *Forty Acres and Steel Mules* by Herman Clarence Nixon examines agriculture in a readable book, illustrated with photographs by the Farm Security Administration. He contends that the plight of the South comes from three causes. *"Farmers are notoriously an exploited class, and the South has half of the farmers in the United States. Unorganized labor is exploited, and the South has more unorganized labor than any other section of equivalent area. Negroes are exploited, and the South has two-thirds of all the Negroes in the United States."* [11] Here, he says, are the major causes of exploitation. A valuable historical survey of the literary reflection of the share cropper is Shields McIlvaine's *"The Southern Poor White: From Lubberland to Tobacco Road."* [12]

An informal, and all the more convincing picture of the situation for that reason, is to be found in the very interesting autobiography of a Washington correspondent, Thomas L. Stokes, in his *Chip Off My Shoulder.* The title gives the viewpoint and "plot" of the record. It is the story of a "Professional Southerner" who started out in life with a chip on his shoulder. His years of experience make him less resentful of any reflection on the South. A most impressive chapter is his powerful story of his revisiting Georgia after many years' absence and realizing with his own eyes and mind the truth of the picture he had so bitterly resented, "the squalor, the poverty, the oppression, the cynical denial of justice, and the brutal self-complacence."

Edwin Lanham's *The Stricklands* is located in Texas, with much background of the tenant farmers, brought in through the story of Jay Strickland, the son of a hill farmer who struggles to organize the tenant farmers of the neighborhood, in order to break the forces which have kept his family and others like it in crushing poverty.

[11] *Forty Acres and Steel Mules* by Herman Clarence Nixon. Chapel Hill: The University of North Carolina Press.
[12] University of Oklahoma Press.

Cranberries and Cape Cod get their day in the sun (literally) in two novels, *Sun On Their Shoulders*, by Elizabeth Eastman, and *Cranberry Red*, by E. Garside. The reading of neither of them will make the Thanksgiving cranberry sauce taste any better. Miss Eastman's novel centers around a Finnish family, while Mrs. Garside records the history of a Portuguese group among others. Each portrays New England serfdom in a feudal empire.

The popularity of Steinbeck's *Of Mice and Men* comes from many sources, among which the author's literary skill ranks high. Its combination of sentimentality and melodrama also helps greatly, in the fresh theme of the protective care of George for the big, powerful, gentle but dangerous, mentally deficient Lennie. But the background, clearly set forth, is the social problem of rootless roaming men in a badly maladjusted agricultural system, of which the Salinas Valley in California is a convincing illustration. Back of the melodrama is the frustration of a natural, almost universal human desire as expressed by one character, "Everybody wants a bit of land, not much, just somepin that was his." Simple words those, "somepin that was his"; yet closely and profoundly related to a central issue in the whole spread of American life.

The human results of the decay of a great rural industry are nowhere more movingly set forth than in Mrs. Louise V. Armstrong's *We Too Are the People*, giving her experience as Relief Administrator in Northern Michigan. Look at the contrast in two quotations. First, the lumber industry in its ruthless, waxing stage:

"The great lumber industry was born and grew to a roaring, roistering and not too honest maturity. It did its gaudy and ribald turn in the pageant of national development and passed on out of the picture, leaving a ruined land and a stranded population to fight off poverty as well as it could." [13]

And here are some of the results of the decay, seen in the Relief Administrator's office:

"The sound of tramping feet in a long hall, the noise of scuffling feet in a big room, the babble of human voices pitched in every key, mingle with other sounds in a ceaseless jazz symphony of human life. A baby cries, a woman's shrill complaints rise above the general theme, the quavering tones of an aged voice become distinct in a sudden lull, to be drowned by the gruff voices of men. Crisp sentences in the brisk tones of busy people cut through at times and are lost again in the surge of angry voices, pleading voices, gentle voices, harsh voices, good-natured voices with jests that ripple the flood of sound into momentary waves of laughter. The click of many typewriters keeps up a steady accompaniment, punctuated by the faint 'ting' of their little warning bells, and at longer intervals by the sharp ring of the telephone. And weaving together this welter of sound, the tramp, tramp, tramp of feet is a neverending thud, thud, like the throbbing of muffled drums." [14]

"Tramp, Tramp, Tramp, the boys, (and the girls) are marching" to the muffled drums of social doom.

[13] *We Too Are the People* by Louise V. Armstrong. Boston: Little, Brown & Company, 1938.
[14] *Ibid.*

Chapter 8

THE DRAMA AND SOCIAL ISSUES

"Literary criticism," writes F. R. Leavis, in *Determinations,* "is concerned with more than literature. A serious interest in literature cannot be merely literary. It is likely to be drawn from a perception of—what must be a preoccupation with—the problems of social equity and order and social health."

These words indicate the direction of the most prominent movement in the American theatre during the 1930's. Amid all the conflicting influences and confusions, the trend in the drama to the more direct and explicit treatment of definite social problems has been the outstanding feature of the ten years' production. This has been manifest not merely in the work of the admittedly "leftist" playwrights, work produced for the most part in the smaller non-commercial group theatres, such as the work of George Sklar and John Wexley. It has marked also the work of dramatists on whom no political or economic label can rightly be affixed, such as Robert E. Sherwood and Sidney Howard.

John Sloan, the artist, has given a bit of advice to young artists, advice which echoes Browning's *Fra Lippo Lippi,* which has a real relationship to the drama. He says, "Don't let the hand fall into a smart way of putting the mind to sleep." [1] That has been a liability of the dramatist, one which finds much illustration in the American drama. The com-

[1] *The Gist of Art* by John Sloan. American Artists Group, New York.

petent craftsman's hand has had a way of "putting the mind
to sleep," as far as facing vital contemporary issues was concerned. The dextrous Clyde Fitch and Augustus Thomas are
good illustrations. In the thirties, the minds of many dramatists
awakened in a fresh sense to the opportunity and compelling
necessity to write plays that go beyond a slick competence,
that go beyond individual themes treated as though lives were
lived in a social and economic vacuum, and deal with the
major forces which condition life.

Dramas dealing with social questions are of course not new.
A number of significant and important ones were produced
during the relatively prosperous years of the nineteen twenties.
Yet it can be said that the thirties were a decade with peculiar
characteristics affecting the production of the drama of social
criticism. This can be put into a concise form by saying that
the atmosphere of the twenties, that of fairly general economic
well being and complacency, was not conducive to the creation of plays of realistic radical criticism; and, from all present
indications, the nineteen forties, with the overhanging shadow
of war, with the resultant fear, and feverish effort for security,
with the inevitable repression of dissent of all sorts, will make
lean years for vigorous social drama. The thirties were an era
between two worlds, a time when the economic and social
disaster furnished conditions and emotional climate favorable
to the production of drama of outspoken criticism, such as has
never been known before and will probably not appear again
for several years. This prophecy concerning the forties is
risky, like all prophecy. Yet, from indications already at hand,
there is a basis for it. It comes not only from the growing
intolerance for any work that can be labelled "subversive" and
"diversive." It comes also from a natural need for the positive
affirmation of the traditional values of American democracy,
at a time when democracy is seriously threatened as never

before in its history. The response to such a play of affirmation
as Sherwood's *Abe Lincoln in Illinois* is an illustration of this
mood and need.

It can be said of the social plays of the thirties that they have
been more explicit in theme and criticism, while those of the
twenties were implicit; they have been more specific in content, while those of the preceding decade were more general.
Many of the plays which had critical content were in what
might be called the tradition of *Main Street*, satire and
parody, and even burlesque, on aspects of the business and
social world which were irritating to the spirit of revolt, not
so much economic or political revolt, but literary and personal. Joseph Wood Krutch characterizes these plays as being
more bohemian than radical. Thus, Marc Connelly's and
George S. Kaufman's *To the Ladies* carried a hilarious and
yet deadly debunking of the windy pretentiousness of business, as exemplified by the Kincaid Piano Company, with all
the hocus-pocus of "service," and the tub thumping over its
reward to workers with a twenty-four year record by awarding
them—a button. Similar shafts of satire, bitter and gay at the
same time, marked *Beggar on Horseback*, by the same authors,
a fantasy making merry with the regimentation of business and
the cult of the efficiency systems, so devoutly worshipped
at the time.

Far more serious were two plays of Elmer Rice. In *The
Adding Machine*, a drama in the form of impressionistic fantasy, his hero, Mr. Zero, symbolically named to represent the
adding machine reducing to a human cipher the man who
runs it, may stand for the unequal battle of man against the
machine. It is the record of a nightmare, but the implication
is realistic enough, that of the flattening out of personality by
the misused machines of a profit-mad economy. Rice's *Street
Scene* was realistic in the traditional dramatic form, a melo-

drama of frustration and conflict in a street in a tenement district, which rises in its climax to tragedy. It deals with individual character, but the ultimate social and economic causation of the tragedy is implied and at least dimly indicated. Even more direct and didactic in pointing a moral was Maxwell Anderson's *Gods of the Lightning*, dealing with the Sacco-Vanzetti case, a theme to which he returned seven years later, in 1935, in *Winterset*, treating it then with distinctly less partisanship and much less passionate indignation at the miscarriage of justice, and less clear realization of the economic motivation in the case. One of the most effective plays of the twenties for clearly presenting the economic problem was Paul Green's *In Abraham's Bosom*.

Coming now to the social plays of the thirties, a mixed report must be made. On the one hand, some of the most serious plays, dealing most directly with social issues, have suffered from having too much of the soap box in them. They have been too didactic and evangelistic in calls for economic repentance, as in Elmer Rice's *We the People;* or they have followed a rigid mechanical formula, where the devils (the employers) are all pitch black, and the angels (the workers) are angels, ever bright and fair, as in Albert Maltz's *Black Pit.* Audiences and critics who share the views set forth by the author have been hasty to judge the value of the play by the distance by which it veers to the left. It is this tendency which gave rise to the sneer that many radicals regarded Clifford Odets as "the little Jesus of the proletarian theatre." A great liability of the hortatory Marxian drama is that of poverty of ideas, so it comes to have no more surprise than a juggler tossing three balls in the air. Two or three formulas, tossed back and forth in speeches, no matter how earnest and noble the speeches, are a poor substitute for a play. Yet it can also be claimed, on the basis of quite a sum of evidence, that plays have been vitalized by the honest and vigorous treatment of political and economic ideas, as in *Stevedore* and *Dead End*.

The Federal Theatre Project made an impressive record in carrying dramatic treatments of social problems to an audience of unprecedented dimensions. It completely refuted the contention which had become a stock cliché among theatrical producers, that "there is no audience for plays about unemployment, lynching, housing or strikes." There may be only a limited audience when such plays are produced at a $4.40 top price on Broadway. The Federal Theatre did discover and draw an audience of over fifteen millions at prices within their means. It has been one of the most notable achievements in adult education in American history. It has had a real effect on the commercial theatre, in demonstrating the popular interest in social questions presented on the stage and the demonstrated possibilities of a social theatre which provokes audiences to thinking. When a reactionary Congress, coerced by reactionary interests, blindly killed the Federal Theatre, it did not stop the cause of thinking on social questions; it merely struck out in futile fashion at a symptom of it.

The great and real service of the group of plays here considered has been well expressed by Anita Block: "The richness of our own lives, creative and receptive, depends on how closely we identify ourselves with the struggles and problems, individual and social, as well as with the hope and ideals of the age in which we live." Plays which enable us to make more close that identification render a service to the enlargement of understanding and the sharpening of the capacities of awareness and sympathy.

No adequate appraisal of the social drama of the 1930's can come merely from an examination of the plays themselves. Recognition must be had of the various theatre groups which originally sponsored many of the best of the plays, and without which many would not have been brought into being at all. A complete survey would have to include amateur productions not above the level of little skits, done in large numbers by workers in the early years of the decade. They were not plays at all; they were the framework for speeches. They were called "agit-props." The climax of *Waiting for Lefty*, the agitator's speech calling for a strike, is the sort of thing in which these "agit-props" specialized. They gave a strong propulsion for more professional productions by radical groups. The Theatre Union, composed of militant labor groups, produced *Peace on Earth* and *Stevedore, Black Pit* and Lawson's *Marching Song*. The Actors Repertory Theatre produced Bein's *Let Freedom Ring* and Shaw's *Bury the Dead*. The Group Theatre produced Odets' *Waiting for Lefty* and *Awake and Sing*. The four year run of *Pins and Needles*, an entertaining hard hitting satirical revue produced by the International Ladies Garment Workers Union, was something new in the theatre, not only for the successful production by a non-professional group, but also for its unusual combination of propaganda and humor.

Quite a number of the most forceful plays were devoted to peace. These are reserved for consideration in a later chapter.

One group of plays is that dealing directly and primarily with labor conflict, usually coming to a climax in a strike situation. The most effective of these, as well as the one receiving the widest attention, is Odets' *Waiting for Lefty*. It had many unpromising features which would seem to give it slight hope for great success. It is episodic, didactic and hortatory and excessively talky. Yet it overcame these handicaps by its vigor, directness and dramatic intensity. The play is short, the movement swift, an adaptation of moving picture technique to the stage. The theme is the natural history of a taxicab strike. The initial scene is the meeting of the labor union to vote on a strike. A corrupt business agent of the union, who has sold out to the employers, counsels no strike, drawing the familiar red herring of radicalism across the real issue. That issue is forcefully set in the center of the picture by Joe, a taxi driver:

"You boys know me. I ain't a red boy one bit. Here I'm carryin' a shrapnel that big I picked up in the war. And maybe I don't know it when it rains! Don't tell me red! You know what we are? The black and blue boys! We been kicked around so long we're black and blue from head to toes. But I guess anyone who says straight out he don't like it, he's a red boy to the leaders of the union. What's this crap about goin' home to hot suppers? I'm asking to your faces how many's got hot suppers to go home to? Anyone who's sure of his next meal, raise your hand! . . . And that's why we're talking strike—to get a living wage!" [2]

After these words, we have a series of six "flash backs" so familiar to the movies, showing how different people were led into the labor struggle. The procedure is remarkably like a dramatization of the old-fashioned church prayer meeting in which one after another rises to tell "How I found the Lord." Here, too, they reveal how they found a new sort of salvation, in active participation in the labor struggle. The first to report is Joe Mitchel. We get the experience of his militant wife who will not take exploitation without fight, and who sees clearly that the struggle can only be won by solidarity. She tells Joe:

"Your boss is making suckers outa you boys every minute. Yes, and suckers out of all the wives and poor innocent kids who'll grow up with crooked spines and sick bones. Sure, I see it in the papers, how good orange juice is for kids. But dammit, our kids get colds one on top of the other. They look like little ghosts. Betty never saw a grapefruit. I took her to the store last week

[2] *Waiting for Lefty* by Clifford Odets. Random House, New York.

and she pointed to a stock of grapefruits. 'What's that!' she said. My God, Joe—the world is supposed to be for all of us." [3]

Other converts are a young laboratory assistant who is disgusted at the attempt of his employer to make a spy out of him; he gets fired and becomes a cab driver. Then a frustrated youngster, unable to marry the girl he loves, is shown, a genuinely moving bit of reality, to be added to the many treatments of this particular situation mentioned earlier. A young actor and a Jewish physician, the victims of anti-Semitic discrimination, are shown in the process of becoming drivers and strikers. The climax comes when the workers learn that "Lefty," for whom they have been waiting, has been shot. The answer is a resounding "Strike!"

In passing, attention should be directed to the treatment of this same conflict, identical in detail, a taxicab strike, in a notable short story of the depression years, *The Scab* by Albert Halper. He probes even deeper than Odets, revealing the inner conflict of the worker, a conflict not often enough dealt with in labor fiction and drama, that of a man who is torn between the desire to provide a living for his wife and children, and the desire to stand with his fellow workers and strike. This inner conflict is a harder one on the worker than the outward one of exciting battle. Halper thus traces that conflict in a cab driver's mind in his own words as he tells his wife of the progress of the strike:

"You'd think they'd let a man work in peace," she said finally. . . . then I got sore as hell. . . . I told her how I had gone to the coffee pots and couldn't eat because I was looked at in a funny way . . . and the first thing I knew I was standing up and screaming at her across the table . . . "Goddam it to hell," I

[3] *Ibid.*

screamed, "I'm through! I'm not the only guy driving a hack with a wife and kids on my hands. I'm through, I tell you. How do you suppose I feel at the wheel of my cab making money with my buddies out on strike? I tell you I'm through. I'm not reporting in the morning, nor the day after. I don't care if we starve. I'm going tearing through the streets with the other drivers because that's where I belong. I'm going to help them burn and wreck every goddam cab in sight!"

And then I told Ethel something I promised myself I would never tell to anybody.

I told her about how just before I started back to the garage I parked in a side street and took out my tire-wrench and bashed in the fenders of my cab and then broke every goddamned window with my own hands. I screamed that out to her. She asked me why I had done it, and I didn't know what to answer.

Then I hollered out, louder than ever: "A man's got to keep some of his self-respect, don't he? What do you take me for, a scab?" [4]

Ranking in dramatic force, as a stage production, with *Waiting for Lefty* is *Stevedore*, by Paul Peters and George Sklar. Produced by the Theatre Union before a sympathetic audience, it had a violent vitality, played with gusto. It presents a labor conflict complicated by the negro problem. The action draws lifelikeness and reality from being based on the New Orleans levee strike, where the play is located, and also on records of race riots in Chicago and East St. Louis. The play is more distinguished as "theatre" than as literature; its spirited playing by negro actors and its degree of "audience participation," both being unusual. The plot has nothing new, being the familiar setting of workers against exploiting employers on a New Orleans dock. A negro labor leader, Lonnie Thompson, is "framed" on the usual charge of assaulting a white woman. He is an intelligent negro with real capacities of leadership, and the Oceanic Transport Company is out to

[4] *American Mercury.*

"get" him and prevent his organizing the dock workers. The efforts to organize and fight supply the action. Lonnie is killed by a lynching mob, but the play ends up on a hopeful note in the evident success in arousing the workers to strike and fight. Two of the freshest and most forceful scenes in the play are those depicting the action of religion as a restraining force tending to a docile submission, and how it is overcome; and the resort to the familiar effort to divide the workers on race lines and break the strike by injecting race prejudice and conflict, a major issue in labor organization. One of Lonnie Thompson's incendiary speeches conveys the atmosphere of the conflict:

"The lowest animal in the field will fight fo' its home. And all you can think of doing is running away. Supposin' you do run away? What you gwine to do? Whar you gwine to? Baton Rouge? Mississippi? Is it gwine to be better dar? You gwine find jobs? You gwine get yo'self a home? Nassuh! You got black skin. You can't run away from dat. Make no difference what you are, dey hound you just de same . . . Every time de white boss crack de whip, you turn and run. You let him beat you, you let him hound you, you let him work you to death. When you gwine to put a stop to it, black man? When you gwine say: 'You can't do dat. I'm a man. I got de rights of a man.' . . ." [5]

Albert Maltz's *Black Pit*, also produced by the Theatre Union, presents a strike in a West Virginia coal mine. It is more of a cut-to-pattern propaganda play, but has the power of an exciting battle, the passion of a sympathetic portrayal of the miners' life and work, and the interest coming from a factual realistic revelation of the processes of mining, such as the "hotmine" with gas in it, the company stool pigeon, the "joy loader," a machine which can be operated by four miners, while it throws twenty-five out of employment. Similar in

[5] *Stevedore* by Paul Peters and George Sklar. Covici-Friede, Inc., 1934.

theme and treatment, though located in a steel mill, was John Wexley's *Steel*, earlier in the depression 1931. Presenting a larger canvas, depicting a representative character and family history, rather than focusing on a labor group, is George Sklar's *Life and Death of An American*, produced by the Federal Theatre Project in May 1939. It is a play of social intelligence and theatrical force. It is not the type of labor play of which a cynical critic writes that in the early thirties "all you had to do was to open with 'workers of the world' and close with 'Arise' and you had powerful, nay biting dramah." Sklar has brought sincerity and wide ranging knowledge of American life in his seizure of the subject of the failure of the American dream. We have a literal following of the title of the play, the life of an American, Jerry Dorgan, born about nineteen hundred. Through a variety of techniques and short scenes, we see him go through youth and young manhood with experiences typical of millions of Americans, the father's hopes for his infant son in this great and free America, the parents' sacrifice to give him an education, his normal happy life at school, his war service as an aviator. His hope of advancement as a skilled technician is blasted by the crash of 1929, poverty follows on the heels of his marriage and parenthood. He gets a job in a steel mill, followed by wage cuts and strike during which he meets death at the hands of the police.

Summarized in this bare form, it sounds dead and trite, "as dry as a remainder biscuit after a voyage." But it is not trite as produced or read. There is truth to American history, a vivid and disturbing picture of the journey from the hope of a land of milk and honey to unemployment and despair.

Very similar in theme was Elmer Rice's *We the People*, a dramatic treatment of a typical American family of a Ford worker, though he does not use the word *Ford*. (It is remarkable in how much of the literature of the ten years Henry Ford has figured under an alias!) The playwright covers too much ground to preserve unity in the play, trying to represent the many ramifications of the economic collapse, from the dismissing of liberal professors from a college controlled by business men to the Foreign Affairs Committee of the Senate, climaxing in the shooting of the father in the "Dearborn Massacre" and the framing of the son on false charges.

The general tone of the play as well as the too didactic nature of much of it are shown in a speech in the last act by the lover of the boy who was "framed":

"It is so with millions. They ask for bread and for peace and they are given only starvation and war. And they must not protest. If they protest, they are shot down and sent to prison. So that a few people can have a thousand times what they need, millions must live in darkness and hunger. And we must be silent. I shall not be silent, not as long as I live. Because my lover was not silent, they told him he must die. Perhaps they will tell me that I must die, too. It is the only way they can make me be silent. Until then, I shall protest, protest, protest! And when my child is born, I shall teach it to protest, too. With my milk, it shall learn to protest. And we shall go on, thousands, millions, the poor and the oppressed everywhere, until we strike off our chains, until we free ourselves of our oppressors, until we win for ourselves the right to live." [6]

Steel is again the theme of the original hard hitting satire with music, an impressionistic musical comedy, Marc Blitzstein's *The Cradle Will Rock*—a steel town dominated by "Mister Mister," the super magnate of the steel mills. John Wexley's *They Shall Not Die* was a play based on the Scottsboro case, with much actual legal record as its foundation and a forceful dramatization of both the labor and the race problems of the South. It has an exciting and impressive trial scene

[6] *We the People* by Elmer Rice. Coward McCann Co., 1933.

as a climax, which leaves the spectator oppressively conscious of the power of phrases, as mouthed out by the demagogic prosecuting attorney, such as "white women . . . rape . . . black dominance . . . outside agitators." The negro boys were not really on trial at all. It was a field day for the defense of prejudice and traditional mores and customs and cherished emotions.

By no means all the plays which have had definite social content have dealt with clash situations, and have had what could be called a definite "message." A large number of plays may be not unfairly regarded as dealing with social problems, even though they are more general in theme and treatment than the conflict plays listed in the preceding pages, and relate themselves to problems more indirectly or incidentally. Sidney Kingsley's *Dead End* is an example of a play dealing with a specific aspect of the social and economic set up, the effect of the city slum on boys. Yet the specific theme is by clear implication related closely to real estate values, low wages, unemployment and poverty.

The play is set at a point where privilege and poverty meet on the East River edge of New York. Gimpty, the young architect out of a job, himself a product of the slums with a leg withered and twisted by rickets, is responsible for the lines which state the philosophy of the play: "The place you live in is awfully important. It can give you a chance to grow, or it can twist you, like that. When I was in school, they used to teach us that evolution made men out of animals. They forget to tell us it can also make animals out of men." "Now, men and women," says Evolution, "I made you walk straight, I gave you feeling, I gave you reason, I gave you a sense of beauty, I planted a God in your heart. Now let's see what you are going to do with them. An' if you can't do anything with them, then I'll take 'em all away."

One of the wealthy women thinks that the nasty boys have inherited their badness, but Gimpty says: "Wooden heads are inherited, but not wooden legs—not legs twisted by rickets."

The contrast, meant to be so obvious as to need no special lines to underscore it, is between the boys as they now are and the gangster who such a few years ago was a boy like them. It will take so little for their most promising leader to slip over the line into that kind of hero. A minor crime, a police record, the reform school, and the wisdom of the slum produces a gangster.

With the starting advantage of the most realistic stage setting the theatre has witnessed in many years, and the talents of a group of boy actors of remarkable naturalness, the play shows the full grown flower of the garden of crime in "Baby Face Martin," a braggart, and a ruthless killer. The end of the play, with one of the youngsters, Tommy, led off to the police court, leaves us wondering whether his life will follow the same vicious cycle.

Robert E. Sherwood's *Petrified Forest* is a romantic melodrama, full of suspense, full of sure-fire dramatic material: tough highwaymen, plenty of shooting, young love and noble sacrifice. Yet underneath the realistic scenery of an Arizona gas station, there is much that can be taken as intended symbolism of an era and way of life that has been weighed and found wanting. Alan Squier, the wandering philosopher and aesthete of the play, indicates the underlying theme of the play in his assertion that he belongs to a vanishing race, the race of intellectuals which "have brains without purpose." He tries in an amateurishly philosophical way to interpret the strange reversion to force and violence going on in the world, a reversion to be illustrated later in the play by the hold-up of the lunch room and gas station by the renowned gunman, Duke Santee. "The impotence of the intellectuals," he says, "is nature hitting back. Not with the old weapons—floods, plagues, holocausts. We can neutralize them. She's fighting back with strange instruments called neuroses. She's deliberately afflicting mankind with the jitters. Nature is proving that she can't be beaten—not by the likes of us. She's taking the world away from the intellectuals and giving it back to the apes." [7]

Those words, "Taking the world away from the intellectuals and giving it to the apes," have a much more terrifying timeliness in this year of Nazi conquest of Europe than they had in 1935 when the play was produced. Sherwood here touches on a theme which appears often in the work of S. N. Behrman, the plight of a liberal in a world of violence, notably in *Rain from Heaven* and *Wine of Choice*. "The Petrified Forest," says Squier, "is a graveyard of the civilization that's been shot from under us. It's a world of outmoded ideas. Platonism—Patriotism—Christianity—Romance—the economics of Adam Smith—they're all so many dead stumps in the desert. That's where I belong. . . ." [8]

France and England and the United States, all the democracies, have exhibited a good many "dead" stumps in the desert!

Maxwell Anderson's *Winterset* is a romantic drama in poetic verse, his second play, as stated above, to deal with the Sacco-Vanzetti case. Left wing critics of the drama, notably Eleanor Flexner, in her stimulating *American Playwrights 1918–1938*, takes this play as an extreme example of a dramatist gone "soft" and muddled, refusing to follow through to their logical conclusions the implications of his theme. It is true that Mr. Anderson does allow his hero, the son of one of

[7] *The Petrified Forest* by Robert E. Sherwood. Charles Scribner's Sons, 1935.
[8] *Ibid.*

the victims of a judicial lynching, to drop his endeavor to have his innocent father cleared of a murder charge. The economic causation of the injustice is left clouded in fog. There is much in the action and character of Mio, the boy starting out to right the wrong done his father, to serve as an illustration of Max Eastman's contention that "all Anderson's heroes are quitters." That is certainly true of the escapist hero of *High Tor;* it is true of Rudolph who flees his kingship in *The Masque of Kings.* Yet it may well be contended that Anderson has a right to write a play dealing with a personal story, as well as with a social indictment. There is much moving poetry and a good deal that is genuine on forgiveness as better than revenge. There is also an interesting portrayal of conscience in the Judge who keeps on repeating so often to himself and to others that his decision was compelled by duty, that it develops into monomania and his mind becomes unsettled.

Two more of Odets' dramas, *Golden Boy* and *Rocket to the Moon,* though the action unfolds personal histories which hold the interest without reference to any economic background, yet are concerned by clear implication with the conditioning of life by economic forces. *Golden Boy* tells the story of a young violinist who, frustrated by lack of economic opportunity to continue with music, turns to prize fighting to make money. (A hand that combines the exquisite sensitiveness of a violin player with the deadly wallop of a Joe Louis would be a remarkable one!) The implication is that this is all the use which a society, blind with acquisitiveness, could make of a fine talent. There is a common inner conflict represented here, set up in people who are deprived of the chance of doing what they like best to do, and unable to become reconciled to a second best or a fifth best. The fault of the social order in this waste is clearly indicated. The young musician thus announces his change of vocation to his father, impelled by financial need and desire:

"Poppa, I have to tell you—I don't like myself, past, present, and future. Do you know there are men who have wonderful things from life? Do you think I like this feeling of no possessions? Tomorrow's my birthday! I change my life!" [9]

Joe is exploited by the managers who get hold of him. They have contempt for Joe's endeavors to save his hand. The climax comes when he accidentally kills his opponent, breaking his own hand in the fight, followed by reckless driving, which amounts to suicide. The author seems to make Joe a prize-fighter in the interests, partly at least, of symbolism, the killing off an artist when he joins under pressure the destructive forces of society.

Rocket to the Moon is a sordid story in its outline—the desire for a young girl on the part of two older men, one of them married. But underneath, we glimpse the emptiness and frustration of the lives out of which the desire for love arises. It seems to be part of the author's theme that despair and loneliness, so sharply conveyed, spring from the barrenness of life, a barrenness which has economic and spiritual roots.

It was inevitable that under the pressure of Nazi threat and war in Europe, and the uncertain future of democracy anywhere, that drama devoted to celebrating the positive values of democracy should appear. Maxwell Anderson's *Valley Forge* is notable for the eloquence with which George Washington is made to speak of the dream of democracy and to declare a faith in its permanent victory. "What I fight for now is a dream, a mirage, perhaps, something that's never been on this earth since men first worked it with their hands, something that's never existed and will never exist unless we can

[9] *Golden Boy* by Clifford Odets. Random House, 1937.

make it and put it here—the right of free-born men to govern themselves in their own way."

Robert E. Sherwood's *Abe Lincoln in Illinois* aroused as much enthusiastic response as any American play ever received. There are so many factors entering into this result that it is hard to estimate their comparative weight. The hold of Lincoln on the imagination and affection of the public played its part; the liberal use of Lincoln's own words helped the impression of reality; the splendid acting of Raymond Massey contributed much. The skill and sincerity of the dramatist in breathing life into an episodical chronicle framework must be given grateful recognition. There was also the element of the timeliness of theme. Here was the great epic of democracy, its greatest exemplar. There is historical knowledge and clear thinking in Sherwood's underlining, through the medium of Lincoln's speeches and conversations, that Lincoln's opposition to slavery came not wholly or even primarily from humanitarian reasons, but from the realization that to deny liberty to any group in the population is to threaten the liberty of all, and ultimately to lose it for all. He sees that the greatest enemies of democracy are not its avowed foes from outside, but those who pay it mere life service, as the upholders of slavery did, and who deny it when they limit its application. No one speaking today could carry more conviction than there is in these words of Lincoln in the past.

CHAPTER 9

SOCIAL POETRY

SHAKESPEARE, WHO IS always contemporary, has pictured one
great trend in today's poetry in the problem which Hamlet
poses:

> Whether 'tis nobler in the soul to suffer
> The slings and arrows of outrageous fortune,
> Or to take arms against a sea of troubles
> And by opposing, end them.

That classic weighing of alternatives can quite legitimately
be made to represent one marked contrast between the bulk
of the poetry of the nineteen twenties and the nineteen thirties: the change from a limp acceptance by many poets of the
outrageous fortune of the post war years to an active positive
struggling mood which takes up arms. It is not only that
personal preoccupations with inward emotions and aesthetic
appreciations of nature—traditional and inevitable themes of
poetry—have been replaced with concern for the outward social scene. The mood is different. A dispirited disillusion and
despair, what has been called the "waste land" school of literature, has given way in many of the most important poets
to a rejection of any kind of "escapism" or self pity, and an
acceptance of a militant part in the social struggle, as a poet's
inescapable responsibility. Muriel Rukeyser, who is one of the
notable exemplars of this mood and spirit, expresses it in her

"Citation for Horace Gregory," in tribute to his refusal to escape:

> These are our Brave, these wrot their hands in on the work.
> hammering out beauty upon the painful stone
> turning their grave heads passionately finding
> truth and alone and each day subtly slain
> and each day born.
>
>   *   *   *
>
> Young poets and makers, solve your anguish, see
> the brave unmedalled who dares to shape his mind
> printed with dignity to the machines of change.
> A procession of poets adds one footbeat to the
> implacable metric line: the great and unbetrayed
> after the sunlight and the failing yellow,
> after the lips bitten with passion and
> gentle, after the deaths below
> dance floors of celebration we turn. We turn
> these braveries and preferment. These gifts
> flare on our lives, clarifying, revealed.[1]

C. Day Lewis has expressed the change in a vivid figure, "A poet makes a great mistake if he thinks of himself as moored halfway up to heaven, away from humanity. When an economic, political or social situation, unfavorable or dangerous to the community, arises, this poet in his captive balloon will be hauled down." A good many "captive balloons" have been hauled down to earth.

Of course, no one trend can ever in any time express the great variety of the sensitive apprehension and expression of the experiences of life by poets. Our attention in this chapter is given to one kind of poetry, that which shows a marked influence by the great economic and social and international events of the period. It is just one part of contemporary poetry.

[1] *Theory of Flight* by Muriel Rukeyser. Yale University Press, 1935.

No greater blunder could be made than to mistake the part for the whole, or even an overwhelming portion of the whole.

The general movement of this particular body of poetry can be specifically illustrated in the poetical pilgrim's progress of Archibald MacLeish, one of the most vigorous and gifted of American poets. He may be said to have changed from an introspective Hamlet to a poet of "public speech." Like many of his generation, he went through disillusionment after the war, and bitterness too, not so much over his own experience as over the death of a brother. An early poem was *The Hamlet of a MacLeish*, proclaiming very definitely that "the times are out of joint"; an expatriate at the time when the much advertised "lost generation" was so vocal, introspective, writing that "the knowledge of ill is among us, and the obligation to revenge" but giving no indication of what positive action such obligation might lead to. He seeks later what seems to be an escape from the social world, standing, as he expressed it, "provisionally before a mirror to subject the hypothesis of subjective reality." He returns in his interest to America as the natural theme of an American poet, expressing in *New Found Land* that return. But, in *Conquistador*, that interest was directed to an older civilization in Mexico, now gone. It was still a sort of nostalgia and escape. But in his poetry since 1935, he has expressed strongly a new spirit, which turns its glance outward to the present world and feels the necessity for a poet's dealing with a social system out of joint, if not actually doomed; also for the necessity of coming out of every sort of an ivory tower to partake in mass action movement to right injustice and save a threatened world.

A less marked but similar movement can be seen in Edna St. Vincent Millay, in her progress from "a privateness of feeling to a world of thought"; from the egoistic preoccupations of her early work, when her candle-burning-at-both-ends seemed a cosmic conflagration to a concern for the outward world, shown in the bitterly savage "Epitaph for the Race of Man" in her *Wine from these Grapes* and the varied social observation and denunciation scattered through *Conversation at Midnight*.

MacLeish has made the most emphatic statements of what he feels to be the necessity of the poet to deal with public questions, to be a part of the social struggle for a better ordered world. "Poetry," he declares, "is a living thing, no longer defending its existence, but challenging to look at the actual world, and saying that poetry is native to the actual world and being aware that the current crisis must be met, not escaped from." He has had the rare courage to admit a change of mind and outlook. When, in 1931, he expressed his scorn for poets who live within themselves and brood with futile indolence over the past, he was passing some judgment on his earlier work. He writes:

"Unless we can not only perceive, but also feel, the race of men to be more important than any one man, we are merely fighting back against the water . . . It is mankind, that which has happened always to all men, not the particular lives . . . not the 'great,' nor the 'leaders,' the brass voices, but these men, these lives, . . . Poetry, which owes no man anything, owes nevertheless one debt . . . an image of mankind in which men can again believe." [2]

Seven years later he writes:

"Never before in the history of this earth has it been more nearly possible for the society of men to create the world in which they wished to live . . . It is the act of the spirit which fails in us. This failure of the spirit is a failure from which only poetry can deliver us . . . Only poetry, exploring the spirit of man, is capable of creating in a breathful of words the common good men have

[2] *Poetry,* July 1931.

become incapable of imagining for themselves . . . Poetry alone imagines, and imagining creates the world that men can wish to live in and make true." [3]

"Politics," he declares, "is a subject for poetry because with us the public world has become the private world. The single individual, whether he wishes so or not, has become part of a world that contains also Austria and Czechoslovakia and China and Spain."

Another poet, Jean Starr Untermeyer, has related this trend to the history of poetry in saying that, "in bad times poets prophesy: poets have been prophets from Isaiah to Auden. They are dedicated to courage and their function, for one thing, is to relate the material world and the moral world, interpreted in no narrow sense." A closely parallel movement in poetry in Great Britain is seen in the emergence and work of such poets as W. H. Auden, Stephen Spender, C. Day Lewis, Louis MacNeice and Christopher Isherwood. This movement in the poet's thought of his art has been marked by the realization that in our kind of a world there is no valid insurance other than social insurance. Men are held together, for richer for poorer, for better for worse, in sickness and in health as long as they all shall live. Genevieve Taggard thus puts that realization in *The Words of a Mother:*

> They come to me talking about your safety,
>   your future. The heavy odds.
> They paint a black picture. How shall our
>   children survive?
> As if with all mothers and fathers, and since
>   the first day of your life
> I had not worried in big ways and small.
>   Knowing the perils. The frauds.
> As if I needed an actuary with slide rule
>   to give me a pang.

[3] *Poetry Magazine,* July 1938.

Insure? How insure against pain? Is there perhaps
    no class-struggle?
How is it with millions of children? With you
    as with them.
A different insurance, darling. One safety,
    one hope, my hope, my resolve:
Your face lifted with a million others,
    laughing, under red banners.[4]

Two general aspects of the work of poets who in bad times
become prophets, must be noted before we turn to a glimpse
of typical poetry which documents the affirmations made
above.

The first is a reiteration of what has already been pointed
out in connection with fiction and drama: the danger to art of
any kind from a rigidly Marxian formula. Poverty is not the
only thing that can "freeze the genial currents of the Soul."
Subscription to a Nicene Creed of the dictatorship of the pro-
letariat can also freeze a poet, and has frozen many. Wilfred
W. Gibson, not rated by criticism at all leftist in his leaning,
is a conservative and traditional poet, and yet one of the first
modern poets to portray effectively the life of labor; he has
said with great truth that "the proper spiritual habitation for
a poet is a half way house between the ivory tower and a soap
box at the corner of the public thoroughfare." Poetry cannot
flourish when the mind is in shackles to any formula. One particular aspect of this is to be noted in the verse, of which there
was much in the ten years, celebrating Russia as the glorious
"Red woman" who was to save the world. It "dates" curiously
and lamentably. Here, for instance, is a poem by one of the
strongest of all the poets of radical revolution, Kenneth
Patchen:

[4] *Calling Western Union* by Genevieve Taggard. Harper and Brothers,
1936.

Watch the massive body stir
Horizon's nearness coming on
In the Kremlin lamp of her eyes
In the iron advance of arms
Like crowds of working men
Exploring bellies of the rich
With thunder of planning,
With the lightning Beauty of Revolution
Grinding out the day's agony
A vast and teeming star.
Comrades, the Red woman!
She is dream's image made real.
She is the timeless Bride of all our loving.[5]

But by 1939, the Red woman had been to Finland and had lost something of the "Bride-of-all-our-loving" look in her eyes.

Another baffling aspect of quite a large body of contemporary social poetry has been the difficulty of the poet finding a means of real communication with the reader. So often he speaks in a private tongue, his images and symbols are confusing and opaque. Often, as in Muriel Rukeyser and Kenneth Patchen and Ben Belitt, the speech goes into a sort of "esperanto." A stanza from the verses in *The New Yorker*, already quoted, has genuine critical value as well as humor:

Rare is the nugget I can fish out
From subtleties the poets dish out
In fact I think it's time we had some
Poets who are plain and gladsome
Who shun the effort it must cost
To seem more deep than Robert Frost.[6]

Sometimes a lack of punctuation seems to be regarded as sufficient atonement for all failures of intelligibility. The search for depth results merely in obscurity. William Rose

[5] *Before the Brave* by Kenneth Patchen. Random House, 1936.
[6] *The New Yorker*, July 8, 1939.

Benét, who has as warm a sympathy for poetical experiment and originality of form and radical content as any critic could have, suggests one cause of this darkness, "I only regret that the great example of James Joyce has done such irremediable harm to so many young poets."

Yet the poetry expressing social interest and influence has been very noteworthy in idea, feeling and art. It has made an effective refutation of the indictment of the poetry of an earlier generation made by Edgar Lee Masters in his *Petit the Poet,* in the Spoon River Anthology; poetry like genteel needlework, "Triolets, Villanelles; Rondels, Rondeaus" rattling inconsequentially like "Seed in a dry pod," while life all around went unnoticed. Today, there is more interest in power than in specious cleverness. This poetry is marked by ethical insight, passionate sympathy with men, women and children, and a deeply religious protest against an order and way of life careless of human consequences.

Since 1935, Archibald MacLeish has published one volume of poetry, *Public Speech,* three plays, *Panic, The Fall of the City* and *Air Raid,* the latter two written for radio production, and *Land of the Free,* a poetical text for the photographs exhibiting the westward pilgrimage of the dispossessed. *Public Speech* illustrates his conviction of the necessity of the poet dealing with public questions. It conveys his strong sense of social disaster, already present and impending. One of the poems, "Speech to the Scholars," first given as a Phi Beta Kappa poem at Columbia University, is a fervent appeal to recognize the threat of the totalitarian attack on the mind of man, in contrast to the older type of military assault alone. "You could be neutral then," he says. Now the battle is carried to the scholar's own home, the mind. There can be no neutrals in that struggle except "the bought historian" and "the lying churchman." The complacent remoteness of the scholar has allowed the word left by the fathers to become "filthy with rust." "Speech to Those Who Say Comrade" rebukes the sentimental spirit of words masquerading as brotherhood. MacLeish's faith in some ultimate verity, as well as his ethical evaluation of love, speak eloquently in one of the greatest poems in the book, "Pole Star for This Year" (1936). The true pole star for guidance he declares is love:

> Liberty and pride and hope
> And every guide mark of the mind
> That led our blindness once has vanished.
> This star will not. Love's star will not.
>
> Love that has beheld the face
> A man has with a man's eyes in it
> Bloody from the sluggard's blows
> Or heard the cold child cry for hunger—
>
> Love that listens where the good:
> The virtuous man: the men of faith:
> Proclaim the paradise on earth
> And murder, starve, and burn to make it—
>
> Love that cannot either sleep
> Or keep rich music in the ear
> Or lose itself for the wild beat
> The anger in the blood makes raging—
>
> Love that hardens into hate
> Love that hatred and as bright—
> Love is that one waking light
> That leads now when all others darken.[7]

Love is not a sentimental emotion. It is built only on shared life and struggle. There is sure ethical and religious insight in his affirmation that "born brothers in truth" are puddlers,

[7] *Public Speech* by Archibald MacLeish. Farrar and Rinehart, 1936.

"scorched by the same flame," veterans out of the same ship and factories; those who have fought and labored together, who "carry the common look like a card."

> Brotherhood! No word said can make you brothers!
> Brotherhood only the brave earn and by danger or
> Harm or by being hurt and by no other.

> Brotherhood here in the strange world is the rich and
> Rarest giving of life and the most valued:
> Not to be had for a word or a week's wishing.[8]

His drama, *Panic*, has for its subject the collapse of the American banking system in 1933. It has been criticized because it neither assigns a cause nor points to a remedy for the crash. Such were not the poet's aims. He himself says that the trouble is too big and far ranging to be readily understood. It does convey the tensity, the despair, the sense of impending doom of the time in rhythm which the poet tries to adapt to the swiftly moving doom. He is no propagandist, he has no class axe to grind; he does express the bewildering chaos of the closing banks. The central figure is McCafferty, the banker, whose bank has gone down in the flood. The scenes shift from a street in which news bulletins of the disasters are given out to the office of the bank where McCafferty tries to inject courage into his fainting partners (in much the manner and even the words of President Hoover's pep talks of the same grim month, February 1933). McCafferty's first words set the key,

> "Things like this don't happen by themselves.
> What's behind it? Who is?"

No one knows the answer. McCafferty tries reassurance. "Easy enough for you," the bankers cry, "but what about the

[8] *Ibid.*

rest of us?" The bankers feel that they are blind; they can't fight because they can't see anything to fight against. With the news that the Detroit Guardian Trust is closing, shouts of panic, both in the office and in the street outside, increase. And, in the crisis, the government and the people call upon McCafferty, the great man, to save them. At this point a small mob of unemployed break through the guards, enter. They tell these 'empire builders' that their days are over:

> Nothing can help you now, Captains. It's our world!
> History's back of us! Time's bearing us!

The bankers retreat: McCafferty mocks them for being afraid. The leader of the unemployed, a Blind Man, seeks out McCafferty and reaffirms his words; these broken, starving and sick men are not to be feared:

> It is not we you have the need to fear!
> It is not we who threaten you! Your ill is
> Time—and there's no cure for time but dying!
> Time's the hurt your hearts have; not our hands.[9]

The banker has no way of even understanding, much less meeting what has happened. His one solution—suicide—was a common one at the time. The blindness of this man, and those of his class which he typifies, is shown in the bitter invective he makes against all humanitarianism, in which he sees nothing but a threat to profits:

> Calling it love of humanity! Love of humanity!
> What's the love of humanity? Hatred of manhood!
> Hatred of one man: love of men by hundreds!
> Love of what's least like a man: unliving:
> Nameless: faceless: sexless: odorless: blank:
> Without breath: unreal: made of words: of numbers—

[9] *Panic* by Archibald MacLeish. Houghton, Mifflin & Company, 1935.

Love as prudes love: love in books: on paper—
Love! Not love but envy—but revenge—
But fear: hatred of life: horror of manhood!
Men who love humanity are men who
Hate the man: who'd first destroy him: that kind!
Their kind shrieking at us!

Stephen Benét's *Burning City*, 1936, contains some of the finest and strongest poetry infused with social feeling and outlook. Imagination, humor and lyric gifts are all brought to the service of a militant skepticism of traditional economic and political codes.

Here is an indictment of complacency in the presence of fascist threats, a warning far more pertinent now than when written four years ago:

> We thought we were done with these
>   things but we were wrong.
> We thought, because we had power, we
>   had wisdom.
> We thought the long train would run
>   to the end of Time.
> We thought the light would increase.
> Now the long train stands derailed and
>   the bandits loot it.
> Now the boar and the asp have power in
>   our time.
> Now the night rolls back on the West
>   and the night is solid.
> Our fathers and ourselves sowed dragon's
>   teeth.
> Our children know and suffer the
>   armed men.[10]

The bankruptcy of the vaunted resources of a machine civilization is thus put in words often quoted. These are from

[10] *Burning City* by Stephen Benét. Farrar and Rinehart.

Nightmare with Angels by Benét—in which a portent appears from the sky:

> He turned blue at the wingtips and
>   disappeared as another angel approached
>   me.
> This one was quietly but appropriately
>   dressed in cellophane, synthetic rubber
>   and stainless steel,
> But his mask was the blind mask of Ares,
>   snouted for gasmasks.
> He was neither soldier, sailor, farmer,
>   dictator nor munitions-manufacturer.
> Nor did he have much conversation,
>   except to say,
> "You will not be saved by General Motors
>   or the prefabricated house.
> You will not be saved by dialectic
>   materialism or the Lambeth Conference.
> You will not be saved by Vitamin D or
>   the expanding universe.
> In fact, you will not be saved."
> Then he showed his hand:
> In his hand was a woven, wire basket, full
>   of seeds, small metallic and shining like
>   the seeds of portulaca;
> Where he sowed them, the green vine withered,
>   and the smoke and the armies sprang up.[11]

That reads like quite a sober history of 1939–1940.

Edna St. Vincent Millay's latest work does not present the clear direction marked in the poetry of MacLeish and to a less extent in Benét. In her book, published in 1939, *Huntsman, What Quarry*, she reverts in a majority of the poems to earlier moods and themes of personal emotion. Indeed, the critical reception of that book indicates the difficult position of a poet. If he follows the content and mood and form of his earlier

[11] *Ibid.*

work, some critics will sigh, "Alas, alas, mere repetition; just the mixture as before." If he turns to new fields, he gets, from some, the counsel to be himself and not make futile efforts to change. In *Wine from These Grapes*, Miss Millay has sharp and powerful expressions of the mood of rebellion and protest which so marked the ten years, and the quickened and enlarged interest in society and its fate. A new planet has swung into her pen, most memorably shown in the bitter "Epitaph for the Race of Man," a passionate protest against the obscene idiocy of war. The poet's concern with a disintegrating world is shown again in the group of poems, "Say That We Saw Spain Die," in *Huntsman, What Quarry*, in which the figure of a dying bull in the ring is made to serve as a symbol of the Spanish Republic, betrayed by the democracies and slaughtered by its fascist enemies. Written before the outbreak of World War II, the poem shows a grasp of the worldwide importance of the Spanish tragedy, which the years following underlined in deep red.

In *Conversation at Midnight*, Miss Millay uses new forms as well as content. Instead of the skillfully carved sonnet-sequence, there is the attempted reproduction of familiar talk, employing the devices of slang, unfinished sentences, even doggerel. Typical figures representing different economic, social and religious points of view engage in a "bull session." A stockbroker, a Franciscan priest, an agnostic painter, a communistic poet, an advertising man and a short story writer are made to express characteristic clashes of opinion and denunciations. The opinions of the author do not emerge clearly; possibly there is some sympathy with many of the divergent convictions. At any rate, there are pungent diatribes against most of the ills of the time, such as the lack of leisure; the living in a bath of barbaric noise which threatens to atrophy the sense of hearing; the bane of meretricious advertisement, "daily slop," in the words of the advertising man; the hypocritical emptiness of religion and also the defense of the church by Anselmo, the priest; the futility of war; indictment of both conservatism and communism.

Horace Gregory, like the other poets named in this chapter, cannot be even partially appraised by a few adjectives or quotations. Repeated warning must be given that there are more things in the heaven and earth of each of these poets than can be suggested by attention to the one aspect of the poetic reflection of the social turmoil and struggle. Gregory, for instance, could be more adequately treated as a poet giving expression to the inner intellectual and spiritual strains and dilemmas of the time. He is a sensitive instrument on which the pulls in various directions are recorded, the struggle between hope and despair, the search for a new hope for human salvation to replace what seems to be the inadequacy of traditional religious faith. There is a strong feeling of the disintegration and chaos of the present order, the urgency of action, the turning to some form of collectivist society as the way out, yet a foreboding that not his generation but that of his son will see (we should say, *may* see) a better day. With a deep appreciation and love for the past, with many of its cherished values either gone or threatened, he still turns to the future, as in the advice to his son in the prologue to *Chorus for Survival,*

> Turn here, my son,
> No longer turn to what we were
> Build in the sunlight with strong men.

The builder's chief foundation is the reality and power of human love, capable of sustaining a new society. The title of an earlier book, *No Retreat,* well expresses his impulse to action, amid all tensions and confusions.

Kenneth Patchen is one of the most revolutionary of contemporary poets, in his faith and outlook. He is also, unfortunately, one of the most difficult. His volumes, *Before the Brave* and *First Will and Testament*, well merit the observation of C. Day Lewis that modern poets have "lost their audience because they began to talk the private language of personal friends." Some, at least, of Patchen's most deeply felt work appears in a sort of a Morse telegraphic code to which the ordinary reader has no key. Patchen is the most thorough going of the radical poets of violent revolution. He lays about him vigorously smashing the idols and most of the ideals of modern civilization. He has the ardor of bitter youth, and when he temporarily emerges out of the low visibility of incoherence into real eloquence, he is much more clear in details than in general theme. Too many of his poems as a whole have the quality of vaguely remembered and confused bad dreams. Yet his specific pictures are sharp and powerful. No one has more vividly expressed the feeling of youth cheated and frustrated by economic pressures and by war. The picture of unemployed youth at "Street Corner College" is forceful:

We are the insulted, brother, the desolate boys.
Sleepwalkers in a dark and terrible land.

* * *

We manage to have the look that young men have;
We feel nothing behind our faces, one way or another.

We shall probably not be quite dead when we die.
We were never anything all the way; not even soldiers.[12]

The same bitterness of defrauded youth is voiced in the "Letter to a Politician in Kansas City":

[12] *First Will and Testament* by Kenneth Patchen. New Directions, Norfolk, Connecticut, 1939.

> I'm not too starved to want food
> not too homeless to want a home not
>   too dumb
> to answer questions come to think of it
>   it'll take a hell
> of a lot more than you've got to stop
>   what's
> going on deep inside us when it starts
>   out
> when it starts wheels going worlds
>   growing
> and any man can live on earth when
>   we're through with it.[13]

Patchen has a strong faith in revolution—in communism as a redeeming Messiah, though he makes no obeisance before Stalin:

Those smug saints, whether of church or Stalin can get off the back of my people and stay off.

The significance of the title "Before the Brave" lies in his faith that "the sun retreats before the brave" in the class struggle:

Who were the property of every dunce and prophet
Of every gust of wind, of every goutish giant on earth,
Are come now to claim ourselves and the profit
Of an ownership what has been our own since birth.
We are not cool; our hate has made us wise, not clever
Beloved listen, the stirring of life from the grave
The heart breaks with the groan and grind of a lever
Which lifts a world whose very sun retreats before the brave.[14]

Here is his lyric praise of the Gun, as the instrument of social salvation:

[13] *Before the Brave* by Kenneth Patchen. Random House, 1936.
[14] *Ibid.*

They too are craftsmen whose fingers close
Over careful triggers, whose targets we are
Set up machine guns over the state bellyaching
                    over our books.

                *   *   *

We have not long: our plays are few
Can we convince you in better speech?
            Yes, guns are loud.
And history has place for orators not
            quite so proud.[15]

Another Kenneth, Kenneth Fearing, writes in a very different language and mood. He leads what might fairly be
called the Jazz attack on modern life and on capitalism, particularly on what Fearing considers its debauching of the middle class. To this attack he brings ridicule, sarcasm, irony and
invective, with a spirited gusto. He has little concern for any
positive alternative order of society which should replace the
present doomed and damned order; at least no outlines, however vague, of such an alternative appear in his work. His
heart is in a riot of debunking. He is not crouching in a corner on the defensive; he advances gaily to the assault on the
forces causing degeneration, a sort of Chesterton in swing
time. It might seem fantastic to claim for Fearing's metrical
extravaganzas the qualities of serious ethical criticism. Yet that
is exactly what they have. There is a strong ethical protest
which runs deeper than the desire for economic redistribution.
He is appalled at what the present system does to the minds
and spirits—to the *souls* of men, to use a word outmoded in
many circles. Life has been reduced to trivial and insignificant
routine, from which beauty and the sense of inherent worth
have been taken away. He is particularly savage in his scorn
for the effects of the instruments of man's demoralization,

[15] *Ibid.*

such as newspapers, the radio and movies. Here is his picture of the life of a typical hustler, whose life has dribbled away in the service of speed, efficiency and profit:

> And wow he died as wow he lived,
> Going whop to the office, and blooie home to
> sleep and biff got married and bam had
> children and oof got fired
> Zowie did he live and zowie did he die.[16]

In *Denouement*, he presents a trial of laborers framed in a case practically the same as that which gives the theme to Levin's novel, *Citizens*, exhibiting the hopeless struggle of workers equipped with "three dependents and a package of cigarettes," against the alliance of owners, police and law courts. Yet his sense of the spiritual impoverishment of middle class life is strongly felt here, as well as his sense of injustice. Mr. Fearing has many resemblances to the technique and motives of the old evangelistic preaching. He is denouncing sin from a strong sense of the ethical and spiritual blight that it puts on life. He is not berating the old fashioned objects of the evangelist Jeremiads, drinking, gambling and card playing. He is on the trail of bigger devils than those, the complex sins of an acquisitive social order. The wages of that sin is death to the capacities of the spirit. The professional exponents of religion could learn much, if they would be so humble, not from Fearing's language or literary form, but from his indignation and insight. He sees clearly, for instance, the essential evil in all that depersonalizes man, showing a sure understanding of the very core of the Christian Gospel. This appears notably in his poem, *Dirge*. A man is killed in the street, as a result of the careless disregard for human life. The police search his

16 *Poems* by Kenneth Fearing. Dynamo Press, 1935.

pockets, and what they find is all essentially impersonal. The poet suggests that these trinkets be given to those institutions which have encircled and conditioned his life to a form of impersonal servitude; thus the small change should go to the People's Gas and the Standard Oil Company; his matches to the Interborough Rapid Transit; other things to Will Hays of the movies, and Al Capone, representing the bootleg industries. "These," says the poem, with irony, "were his pals."

Muriel Rukeyser, one of the most promising of the younger poets of today, combines a radical social criticism and a revolutionary ardor and faith with poetic techniques of rare skill and imagination, particularly in treating the contemporary environment, but which sometimes make the meaning difficult to grasp. Her three volumes, *Theory of Flight, U.S. 1,* and *A Turning Wind,* are marked by a sensitive sympathy and an indignation at social injustice. Her "Book of the Dead" in *U.S. 1,* a detailed poetic record of the victims of silicosis, the deadly disease from preventable mine dust, at Gauley, West Virginia, and the trial which failed to remedy the wrong, is a most effective handling of a theme of great human and social importance.

Joy Davidman, whose *Letter to a Comrade* was published in her twenty-third year, writes, for the most part, much more directly and clearly than many "modern" poets, and shows a clear-eyed awareness of social and economic issues, a strong interest in the whole spread of American scenes and life, and genuine poetic gift. She speaks for the generation "that knew the depression in its teens, and the war not at all." She herself says, "I am of this depression generation and I know what we face." Her spirit is well conveyed in one poem, in which she makes her petition, not for that *summum bonum* of so many young women poets, the gift of love. She makes instead *A Prayer Against Indifference:*

When wars and ruined men shall cease
To vex my body's house of peace,
And bloody children lying dead
Let me lie softly in my bed
To nurse a whole and sacred skin,
Break roof and let the bomb come in.

Knock music at the templed skull
And say the world is beautiful,
But never let the dweller lock
Its house against another knock;
Never shut out the gun, the scream,
Never lie blind within a dream.

Within these walls the brain shall sit
And chew on life surrounding it;
Eat the soft sunlight hour and then
The bitter taste of bleeding men;
But never underneath the sun
Shall it forget the scream, the gun.

Let me have eyes I need not shut;
Let me have truth at my tongue's root;
Let courage and the brain command
The honest fingers of my hand;
And when I wait to save my skin
Break roof and let my death come in.[17]

Her *Letter to a Comrade* is a description of America with
the eye of a poet with a rare gift for picturesque phrase, a love
for the land of "breasted and milky earth." But it is also seen
with a realistic eye, keen to detect economic and human devastation. Yet she sings with an ardent revolutionary faith that
from a devastated land there shall be a new growth. Here are
two contrasted pictures, one a detail of the economic blight:

[17] *Letter to a Comrade* by Joy Davidman. Yale University Press, 1938.

". . . but pray for us
       pray for us; we are the sons of the
              French adventurers
       salt and dry codfish beside a salty stream
       here with no buyers; here our bread
       stands to the flies; here our children
       have no teeth, live on the thin flesh of
              fishes
       and the pallid taste of Christmas berries
              plucked by the roadside
       while waiting for the cars and money of
              tourists;
       and because we have no teeth in our heads
              with which to bite." [18]

The other is the faith in the outcome of struggle:

"But he has said, this man, I have
       heard him speak.
       He will come out of the black hell
       of the mine.
       He will come out of the fire and
       forging steel,
       the hell of the boiler room, the
       prison hell,
       the whirring hell of the factory; and
       when he comes
       we shall not need archangels. We shall
       need
       only the salt and human loins of this
       man
       and the sweat marking with grime the
       lines of his palm,
       the brutal stone, the sea, the supple
       water,
       the iron mountains and the fertile soil
       the everlasting image of this man." [19]

[18] *Ibid.*
[19] *Ibid.*

Genevieve Taggard is a poet whose work shows many moods and changing interests, being sharply marked into two general periods, before the depression and after. Her poetry of social interest and protest is forceful and clear, if not marked by the same lyric quality of her early work. Here for instance is a post-mortem with realistic detail and a bitter fire:

. . . the child died, the investigator said, for lack of proper food. After the funeral the mother went back to the mill. She is expecting another child . . .

> . . . then fold up without pause
> The colored ginghams and the underclothes.
> And from the stale
> Depth of the dresser, smelling of medicine, take
> The first year's garments. And by this act prepare
> Your store of pain, your weariness, dull love,
> To bear another child with doubled fists
> And sucking face.
> Clearly it is best, mill-mother,
> Not to rebel or ask clear silly questions,
> Saying womb is sick of its work with death,
> Your body drugged with work and the repeated bitter
> Gall of your morning vomit. Never try
> Asking if we should blame you. Live in fear. And put
> Soap on the yellowed blankets. Rub them pure.[20]

Here is a typical "comrades-over-the-barricades" bugle call, in a formula becoming hackneyed, yet withal with spirited vigor and representative of much poetry with a resolve "to do something about it" produced during the thirties:

O people misshapen, hugging bones in old coats,
Wavering as you walk, hurrying on mean streets and stairs,
Poor eaters, with bodies the clinics hastily patch
And push out into dark, dirt, roar and lack again. . . .

[20] *Calling Western Union* by Genevieve Taggard. Harper and Brothers, 1936.

Come close-up, faces, showing sunk eyes and skull forehead,
Blinking with light and the horror of being seen.
Brothers, Comrades, pool the last strength of men
In party, in mass, boil into form, and strike.

We will see you change,—shoulders swing broad and slow.
Your coats will not change this winter, no. But you
In ranks no distant day, clad and alert,
As resolute as storm, born of this bad extreme.[21]

Babette Deutsch, Ben Belit, Willard Maas and Sterling
Brown should not be omitted from any roll of the poets of
radical feeling and content.

Carl Sandburg's *The People Yes* will not fit into any Marxian pattern. It cannot be crowded into any shrill—"workers of
the world unite" music. It is Sandburg—a song bag of genuine
America, a motley collection of legends, old jokes, folk traditions, fused into a strong faith in the survival and triumph of
the people and democracy, bitingly scornful of the blind and
the vicious who exploit and disdain the people. Here is his
version of the economic Alice-in-Wonderland which the hungry thirties created:

"I came to a country,"
said a wind bitten vagabond
"Where I saw shoemakers barefoot
saying they had too many shoes.
I met carpenters living outdoors
saying they had built too many houses.
Clothing workers I talked with,
bushelmen and armhole-basters,
said their coats were on a ragged edge
because they made too many coats.
And I talked with farmers, yeomanry,
the backbone of the country,
so they were told,

[21] *Ibid.*

saying they were in debt and near starvation
because they had gone ahead like always
And raised too much wheat and corn
too many hogs, sheep, cattle.
When I said, 'You live in a strange country,'
they answered slow, like men
who wouldn't waste anything, not even language:
'You ain't far wrong there, young feller.
We're going to do something, we don't know what.'

I raise hogs and the railroads and the banks take them away
    from me and I get hit in the hind end.
The more hogs I raise the worse my mortgages look,
I try to sleep and I hear those mortgages gnawing at night
    like rats in a corn crib.
I want to shoot somebody but I don't know who." [22]

He has real faith in people and he writes with a biting anger of the suave folk who pay themselves higher salaries while they cut wages, of the "profiteers" whom Lincoln called "respectable scoundrels," of all who deny, debauch, oppress, mock and enslave the people, of all those who say, "Your people, sir, is a great beast," overtly or covertly.

Here is his democratic faith:

The people will live on.
The learning and blundering people will live on.
They will be tricked and sold and again sold
And go back to the nourishing earth for rootholds. . . .

. . . This reaching is alive.
The panderers and liars have violated and smutted it.
Yet this reaching is alive yet for the lights and keepsakes.[23]

These poets have a function like that of the spies who reported on the land of Canaan. This poetry has been a return

[22] *The People Yes* by Carl Sandburg. Harcourt Brace & Company, 1936.
[23] *Ibid.*

of the spies, a report, they have been exposed to the storms and stresses.

These poets have turned away from the private world of self-centered esthetes, who have been called, "The frivolously decorative or elaborately erudite." A headlong enthusiasm for life is returning. There has been immediate and emotional contact with people. Poetry today is returning from the desert of the waste land to the life of men.

Even the extremely limited excerpts in this chapter give evidences that a great deal of contemporary poetry joins hands with religious and moral insight in one important respect—it refuses to believe that the new order can be brought about by the simple economic struggle proposed by the Marxists. Fuller resources and a deeper plumbing of human life are necessary.

CHAPTER 10

RELIGION—IMPLICIT AND EXPLICIT

THERE HAS BEEN much comment that in the book on the 1930's, purporting to take in the whole survey of American history and life, *America in Midpassage*, by Charles A. and Mary Beard, there is no mention of religion as a factor in the life of the period, except in the most minor, incidental references. Whole pages are given over to very unimportant novels, a chapter of 125 pages is given to entertainment, including stage, radio and movies, a whole chapter of 76 pages to art. In the 950 pages, not a line to religion!

What is the answer? John Haynes Holmes has one, brusque and to the point. He says that the Beards "were either careless, ignorant or prejudiced." We are not limited to one choice among these three vigorous adjectives. We can take all three and add some. The judgment of Dr. Holmes, however, covered a very much wider territory than just a comment on one book. It provides a clue to a large question—why does religion, either as thought or organized church, play so small a part in the literature of the time? For we need have no doubt about the fact. From great areas of life repeatedly presented in novel and drama in multitudinous detail, the impression might be gained that Christianity had completely passed from the earth. If it were not for the generous profanity, we might wonder if God had ever been a subject of speculation by the human race, or if a man named Jesus had ever lived.

There is no ready or complete answer to the question, but merely raising it opens up avenues into the whole cultural life of America, its literature and religion.

It is hard to see how anyone who has lived in normal touch with the broad range of life in this country can fail to admit that this relative absence of religion as a definite concern or aspect of life, represents a badly distorted picture. This is due partly to carelessness, ignorance and prejudice on the part of many writers. For one thing the majority of those hailed as most significant writers are entirely outside the ranks of organized religion. There is a familiar literary judgment on novels written about Oxford, doubtless made by an Oxford man at the end of his patience: "most Oxford novels have been written by elderly ladies on the basis of a one-day visit thirty years before, to Cambridge." The knowledge of religion possessed by many writers rests on the same massive foundation.

Interesting data on the relation of writers to religion are given in the results of the questionnaire of Professor James H. Leuba on religious belief. In the group designated as 'writers,' the returns he received show that of those who replied, only 32 per cent stated that they believed in "A God to whom one may pray in the expectation of receiving an answer," while 62 per cent said they did not believe. Forty per cent expressed belief in immortality, twenty-eight per cent disbelief, while thirty-two per cent stated that they had no definite belief on the question.

Other obvious facts have a bearing on the result. Among many writers, there is a tendency to take normal processes and interests for granted. The result is often an undue prominence of the unusual or abnormal, which gives a distorting effect. Then it is also true that religion, either in its intellectual or institutional aspect, does not lend itself readily to the dramatic. It is much more exciting to describe an explosion than summer rain.

An editor of a religious journal defends the Beards, and, presumably, this larger absence of consideration of explicit religion, on the specious ground that religion was not doing anything worth recording. There are two answers to that. One is that religion is part of the life of the time, whatever it is doing or not doing. As Dr. Holmes has put it, "Religion holds the allegiance of some 50 millions of American citizens, who spend hundreds of millions of dollars in its support. It has thousands of adherents who are among the outstanding intellectual leaders of the time. Doesn't this rate along with half-forgotten best sellers, or trends in architecture, or the discount rate?" The other answer, at which we shall glance briefly later, is that religion has been doing plenty that is worth noticing.

There are two cautions to be kept in mind as we try to survey religion, both explicit and implicit, as reflected in American literature. The first is to refrain rigidly from finding more than is there. The literature of the 1930's is no promising garden in which to find "every common bush aflame with God." God does not flame through the shrubbery. We cannot, on this excursion, take as our theme song, "Wishing will make it so."

On the other hand, we must guard just as carefully against missing the real thing when it appears—as it does appear, emphatically. By the "real thing" in this connection we mean attitudes and cherished values which find a place in religion. The term legitimately includes evaluations of the worth of man which have an overtone of a universe of spiritual values; the spirit which cares desperately for "the least of these," and the sense of sin, though it is rarely called by that theological term, the sense of missing the mark of man's high calling; in a word, the deep dissatisfaction of the prodigal in the pig pen, even though there is no explicit declaration, "I will arise and go to my Father."

There is also to be considered as belonging in the field of religion the negative aspects, expressions of the strong sense of the tragic nature of human existence, the rejection of traditional beliefs which are felt to be inadequate, the substitution of other faiths, or hopes, or the rejection of all faith and hope. In addition to that, there is much more of definite treatment of positive religion than appears at first glance.

If we ask why there is so little religion, we are on our way to explore some leading characteristics of our time, speculations we cannot pause to follow here. Bliss Perry, in his *And Gladly Teach,* points to one cause when he says, "The war took it out of our generation, exhausting our capacity for emotional and moral reaction to events." Writers with an entirely secular outlook have become the guides, philosophers and friends of a large reading public. Art of one sort and another has to a large extent replaced religion and metaphysical thinking. It is no doubt easy to exaggerate the number of people who deliberately go to a particular novelist for their philosophy, but the fact cannot be overlooked that it is to imaginative writers that the public, whether consciously or not, is more and more inclined to turn. We see often the uncritical acceptance of the artist's wisdom as though it were a complete philosophy, without any reference to first principles. It is because the reading public to a large degree is without any body of principles of this sort, as T. S. Eliot has pointed out, that it is today at the mercy of an army of writers whose chief effect is to impose on it a secularist outlook. "What I wish to affirm," Mr. Eliot writes, "is that the whole of modern literature is corrupted by what I call secularism, that is simply unaware of, simply cannot understand, the primacy of the supernatural over the natural life: of something which I assume to be our primary concern." [1]

What about the movement of religion itself during the decade? That would be an exploration that would take us on too wide a detour. Only the most general suggestions can be made, and those very briefly.

For one thing, there was no great turning to religion, or to the church. There was nothing to compare with the religious revivals following the panics of 1857, 1873, or even 1893. Much fervent exhortation was given to 'get back to God,' whatever that might mean. But in the absence of any sharper definition, there were no augmented crowds streaming into the churches. This is not to say that the period was without deep religious and ethical thinking. There was close scrutiny of the economic and social traditions that had eventuated in so great a catastrophe, and scrutiny from the point of view of ethical qualities and social results. Many said not, "Lord increase our faith" but, "Lord increase our doubt"—our doubt about a much vaunted American way of life that furnished such meagre provision for millions, doubt about the orthodox creed that our present way of life is just about the best that can be expected. And that had great religious values. A preliminary step to worshipping God is to stop worshipping idols. A great many idols were toppled. Right there lies one big thing: There was more spiritual devastation in the prosperous 1920's than in the hungry 1930's. Lord Elton's phrase for the 1920's in Great Britain is just as true of the United States. He calls it "that devastated area of the spirit."

The primary movement in religious thinking—so clear that even the hasty runner can read, is the movement from more or

[1] *Essays Ancient and Modern* by T. S. Eliot. Faber and Faber, Ltd., London.

less man-centered faith to a God-centered faith. That has been due to European continental influences in part, and in part to the economic collapse furnishing a climate in which that emphasis flowered. In crude language, a theologian recently said, "Barth wouldn't have got to first base in America in the 1920's." In equally crude language, we can record that he did get to second base in the 1930's! There has been a shift from a faith that was so largely an appendage to the culture of its time, intellectual and economic, to a faith more solidly standing on its own feet to confront the world with revelation.

It is not too much to say that at the beginning of the decade Protestant Christian theology was somewhat generally diluted to an ethic which was supposed to be in the process of realization with the same march of time as the general march of progress. There was much talk about God, of course, and about sin, but it was not sharp enough to disturb the orderly parade to Zion. The emphasis on a God of judgment which is a theological commonplace today would have been complacently dismissed in many quarters ten years ago as an inevitable, but temporary, survival of fundamentalism. For, ten years ago, the slide to Avernus was just beginning.

All this is commonplace, and was one powerful force in bringing about a changed outlook in Christian thinking. Indeed, there may be data here for some future Marxian philosopher to use in a thesis demonstrating the economic determination of theology. The economic system, following a war, is stalled; the flow of dividends is dammed; consequently, theology follows the advice of Paul and turns "from these vain things to the living God." But the history is too deep and wide to be crowded into any merely economic explanation. It is part of the universal pattern of faith shaped by experience. In the religious view of the calamity as the judgment of God on sin, there has been the spiritual experience recorded in the 107th

Psalm: "Their soul melted away because of trouble. They reel to and fro like a drunken man, and are at their wits' end. Then they cry unto the Lord in their trouble."

As has been frequently observed, in times of prosperity Christians tend to become Greek in their theology; in times of adversity, they again become Hebrew. The movement from Greece to Judea has assumed the proportions of a great trek. Out of experience the emphasis has shifted from the immanence of God to His transcendence; from rationalism to revelation. The process might be put into old words, that "man's extremity is God's opportunity." There has been a compulsion to find other sources of salvation than those we have looked for in the mechanical skills of a secular civilization.

There has been a sharpened and deepened sense of evil which, as we shall see, has been impressively paralleled in literature. To use again the phrase of an earlier chapter, the 'candid camera' has been moved up closer to man himself—resulting in a new awareness of the evil, both actual and potential, in man. Reinhold Niebuhr says of the popular thinking of the early 20th century, "Whatever was wrong with man, the cause was some deficit in his social organization, or some imperfection in his education which further social history and cultural development would correct." That easy way out has been closed for many.

As we turn to look at the literature in America which has come out of this era marked by such trends in religious thinking, we find some features supported by evidence large enough in amount to give them, we hope, some value as interpretation.

One element of genuine religious implication has been the persistent search for values in a time when many traditional faiths and reliances, including religious ones, have been badly shaken. There has been a search for something to cling to, which is at heart a religious quest. There has not been much that could be called a reaffirmation of the Apostle's Creed or the thirty-nine Articles of Religion. The search has been expressed in thinking and feeling rather than in dogmatic expression. But there has been more real religious searching in tentative hopes and wonders than in many orthodox expressions. This generation may have been born without faith, but it was not without the need of it. Evelyn Underhill writes accurately, and her word applies to America as well as England, "Our generation is remarkable, or seems remarkable to those who have known no other, for the number of persons who must believe something, but do not know what." Hence, the emptying of the churches is accompanied by a vigorous growth of amateur theologians. Saroyan's *Daring Young Man on the Flying Trapeze* is a real symbol—for the hero wanted to get a flying trapeze to God—to some sort of eternity. This search, which finds so many expressions, is in itself impressive evidence of the depth of the religious capacity in man. It is as deep as sex or hunger. In one of Robert Frost's poems, a farmer speaks as he lovingly touches an axe handle:

> "The lines of a good axe helve
> Were native to the grain before the axe expressed them.
> And its curves were no false curves
> Put on it from without. And there its strength lay
> For the hard work." [1a]

There is much evidence that the lines of man's capacity for God are "native to the grain." They are no false curves put on it from without.

A story appeared in 1938, in the magazine *Story*, which has some allegorical value in this connection. It describes the state of mind of a postman who, after many years of walking, was seized by the fixed desire that he wanted to become a tree. He

---

[1a] *New Hampshire* by Robert Frost. Henry Holt & Co., 1923.

longed for fixed roots. The story is fantastic, yet it may serve as a sort of picture of a rootless generation. Man cannot live by movement alone. The search for fixed meaning is felt in many forms of literature. It appears in the revolutionary poetry of Patchen, much of which is concerned with recovering a meaning in life. It is expressed in the very original novel of Claude Brion Davis, *The Anointed*, giving the sea-going and spiritual odyssey of Harry Paterson, whose quest pursued through jails, forecastle and shipwreck was a search for an understanding of God. Man cannot rest in "loud days that have no meaning and no end," as one "seeker," Edna St. Vincent Millay, describes life. James Broughton's poem, *When in Diversity*, urging to "look deep to the roots," expresses well this search for some enduring values:

> When in diversity
> patterns make only diffusion,
> when even railroad trains
> disconnect, never leave,
> and canaries, like flowers,
> are remote from men's eyes
> and the hearts of faces you know,
> when without purpose
> leaves turn in your book
> and the chapters are meaningless,
> look to the roots,
> look deep to divinity,
> seek to the way and the woof
> that are one woven unity.
>
> When in diversity
> lives of others, and yours,
> only meet in confusion,
> in crossed figure and line,
> when, for your bread,
> no yeast can be found or contrived,

for your wine no sap that has strength,
for your mind and your blood no consent,
look to the roots,
look down to the root womb
and the kinship that bred these,
gave wholeness with difference
to brick and magnolia,
pickle and peacock.[2]

A second characteristic of a large amount of the literature of
the decade in fiction, poetry and drama is the strong, often passionate expression of the inadequacy of the Christian religion
and the church to meet contemporary needs of the individual
or society. This is largely a negative treatment of religion, the
judgment that it has been weighed in the balance and found
wanting. It would be hard to exaggerate the importance of the
work expressing this feeling, either as major mark of the writing of the time, or as required study—a required, not an elec-
tive course, for all people devoted to the progress of religion
and the church. For this varied bill of particulars, drawn up
against a religion charged with impotence for its task, is not
the old oratorical onslaught of the complacent and evangelistic
"village atheist" type of mind. The Bradlaughs and the Inger-
solls have become museum pieces. Nor is it the exuberance of
bad boys joyously hurling rocks through the church windows.
It is rather the thoughtful, often reluctant and saddened rejection of the Christian faith as an insecure foundation; or a
rejection of its adequacy as a force for necessary social change;
or a protest against its organized forms for failing to realize its
potentialities.

Often the feeling is reflected that conventional religious belief is too superficial, too much a comfortable support for the
well-fed to face the ugly realities of the world. Mio, the cen-

[2] *Saturday Review of Literature.*

tral figure in Anderson's *Winterset*, puts this with a stinging
bitterness:

> "Tell them when you get inside where it's warm, and you love
> each other, and mother comes in to kiss her darling, tell them to
> hang onto it while they can, believe while they can it's a safe
> warm world, and Jesus finds his lambs and carries them into his
> bosom. I've seen some lambs that Jesus missed." [3]

From a different quarter is reflected the feeling that there is
"nothing" in church for the down and out. Thus, Bigger
Thomas, the young negro murderer in Richard Wright's *Native Son*, gives his judgment when cross-examined by his
lawyer:

> "Did you ever go to church, Bigger,
> Yeah, when I was little. But that was a long time ago.
> Your folks were religious?
> Yeah, they went to church all the time.
> Why did you stop going?
> I didn't like it. There was nothing in it. Aw, all
> they did was to shout and pray all the time. And it
> didn't get 'em nothing. All the colored folks
> do that, but it didn't get 'em nothing. The
> White folks got everything.
> Did you ever feel happy in church?
> Naw. I didn't want to. Nobody but poor folks
> get happy in church.
>   But you were poor, Bigger.
> Again Bigger's eyes lit with bitter and feverish pride.
>   I ain't that poor, he said." [4]

There is pertinent religious and social comment in the
proud declaration—"I ain't that poor."

A similar judgment is uttered by the young Italian boy in
Di Donato's *Christ in Concrete*, when he sees his mother de-

[3] *Winterset* by Maxwell Anderson. Anderson House.
[4] *Native Son* by Richard Wright. Harper and Brothers, 1940.

voutly praying before a crucifix and explains his refusal to
share such piety by saying, "I want salvation now." The same
disdain for conventional piety appears in James T. Farrell's
description of the religious practices of his Irish characters in
No Star Is Lost. Old Mrs. O'Flaherty has visitations from
heavenly beings, but, to the author, the chief effect seems to
be an improvement in the force of her cursing. It is superstition and no source of strength to any of the characters who
resort to the church. In Eugene O'Neill's *Mourning Becomes
Electra,* the Christian religion is shown as an outworn empty
thing in any manifestations visible in the play.

One of the most common indictments of the church is that
it purveys a gospel designed to minister to the complacencies
of a privileged class, that it is stirred to no passion for righteousness, carries no disturbance to the mind, or rebuke to the
conscience. Kenneth Burke's bitterly sarcastic verses, *For a
Modernist Sermon,* carry a feeling which has had voluminous
expression:

> You'll have an eight-cylinder car in heaven—
> Air conditioning—
> Indirect lighting—
> a tile bathroom and a white porcelain kitchen.
>
> Despite the phenomenal growth of population,
> there'll be no traffic problem,
> if you would drive out
> to the Garden of Eden
> for a week-end.
>
> O the celestial sundaes—
> all flavors made with the purest chemicals.
>
> No strike—no speed-up—no lay-off—
> everybody a coupon-clipper in heaven,
> living in peace, on the eternal drudgery
> of the damned.

All will be fragrant and quiet in heaven,
like the best real estate in Westchester.
All noise and stench segregated
to the under side of the railroad.
In heaven,
when you want something,
you just fill out an order
and your want is met like magic,
from the Power-plants
Assembly rooms
Factories
Presses
Forges
Mines
Mills
Smelteries
and Blast-Furnaces
of hell.[5]

An amusing picture of religion used and welcomed as a means of escape from a challenging social demand is to be found in Ruth McKenney's study of industry and labor in the rubber city of Akron, Ohio, *Industrial Valley*. In the midst of a strike, the Buchman traveling group comes to the city. Thus she reports it, with a keen eye for the relationship of the new "dress shirt evangelism" to the strike situation:

"Akron's *haut monde* suffered an acute attack of religious hysteria this week. For five exciting days, rich rubber men publicly confessed their sins, and luxurious and famous ladies, in full evening dress, told the world they were 'converted.'

Ever since the importation of the Southern hill-billy by the rubber shops, Akron had been rich pickings for itinerant evangelists, but until the arrival of Frank Buchman, a society Billy Sunday, the revivalists had pretty much confined their activities to East Akron and Kenmore Hill. Now, however, the Mayflower

[5] *The New Republic*, December 7, 1938.

Hotel rang with 'amens,' and bewildered traveling salesmen had to dodge prayer meetings at the town's best hotel.

The whole affair, which afterwards proved so embarrassing to many of the town's leading citizens, began on a Monday morning when the newspapers printed advance notices of Buchman's arrival with his troupe of evangelists. Most traveling revivalists were lucky to get two paragraphs on the church page in Akron newspapers, but Dr. Buchman's Thursday night prayer meeting was heralded on page one with big headlines and columns of respectful type.

The headlines, however, were no surprise to Akron. It developed, from the breathless newspaper accounts, that Dr. Buchman's local appearance was sponsored by the Firestone family, including Mr. and Mrs. Harvey Firestone, Senior." [6]

Miss McKenney preserves for posterity a marvelous insight into the significance of Jesus, made by the younger Mr. Firestone:

"But cynics were disappearing by Saturday morning. One after another of Akron's leading society matrons were more or less converted to the new cause. Their husbands went sheepishly to prayer meetings, but emerged proudly in the company of Akron's leading lawyers and rubber executives.

Bud Firestone led the Saturday night businessman's meeting. 'A man with Christ in his heart,' young Mr. Firestone said, 'can outsmart all others.' " [7]

If a man "with Christ in his heart" can "outsmart all others," who could be skeptical of the value of religion? The radical comment on the inadequacy of traditional religion finds vivid expression in Kenneth Patchen's phrase, "sightless old men in cathedrals of decay."

One particular aspect of this indictment of religion as impotent for social welfare is the portrayal found in many novels

[6] *Industrial Valley* by Ruth McKenney. Harcourt, Brace & Company, 1939.
[7] *Ibid.*

dealing with labor of the churches as a force antagonistic to the cause of labor, a repressive, deterrent influence playing into the hands of the employers resisting demands for wage increases. It is not merely that a favorite means of the owners in fighting a strike has been to send for an evangelist to distract and befuddle the workers, but also that religion as interpreted in the churches in mill towns makes for docile resignation. In *A Sign for Cain,* Grace Lumpkin gives many examples of this influence. Thus, a young worker, active in union organization, talks to the preacher:

"I hope to see you at Church," the preacher said cordially. His voice was rich with feeling. "I love your Ma. She is one of the finest in my little flock."

"How are your people getting along?" Denis asked. "Are they having a hard time getting enough to live on?"

"Well, there are some complaints. But I tell them 'keep your minds on the Bread of Life and not on the needs of this earth. The Lord will provide'."

"Some," he went on in a gently complaining tone, "think they don't get enough pay from the white people. They think it's the fault of the white people. But I tell them that isn't the way to think. Heed the words of the Lord, 'Love thy neighbor as thyself and all these things shall be remitted unto you'."

"Bless God!" Hancy exclaimed just as if she was in church. She looked at Denis and Ed one after the other triumphantly, as if to say, "See, the preacher says this. It must be so. It is so."

Ed saw her look and some words blurted out of his mouth. "Do loving your neighbor," he asked, "mean letting him walk over you and shoot you?"

"Nobody is going to walk over or shoot a good colored person, Brother Clarke," the preacher said patiently. "Not one that's got the love of Jesus in his heart. Look at me. Am I walked over or shot at?"

"You sho-o-o ain't," Ed told him.

"What would you advise us to do?" Denis asked. "We are poor and . . ."

"I ain't denying that," the preacher said hastily.
"You think we ought to just lie down and be like that? Most of us work for white people. What should we do?" [8]

There is a memorable passage in Fielding Burke's *A Stone Came Rolling*—in which the heroine, Ishma, considers that a first step toward the winning of justice for the workers is to free them from the bondage of inhibiting religious ideas—and that not in Russia but in North Carolina:

"But she could not keep herself from thinking of the long road of time that the human race had so yearningly traveled. It had been so many years since it was written, 'The poor and the needy seek water and there is none . . . I will open for them rivers on the bare heights, and fountains in the midst of the valleys . . . I will put in the wilderness the cedar, the acacia, the myrtle and the oil-tree; I will set in the desert the fir-tree and the pine . . .' . So long since the promise; yet every year more and more millions were tramping the roads with throats that were parched, with feet that would never be healed. For them no fountains in the valley, no oil-tree and myrtle in their desert; was it because men had put their cry in the mouth of Jehovah—content to wait ages on his humor? But now . . . It would be different. Their cry would be from their own mouths. They would not wait for an unmoving God to translate their vision into life." [9]

Ishma's one hope was that a minority of the working people would question the religious dogmas that held them inactive and helpless and lead the rest. One of the workers reasons with himself thus:

"No matter what happened they had done right. The Bible said so. Then why did God make it so hard for him? Take away his wife and his job and leave him helpless with two little babies?" [10]

[8] *A Sign for Cain* by Grace Lumpkin. Lee Furman, Inc., New York, 1935.
[9] *A Stone Came Rolling* by Fielding Burke. Longmans, Green & Company, New York, 1935.
[10] *Ibid.*

Any suggestion of an attempt to improve the status of the workers was interpreted by some of them as impiety. Mrs. Boardman, an old woman who has been able to endure her almost unbearable misery because of her faith, resents Ishma's efforts in her behalf:

"Don't you say anything about my God! I've worked for Him all my life, I've took poison out of the devil's hand, I've stood for ever'thing a human bein' can stand, an' I'm goin' to have what I've worked for! I've got a place waiting for me in heaven, not at anybody's feet either! I'll be right up in the row with Jesus! An' you ner nobody's going to take that away from me. My God is a just God, an' He'll give me my rights!"
"I only meant that you deserved more in this world. Why should you have to wait until you die before you can have any of the fruits of your toil and faith?"
"Because it's God's way, that's why. If he wants me to wait, I'll wait. I'll go on working for Him and praisin' Him till I kain't turn in my bed an' death's a-rattlin' in my throat. I'm not goin' to take any chance. Heaven is mine! I've bought it over and over, day after day, year in an' year out! I've given up everything for that. I ain't had nothin'. . . . The harder I've got it here, the better I'll have it there. I can hold out." [11]

On the more positive side, there has been continuous evidence of the need for religion. This has been expressed in many ways and by many authors of very different qualities. A poem of Marion Canby affirming that "man is heaven-starved" and that "earth is not enough" is representative of much literature, both poetry and prose, of similar content:

> And here at last we find
> Strict diagnosis of our malady,
> Which is, in short, that man is heaven-starved!
> Earth cannot satisfy, when all is said,
> Spirits possessed of vision by good right

[11] *Ibid.*

Of unremembered eons spent within
The impervious round of majesty, revealed
At last by conscious clarity of seeing—
Men are born thirsting for infinity!
(Still dazed by their own miracle of sight
They have not yet looked squarely at the sky.)
And if they heed the narrowed earth alone,
Their spirits sink in illness through their flesh! [12]

The collapse of the humanistic optimism which so strongly
marked the post war years, and in some degree also the nineteen twenties, has sharpened the recognition that man has
need for resources and reliances beyond those of his own creation. The assault of totalitarianism, both in its philosophy and
in its political and military power, on the dignity and worth
of the individual has brought reminders of the roots of the
conception of the value of personality in religious faith. S. N.
Behrman in his drama, *Rain from Heaven*, has given characteristic expression to this re-discovery. One of the characters in
the play exclaims, "I see now that goodness is not enough,
that charity is not enough. I'm sick of evasions. They've done
us in. Civilization, charity, tolerance, progress,—all catch
words. We'll have to redefine our terms." That is all. Too
much must not be read into the words. They are no equivalent for the declaration, "I believe in God the Father Almighty." But they do indicate a fresh movement and direction
of thought. A great many people, when they have come to redefine their terms, have come to consider hospitably the need
for a cosmic guarantee for the most deeply cherished human
values. It is not theologians and preachers alone who have
perceived the need for a spiritual basis for a defense of man
against totalitarian assault. The same word which was used by
the playwright, Mr. Behrman, is used by Vera Micheles Dean,

[12] *On My Way* by Marion Canby. Houghton, Mifflin & Company, 1939.

of the Foreign Policy Association: "If the West is to prevail over Germany it must do more than perfect its armaments. It must redefine, in equally dynamic terms, the economic and spiritual concepts which it offers as an alternative to Nazi ideology." In similar words, Professor G. A. Borgese, of the University of Chicago, calls for "a new theology." "It seems," he writes, "that no anti-fascist or anti-machiavellian movement can become socially effective without a new theology; or, if the word is unwelcome, without a unitary, and therefore, religious, conception of the world and man." [13] Walter Lippmann writes to the same effect more explicitly in words that seem a bit strange from the author of *A Preface to Morals*:

"The liberties we talk about defending today were established by men who took their conception of man from the great central religious tradition of western civilization, and the liberties we inherit can almost certainly not survive the abandonment of that tradition. And so, perhaps, the ordeal through which mankind is passing may be necessary. For it may be the only way in which modern man may recover the faith by which free and civilized people must live." [14]

These quotations are a parallel in more philosophical and political language to the words Miss Millay puts into the mouth of Ricardo in *Conversation at Midnight*, "Man has never been the same since God died. He has taken it very hard." Gamaliel Bradford has voiced the same idea in his poem, "I Sometimes Wish That God Were Back." There has been much fulfillment in literature during the fourth decade of the twentieth century of the profound prediction of Ernest Renan that the twentieth century would spend a good deal of its time picking out of the waste basket things which the nineteenth century threw into it. There has been a good deal of searching in the waste basket

[13] *The New Republic*, December 4, 1938.
[14] *The New York Herald Tribune*, 1939.

for something resembling the God who was so lightly discarded by many in the hey-day of scientific optimism. The farewell party for God did not prove to be such a howling success. Waldo Frank's *Chart for Rough Waters*, published in 1940, traces the rise of Nazism in part, at least, to the abandonment of what he calls "the great tradition," meaning the Judean-Christian religious tradition. "The individual soul," he writes, "fed and grown great by its awareness of the divine within it believed it could dispense with the divine. . . . This rebellion of the ego brought about man's humiliation." He thinks of salvation for the world in terms of that religious tradition; we must be saved by an act of religious faith, by becoming aware of God beyond and within us. Frank's book brings a lengthy and impassioned, if at times cloudy, argument, supporting the statement in Millay's *Conversation at Midnight*, "Man has not been the same since God died."

There has been a very definite religious spirit expressed in the large body of writing showing an aroused awareness of social injustice, descriptions of its effect on human life and protest against it. The novelists portraying the labor struggle, the poets and dramatists writing with sympathy and indignation, are not ordinarily numbered among the twelve apostles, and we are not trying to baptize them here. All that is asserted is that this literature is a legitimate part of a great prophetic tradition, coming down from the eighth century Hebrew prophets, through Jesus, including the prophetic witness of Judaism, Catholicism and Protestantism. There is evident in scores of novels and hundreds of poems the definite sense that in the exploitation of man something precious, even sacred, is being violated. And the sense of sacredness of personality, however loosely the words are used, is at heart a religious conception. This literature in the prophetic succession has been a large portion of the characteristic output of the period. More than that, it has been more deeply religious than much of the action and expression of organized religion in its more jittery manifestations. There have been noble and sincere expressions in word and action coming from religious groups, too numerous to be mentioned here. One characteristic sample is the statement of the House of Bishops of the Episcopal church made in 1933:

"No mere reestablishment of an old economic order will suffice. Christ demands a new order in which there shall be a more equitable distribution of material wealth, more certain assurance of security for the unemployed and aged, and above all else, an order which shall substitute the motive of service for the motive of gain.

Love of country must be qualified by love of all mankind; patriotism is subordinate to religion. The Cross is above the flag. In any issue between country and God, the clear duty of the Christian is to put obedience to God above every other loyalty."

Such a statement could be substantially paralleled by the actions of many official church bodies. What has not been recognized as it should be is that this body of literature of sympathy, protest and struggle has been an unorthodox but genuine expression of that spirit and understanding. One large hindrance to that recognition has been the habit of many religious people of being so shocked at vulgar language that they have failed to be shocked at the far more important things. No doubt, thousands of readers, for instance, were so shocked at the offensive expressions in the early part of *The Grapes of Wrath* that they failed completely to respond to the tremendous meaning of the book. One urgent need of Christian education is that of getting people to be shocked at the right things, the big things which are truly shocking, the violations of human dignity. The emotional reactions of Jesus have much contemporary relevance in this connection. He was shocked by different things from those which appalled the churchmen of his day. He was never bothered a bit by ceremonial impurities or any form of words; he was profoundly upset by wrongs to man, such as devouring widows' houses, over which others never blinked.

No survey, however brief, of the relationship of current literature to religion could omit the negative aspect of the substitutes for traditional religion which are found. If nature abhors a vacuum, the nature of man also abhors a spiritual vacuum. Something must be put into the place left by the "God-shaped blank." Nothing has more abundant evidence from contemporary writing than the dictum already quoted that modern man is without a religion, but not without the need of one. The phrase in that statement, "modern man," is far too vaguely inclusive, of course, but let it stand. The fact that man is not without the need of a religion and the consequent necessity to find some substitute for a theological creed has abundant data for its support. There are many varieties of these substitutes, the only common feature being that they are an alternative faith. Sometimes it is a faith in revolution and mass social action. This is set forth in Muriel Rukeyser's *Night Flight,* in which the hope of immortality with its traditional "gold and harps and seraphs" is discarded. "We surrender that hope," she says, "in favor of a revolutionary hope that rises above time, on surer wings than those of angels, wings of self confidence; believe that your presences are strong." [15] Sometimes the substitute seems to be a faith in "love" without religious roots in the theological sense, as in MacLeish, and in Willard Maas in his *Concerning the Young.* He discerns the clouds that threaten youth today, "obscene" poverty and war, "no season but we fear the shrapnel dream." Yet there is a faith. "Defeat," he writes, "is no word for the

[15] *Theory of Flight,* by Muriel Rukeyser. Yale University Press.

young." That faith is not the religion which has sustained men in times of disaster, but something vague yet to the poet real, the love of men. "Love is here to stay." "We pin our faith on the new-discovered star."

Often the substitute is a religion without God, with a sensitiveness to spiritual overtones of the world, a religion which rejects a naturalist philosophy as definitely as it rejects the personal God of orthodoxy. Thus Arthur Davison Ficke makes his sincere prayer to what he calls, "Lords of the Lake":

> Lords of the Lake . . .
> Give us strength to forgive our-
> selves our sins;
> Fortify our courage—that we may
> love life
> And fear not pain and old-age and
> death,
> And that we may walk quietly in
> our path without evil. Amen.[16]

Another substitute frequently met, perhaps as frequently as the Marxian creed acting as a religion, is that of Fate, as a blind and inescapable determiner of destiny. That God as it appears in Eugene O'Neill will be noted shortly. It is a God with many worshippers, convinced, if not particularly reverent. Social forces as well as Nature are regarded as Fate in many novels and plays. It is a determinism as rigid as the theological foreordination of Calvinism. Here again we find an echo of Renan's prediction. Calvinism goes firmly into the waste basket, and the twentieth century fishes out an economic and physical determinism to take its place. There is often a competitive rivalry between two substitute religions here. The devotee of faith in economic revolution finds that an accept-

[16] *The Secret and Other Poems* by Arthur Davison Ficke. Doubleday Doran Co.

ance of "fate" is sabotage in the revolution; it negates the individual will. The native hue of revolution is sicklied o'er by a pale docility and helplessness which cannot answer the reveille from the barricades.

On a much lower intellectual level, there is a popular religion of large masses, which is merely a belief in wishing, perhaps the most primitive and foggy of all the religious substitutes, but one with many devotees. The song, "Wishing Will Make It So," could serve both as the Hallelujah Chorus and the Athanasian Creed for this cult. James T. Farrell, in *A World I Never Made*, has pictured in life-like detail this faith in wishing.

Taken altogether, these substitutes afford interesting comment on the thesis of Aldous Huxley that one strange result of scientific progress has been "the reversion from monotheism to local idolatries." He thus traces the movement:

"For a large part of the population science has made the Christian dogmas intellectually unacceptable. Contemporary superstition is therefore compelled to assume a positivistic form. The desire to worship persists, but since modern men find it impossible to believe in any but observable entities, it follows that they must vent this desire upon gods that can be actually seen and heard, or whose existence can at least be easily inferred from the facts of immediate experience. Nations and dictators are only too easily observable. It is on these tribal deities that the longing to worship now vents itself." [17]

One author who has continually revealed an intense preoccupation with finding a substitute for a discarded religious creed is Edna St. Vincent Millay. In an early poem, *The Blue Flag in the Bog*, there is an aspiration, at least, toward the faith into which she had been born. The woman in the poem prays to "Father, Son and Holy Ghost" to "reach a hand and

[17] *The Olive Tree* by Aldous Huxley. Harper and Brothers.

rescue me." Her cry is heard and she receives "the whole of His white robe, for a cloak against the night." There is nothing to parallel that in the later poems. Instead, the dominant themes are a despair about humanity, a preoccupation with death, and also a devotion to beauty and human love as the only substitutes she can find for a religion. She finds no guiding hand in the universe. She resents death, sees in it "unpatterned blackness without horizons," but there is neither evidence of nor desire for immortality. Beauty is the high value; "cleave henceforth to beauty." She seeks "beauty where beauty never stood." It is usually the beauty of nature which she feels and for which she has a sensitive appreciation. "O world I cannot hold thee close enough." Yet occasionally there is a recognition of abstract ideal beauty as in the much quoted sonnet, "Euclid alone hath looked on beauty bare." The other pole star is human love. Yet both fail as sources of lasting hope, faith or joy, or as a fortification against futility or despair. The years return, "like one hack following another in meaningless procession," ("The Harp Weaver"). When love is gone, "there's little use in anything as far as I can see." ("Ashes of Life").

One of the most important dramas of the ten year period, Eugene O'Neill's *Mourning Becomes Electra*, is too large and varied in its significance to be compressed into an instance of any one theme, such as the one here discussed, that of modern substitutes for traditional religion. Yet it is entirely legitimate to consider it in this connection, for one of its many aspects is exactly that. The drama retells the old story of Aeschylus, that of the murder of her husband by Clytemnestra and her resultant murder by her children, Orestes and Electra, all done in modern clothes and in the language of Freud. But the Greek Gods are absent, all transcendent gods are absent. Modern gods with a little "g" take their place, the laws of heredity and environment. The characters are defeated and doomed by these substitute deities, however, just as surely as the similar characters were doomed by the more august Gods of Greek mythology. It is the same gory story, not inaccurately described in a comment on Greek drama quoted by John Jay Chapman, "Oh, it was one of those Greek tragedies where one of the characters on the stage says to another, 'If you don't kill mother I will.'"

Whether these substitute gods are sufficient to support real tragedy in the classic sense has been a question much debated. About the seriousness of O'Neill's intentions, or about his skill in writing dramatic speech and dramatic narrative, or the value of many incidental insights into the unconscious and his favorite bogey "puritanism," there is no question. But his interpretation of personality and life in terms of sexual impulse is so extreme as to result in violent distortion. When clear meaning emerges out of the Freudian fog, it often resembles much worn platitudes. Bernard de Voto brings back a harsh verdict, "the greatest wind machine in our theatrical history is used to assist the enunciation of platitudes."[18]

Another critic returns the same verdict: "of what use is the fantastic world of the unconscious when the secrets brought back are of no more value than this dried sea weed of desire, and these broken shells of lost hope. O'Neill has found no buried treasure in this Sargasso Sea of the soul."[19]

It is a matter of great interest that O'Neill contends that life is not explicable in scientific terms alone. He seems to feel that he must go beyond them and search for an ultimate meaning which will justify suffering as well as explain it. So far, that is a real religious value, but we are brought into a vague and mystical sort of pantheism. In addition he specializes so in the abnormal that his plays have often chiefly a

[18] *The Saturday Review*, November 21, 1936.
[19] *New Theatre*, September, 1935.

clinical meaning, case histories for the records of an insane asylum. It has been pointed out that there are only two plays of O'Neill, *Marco Millions* and *Ah! Wilderness* (neither of them typical of O'Neill plays) in which one or more of the leading characters do not succumb to madness or hysteria or both.

The great common religious experiences of the human race have found continued and varied portrayal. In the midst of all the changes in the world, the ancient themes of the centuries have held the attention of men and found expression in the recording of the experience of men. There is evidence of the pondering of ultimate questions concerning man's nature and destiny, his sense of insecurity, his bewilderments and doubts, the disturbing experience of conscience and the dark problem of evil.

In Eugene O'Neill, for instance, in spite of the absence of familiar theological presuppositions and vocabulary, there is a strong grappling with what are ultimately religious as well as psychological questions, the consciousness of guilt, the sure wages of sin, the visitation of the sins of the fathers on the children. O'Neill's play dealing most explicitly with orthodox Catholic Christianity as a refuge and salvation over modern man may be disappointing dramatically and inadequate in its representation of Christian experience, yet it testifies to an intensely serious interest in religion and contains many acute insights into man's spiritual struggle and quest for redemption. The common idea that the sense of sin is a belated hangover from all earlier unenlightened day finds no support in O'Neill.

Days Without End is the story of a boy nurtured in Christian teaching who loses his faith when his prayers fail to produce a miracle and save his parents from death after an accident.

Then followed a pilgrimage into atheism, anarchy, communism. Then marriage, followed by unfaithfulness to his wife, her discovery of his infidelity and a critical illness, and the hero is reconciled to religion. His wife recovers and apparently they are to live happily ever after. So much of the plot had to be given in order to evaluate the religious insight, if any. We can be glad of the conversion, but had better be suspicious in welcoming O'Neill as an interpreter of Christian theology or religion. The dramatic critics who rejected it as superficial melodrama have a far surer religious insight than the Catholics who welcomed O'Neill, not only as a returning prodigal worthy of the fatted calf and gold ring, but as a great dramatist.

This joyous welcome of O'Neill as theologian and evangelist is evidence of the curious inferiority feeling of many church people. They seem so glad and flattered to have any literary recognition of religion as something to be taken seriously that they are ready to acclaim most any work approving religion, no matter how tawdry it may be.

Yet, the play has in it some very effective insights. The divided self, in the stage presentation, gives a very moving portrayal of the "war in the members." The hero, John Loving, is represented on the stage by two persons, one called John, and the other, Loving. The play carries on a dialogue between the better and the worse self, the idealist and the scornful mocker. There is a fine dramatization of the integrating force of religion, in which the divided self becomes one. The sneering, cynical lower self expires at the foot of the cross.

The essentially religious experience of a genuine fellowship is met with again and again as the reader goes through the fiction and poetry of the time. There is, for instance, a profound religious insight into the meditation of the ex-preacher,

Casy, which Steinbeck records in *The Grapes of Wrath*. The religious idea of holiness is traced to roots in wholeness, in solidarity, in brotherhood.

"I ain't sayin' I'm like Jesus," the preacher went on. "But I got tired like Him, an' I got mixed up like Him, an' I went into the wilderness like Him, without no campin' stuff. Nighttime I'd lay on my back an' look up at the stars; morning I'd set an' watch the sun come up; midday I'd look out from a hill at the rollin' dry country; evenin' I'd foller the sun down. Sometimes I'd pray like I always done. On'y I couldn' figure what I was prayin' to or for. There was the hills, an' there was me, an' we wasn't separate no more. We was one thing. An' that one thing was holy.
"An' I got thinkin', on'y it wasn't thinkin', it was deeper down than thinkin'. I got thinkin' how we was holy when we was one thing, an' mankin' was holy when it was one thing. An' it on'y got unholy when one mis'able little fella got the bit in his teeth an' run off his own way, kickin' an' draggin' an' fightin'. Fella like that bust the holiness. But when they're all workin' together, not one fella for another fella, but one fella kind of harnessed to the whole shebang—that's right, that's holy." [20]

The reader can only answer—"That's right, that is holy."

A poetical expression of the great moral and religious experience of fellowship is found in Joy Davidman's "Survey Mankind," a panoramic picture of America with expressive detail, loving it in its various aspects, the grass roots, the roads, the tumbleweed, jack rabbits, "We have understood all these things and held them in our minds." So with the people, "We have spoken to them one by one."

The tragedy of Job, the problem of evil, has inevitably had consideration in a decade of evil. One of the most specific treatments of evil has been done by Phillip Barry, a playwright whose name has been associated with a very different type of theme, that of bright sophisticated comedy. His modern ver-

[20] *The Grapes of Wrath* by John Steinbeck. The Viking Press, 1939.

sion of Job appeared as a novel, *War in Heaven,* and as a
play, *Here Come the Clowns.* The author chooses a group
of people who will furnish a strong case for the interpretation
of the world as a product of blundering, or malignant evil. A
group of vaudeville actors are shown in an actors' restaurant
after a performance. Each has a tangled history in which
trouble and sorrow have played major parts. Some are freaks,
started off in life with bad handicaps. Clancy, a stage technician, who has met many disasters, losses and betrayals, puts
up his case to the Almighty, in the forthright manner of Job,
with impressive particulars and eloquence. A mysterious Pabst,
masquerading as a conjurer, gives all the traditional dust-
covered answers to the problem of evil. Clancy reaches no
solution, unless his death at the end of the play proves a
solution for him, other than the one of Job, to go as far in
argument as reason will carry him and trust in God for the
unexplained remainder. That is substantially the answer in
Antigone also. Barry's play is notable for its serious, moving
treatment of a tremendous theme. The speeches of Clancy are
powerful expressions of the sense of life's evil.

"I've been tramping the country over. Good God, Almighty, it's
terrible."

"It is—for all its pretty scenery, the earth is full of human
misery, of death, and tyranny and torture. Wherever I've been,
for one contented individual, I've found a dozen who suffered
and sweat and strained—for what to get their backs broken and the
hope put out of their eyes." [21]

Again Clancy stands up to God:

"Have you not said you'd come when we called you? Then
where are you keeping yourself? What are you to lose by passing

[21] *War in Heaven* by Philip Barry. Coward-McCann Company, New
York, 1938.

a moment or two with a man of your own making in such unholy need of you?"

        *   *   *

"Still there must be good reason for such things. I wish God would see fit to make them plainer. I wish He could come down from His high perch for a moment only and explain his ways a little."

"Hush, Dan," repeated Connie. Suddenly he struck his fist upon the table making the ice filled water glasses jump and clatter. "I'll not," he roared. "There's too much hushing done. We hush when we should be—"

He then threw back his head and shouted to the ceiling,

"You up there. Why do you send such blank confusion on the world? What's the earthly good of half the things that happen, things that on the face of them are blundering injustices with no sense or purpose—What's the reason for them?" [22]

The final resting place of the tortured mind is an old one, never entirely satisfactory, calling for an act of faith. God exists, but man has free will and because he uses that will perversely, man and not God is responsible for evil and suffering.

Lillian Hellman has given powerful pictures of evil in action in two plays, *The Children's Hour,* portraying malice in devilish children, magnified by gossip, and *The Little Foxes,* giving the history of a family of the most accomplished villains recently paraded on the stage, depicting the love of money as the root of all sorts of evil.

The poetry to which has been attached the descriptive noun "negation," though not large in volume, is important as a symptom of contemporary moods and attitudes. In its most violent form, this is found in the poetry of Robinson Jeffers, though it is reflected in the work of other poets, including the obscure and tormented Hart Crane. Amos N. Wilder, in his *The Spiritual Aspects of the New Poetry,* has discussed this

[22] *Ibid.*

poetry of negation as well as other aspects of the "new" poetry, a book which no one interested either in present day poetry or the temper of the times can afford to neglect. It is as noteworthy for its insights into the problems of religion as for its sympathetic interpretation of contemporary poets. Mr. Wilder stresses the reflection of spiritual insecurity in this poetry, which has the merit of depth. Jeffers, for instance, inhabits a strange and violent world, in which all the values of our religious and cultural tradition are reversed. Yet "it sees the dimensions of life if only in negative terms." This poetry of denial exhibits an awareness of the tensions and difficulties, of the dark abyss under the surface of life, the "upswing of savagery or brutal egoism in supposedly civilized man." It is this tragic sense of life which is so often lost in the fog of sentimentalism of much traditional religion. This poetry of robust negation of Christian values renders two great services which those who accept the traditional religious creeds and outlook greatly need. It sharply reflects what a British critic, Ruth Bailey, points out, "it is a winter world for these poets, one which has no cause for rapture or the singing note. The poet believes himself caught in the death throes of a civilization. Today human consciousness is passing through a major crisis. It is not merely the traditional forms of life and thought which are disintegrating, but the ego itself which is on the rack." [23] It is a great service to religious thinking to have that sense of disaster and danger sensitively recorded. The other service which this type of poetry renders is the demand for thinking and rethinking which a forthright denial always imposes on religion. Mr. Wilder points out that we ought not to be surprised that so many poets who deal seriously with ultimate themes do so in terms of violent denial. He ascribes part

[23] *A Dialogue on Modern Poetry* by Ruth Bailey. Oxford University Press, London.

of the responsibility for this to the poetic inadequacy of poets "writing out of the Christian inheritance." "They do not explore," he writes, "that inheritance deeply enough to tap springs of unmistakable power, they do not relate that inheritance to the modern mood and its ills." Then he adds with genuine religious insight, "We will have greater religious poetry when the devout and mystical poets among us enter as deeply into the experience of grace as our poets of negation enter into the experience of perdition." [24]

No one has had a more convulsive sense of the experience of perdition than Robinson Jeffers. It is probably only a slight exaggeration to say that his poetry has had more commentators than readers. Here only one of the most obvious aspects of his work may be noted, and even that only as it appears to one ill-equipped to find a path through the dark forest of this poet whose favorite symbols are incest and murder.

The sub-human forces of life, the unconscious, the irrational, all are accepted as realities above the rational. (Incidentally, this is an outlook understandable when the most prominent feature of our civilization is the reversal to savagery in the march of a mechanized barbarism). In such a poem as *Meditation on Saviours,* to choose one of Jeffers' poems in which meaning is most clearly communicated, there is the proud and emphatic rejection of salvation not only through the Christian God, but also through social reform of any sort. "The apes of Christ lift their hands to praise love," he writes. He disdains love, preferring "wisdom without love" as a savior. He calls for a "mind like a many bladed machine subduing the world with deep indifference." (Would not a suitable comment on that be, "Heil Hitler"?) In his poem, "Night," in *Roan Stallion,* he celebrates joyfully the violent and massive forces of nature, with which he identifies himself in a kind of pantheistic worship. These violent forces of nature demand a violence in man if he is to be in accord with the ultimate reality in the universe. He acclaims the superman, rejects the Christian God, the Christian and humanitarian scale of values. He has incidental criticisms of the devastation which the pursuit of money has brought about in life. But when one asks to what Jeffers' glorification of violence leads, the familiar outlines of fascism appear, including faith in a strong man, a "Fuehrer" inhibited by no weakening ethical superstitions. Surely Jeffers is a supreme example of Walter Lippmann's phrase, "trading a majestic faith for a trivial illusion."

To turn again to fiction and drama, the merest mention must be given to some of the many treatments of specifically religious themes. In *Men and Brethren,* James Gould Cozzens drew a portrait of a clergyman who was neither a prig nor a fool, a life-like picture of parish work in a city. Thornton Wilder's *Heaven's My Destination* was a baffling book, largely because it was hard to understand the author's own attitude to his hero, George Brush, a naive "fundamentalist" with a closed mind, who goes through grotesque adventures when his earnest evangelistic spirit and brittle uncompromising idealism meet the world, the flesh and the devil. Yet the novel is obviously not a satire or burlesque, for the hero is a far better man than any of the people to whom he is merely the butt of a joke. Don Marquis in his short stories, *Chapters for the Orthodox,* is strongly satirical on the compromises of the church and orthodox religious minds with evil. Ben Hecht's *A Book of Miracles* is almost wholly concerned with religious themes in which humor and burlesque alternate with genuine spiritual insight.

Clarence Day's *God and My Father,* and *Life with Father*

are, of course, not primarily devoted to religion. His work in those books is a delicate and artistic achievement in character- ization, not only of persons, but also of a period. The pictures of Mr. Day's father and mother rank high in American de- lineations of personality, done with rare insight and humor. The play, *Life with Father*, by Howard Lindsay and Russel Crouse, based on Mr. Day's books, was extremely successful, bringing to thousands laughter and the joys of recognition of features of a bygone generation, including both mental traits and overdrapes. The books, however, have very real value for understanding the religion of a generation past, as well as a good deal of the religion of the present. If one wishes to know what is the matter with much American religion, he can find it in *God and My Father*. "Father" was a man of the highest integrity and had loyal affection under the covering of bluster and domineering. But in his attitude to religion and the church he displayed attitudes common then and now, including patronage, indifference, indignation at any claims of religion that would cause the slightest inconvenience. On the other hand, the picture of his wife shows her religion as never having emerged from a strict form of literalism that often is not much above superstition.

Sir Robertson Nicol wrote in the early 1900's, "For count- less multitudes in these days the literature of fiction is their daily bread. I believe there will yet arise some great modern novelist as a chief apostle of God." That prophecy has been entirely unfulfilled—perhaps in the very nature of fiction it could not be. Story telling succumbs to didacticism. A novelist who has written most directly of religion, Lloyd Douglass, cer- tainly could not be called a chief apostle of God or a chief novelist. It is rather strange why he has not been taken more seriously as a novelist, for he has a real gift for narrative and conversation. His books contain a large sum of definitely

Christian ideas; *Magnificent Obsession*—illustrating the truth that he that loseth his life shall find it; *Forgive Us Our Trespasses*, contending that even with a great injustice, hatred can be healed by forgiveness; *Green Light*, illustrating that what looks like a tragic ruin of a life can be overcome; *Disputed Passage*, the commonplace that struggle for mastery is good for the soul.

All these are accepted axioms of religious thinking and teaching. He shows two lacks: the religion is thin and diluted and watery. It is the sort satirized by Arnold Lunn, "God so loved the world that he inspired a certain Jew to inform his contemporaries that there was a great deal to be said for loving one's neighbor." Second, there is a lack of social depth and economic awareness. Like many "coated paper stories," there is little evidence of ever having glimpsed social and economic conditioning of life. One critic, W. E. Gilroy, writes:

"I am inclined to believe that the thousands of readers of Douglass' novels are recruited chiefly from the people who are more concerned about their own spiritual ingrown toe-nails and stomachaches than about the deeper problems and tragedies of life, and that the people who are really aroused and on the march are either in the radical camps or among the Christians who find a place in their knapsacks for the Gospels and the New Testament that they are not likely to find for the sentimental elaboration of ideas that are largely divorced from their source and their most powerful mediums of expression."

The later years of the decade saw many plays on religious themes. John Anderson the dramatic critic has made the interesting suggestion that possibly the reason was that the public, despairing of any help from the jittery churches, are turning to their original ally, but later enemy, the theatre, for comfort and consolation. Some of the most notable religious plays, such as *Shadow and Substance* and *The White Steed* by Vincent Carrol, and *Murder in the Cathedral* by T. S. Eliot, were by British authors.

Rachel Crothers' *Susan and God* is a comedy dealing with Buchmanism in a kindly spirit, even though with many a mischievous and well aimed thrust. Its theme is: what would happen if a sophisticated cocktail crowd, with lives all messed up with gin and sex and triviality, were confronted with religion? Into such a crowd comes Susan, beautiful and bubbling, who has gotten religion in the form promoted by the Oxford Group, and talks of God with the familiarity of one who has a private wire to the Almighty. She has a passion for changing lives. However, she finds it hardest to begin at home. Her husband needs her in his fight against drink. Her daughter needs her badly. But Susan finds meddling in other's lives more thrilling and evades her immediate responsibilities for a more exhilarating mission.

Miss Crothers is not burlesquing religion. She does give incidentally a strong picture of a "preacher" who does not really believe her own message of salvation, when she refuses to accept back her husband who is impressed by her eloquence about the power of God to "change lives."

Thornton Wilder's *Our Town* is suffused with religion. It is the simple but impressive picture of a small town in the New Hampshire of a generation ago, an order of life shaped by the church and definitely expressing Christian standards and values. The effect which the play had on large numbers is illustrated by a remark overheard at the close of a performance. A prosperous New Yorker and his wife, who had evidently grown up in a small town like Grover's Corners, were talking. The man said to his wife complacently, "Well, that's where we came from, dear." She returned an unexpected answer: "Yes, and I'm wondering where we've got to." The play compelled a fresh appraisal of life. *Family Portrait*, by

Lenore Coffer and William Joyce Cowen, is a beautiful and impressive play on the family of Jesus.

This chapter may well close with one poem which has a representative value. A poet writing in the classic tradition and form, Lizette Woodworth Reese, in her *Prayer of an Unbeliever*, has well conveyed the reality of religious interest and aspiration characteristic of many whose thinking is tentative and confused:

> Draw closer to me, God, than were I one,
> With the hedged comfort of a creed about.
> With not a shadow's shadow of a doubt
> That you are father, and each man a son.
> Because I halt means not the will to roam,
> But through the stubble a surer track to find:
> Confused of foot, the ear, the eye less kind,
> One fears to miss the steps which lead to home.
> Who gives not to a wayfarer at the end
> A roof? To beggar a sustaining cup?
> Else waits the crumbling ditch from dew to dew.
> Even this to me, if by what I mend,
> By such a bitter hand be lifted up,
> To stumble to that lodging which is You.[25]

Professor Wilbur Urban of Yale has written: "For some generations now man has been trying to decide whether he is merely a high grade simian or a son of God."

Now in another war era there will be great argument on the simian side. But the argument on the side of the child of God will never be without the support of literature.

[25] *Pastures and Other Poems* by Lizette Woodworth Reese. Farrar and Rinehart, 1933.

CHAPTER 11

WAR AND PEACE

THE YEAR 1940 is a difficult time in which to try to evaluate
the influence of the great volume of literature dealing with
war, preponderantly anti-war in spirit and content. With a
large part of the world in the most destructive conflict ever
known, and the rest of the world, including the United
States, preparing for war with a frantic expenditure running
beyond the power of the imagination to conceive, there is
strong temptation, to which many have yielded, to rub out
cynically the ten years' literary argument against war, as a
total loss. Concerning this body of writing, so great in extent
and variety, the old question of little Peterkin is asked, "But
what good came of it at last?"

It is no part of the field of this book, fortunately, to attempt
the impossible task of measuring the effect of the discussions
of war in fiction, drama and poetry on the thinking and action
of multitudes of people. Here can be undertaken only the
briefest listing of some of the more prominent works in this
field, with some consideration of the elements of moral, as
well as of economic and political, judgment.

Some preliminary observations may be made with some
confidence, however. There is much evidence that the effect
of this literature on war has been both overestimated and
underestimated.

Strangely enough, it has been overestimated both in advance and in retrospect. There was abroad a rather strong, though unfounded expectation, in the nineteen twenties and thirties, that the realistic pictures given of the horrors of war, its futility, as shown in the demonstration that one war led to another, and of its economic and political insanity, might create such a permanent revulsion against war as to make it improbable or even impossible. That expectation has been proved an illusion, and for many reasons. For one thing, war is never prevented by picturing its horrows, no matter how realistically. The indictment against war in creative literature has been largely emotional, and emotion is an inadequate insurance against the recurrence of war. Also, in the very process of revealing the horrows of war, there is an almost inevitable effect of an unintended tribute to its excitement, its daring and heroism. This was found to be particularly true in the motion picture films made from such books as *All Quiet on the Western Front.* The effect, particularly on the young, was quite other than building up a tough opposition to war. The excitement seemed to be of stronger and more lasting quality than the revulsions.

The exaggeration of the effect of war literature, of the debunking sort, when viewed in retrospect, was given its most prominent expression by Archibald MacLeish in an address in June, 1940, just after the Nazi victory in Belgium. He expressed great disappointment over what he considered the unsatisfactory reluctance of the youth of America to welcome participation in war, particularly its tendency to distrust all "slogans and tags." He professed great alarm over this skeptical spirit. "If the young generation of America," he said, painting the picture more extremely than any facts supported, "is distrustful of all words, distrustful of all moral judgments of better and worse, then it is incapable of using the only weapon with which fascism can be fought—the moral conviction that fascism is evil and that a free society of free men is worth fighting for." He blamed this attitude almost entirely on the effect produced by anti-war literature.

He wrote:

"A large part of the responsibility for this state of mind in the generation of men and women now young belongs to the writers —belongs specifically to the best and most sensitive and most persuasive writers—of my generation who created in many minds this distrust not only of the tags, not only of the slogans, but of the words themselves. The war books of men like Barbusse, Latzko, Dos Passos, Ford Madox Ford, Ernest Hemingway, Erich Maria Remarque and Richard Aldington were not only books written against the hatefulness and cruelty and filthiness of war. They were also books filled with passsionate contempt for the statements of conviction, of purpose and of belief on which the war of 1914–18 was fought. And they left behind them in many minds the conclusion that not only the war and the war issues but *all* issues, all moral issues, were false—were fraudulent—were tended to deceive. You can open the pages anywhere and find this." [1]

He gives two supporting quotations, one from Dos Passos and one from Hemingway.

The voluminous and spirited rebuttal which this speech called forth made clear two things. The first was that he had ridiculously overestimated the extent to which such authors had been read and the consequent influence they had had. Most of the young people whom MacLeish pictured as having been corrupted by these books had never even heard the authors' names. One of the bitterest of the anti-war writers, the British novelist, Richard Aldington, puts this strongly:

"It is typical highbrow delusion to suppose that authors influence anyone but the intellectuals and that intellectuals count for anything in the formation of national policy and the state of the mass

[1] *The New Republic*, June 10, 1940.

mind. Most people in America have never heard of the writers MacLeish mentions and could not have been influenced by them." [2]

The other flaw pointed out in MacLeish's indictment was its superficial character. He yields to the common temptation to find some kind of a villainous witch responsible for a condition that had complex economic and social roots. In other words, the apathy of youth to slogans and its disillusionment with war were not due so much to wicked debunkers as to the experience of the depression. Having undergone the consequences of one war to make the world safe for democracy, their appetite for another was somewhat less than voracious. Robert E. Sherwood points out the roots of this attitude, insofar as it exists in hard experience:

"It seems that now the more articulate representatives of American youth are not so much anti-war as pro-revolution. They consider democracy a decadent mess—and no wonder, in view of the environment in which they grew up: the jazz age of the early 20's, the hypocrisy and crime of prohibition, the drunken-sailorism of the Coolidge boom and the wailing defeatism of depression." [3]

Dalton Trumbo, author of *Johnny Got His Gun*, is even more explicit:

Writers do not create war and injustice, they merely tell the truth about them. Hence, if writers are to emphasize those "final things for which democracy will fight," such final things must first exist in fact. If youth believes it possesses an actual economic and spiritual stake in American democracy, it will smash all who seek to subvert democracy. If youth believes it does not possess such a stake, it becomes an immediate imperative for us to broaden our democratic base. A program of economic security, political honesty and civil liberty is our most impregnable defense. [4]

[2] *Life*, June 24, 1940.
[3] *Life*, June 24, 1940.
[4] *Ibid.*

On the other hand it is easy to underestimate the effect of realistic war literature. True, a world is again at war. But there is evidence everywhere that it is hard to invest war with the glamor that it once had. Even with all the hysteria manifested in the United States in the summer of 1940, there was evidenced a hard core of skepticism about war as a way of salvation, as far as joining a war in Europe was concerned. And at least a small part in achieving that result, though nothing like the effect hastily ascribed by MacLeish, can be set down to a literature dealing with war of which history has no parallel.

Of course there has always been literature dealing with war, from Homer down. There has been literature paralleling Goya's paintings. But, for the most part, it has been in the romantic tradition. Even when it has not been in the *Dulce Et Decorum* mood, there has been a traditional glamor evident. The thirties brought, in the United States as well as in Great Britain, writing in the violently skeptical school. Not often has it reached the bitter cynicism of Ezra Pound's

> There died a myriad
> And of the best among them
> For an old bitch gone in the teeth
> For a botched civilization.

Yet there has been a continuous expression of freedom from any lingering romantic illusions about war. The quotation which MacLeish makes from Dos Passos' *Three Soldiers*, in the address just referred to, expresses the spirit of a wide range of literature, "So was civilization nothing but a vast edifice of sham, and the war, instead of its crumbling, was its fullest and most ultimate expression. Oh, but there must be something more in the world than greed and hatred and cruelty. Were they all shams, too, these gigantic phrases that floated like gaudy kites high above mankind? Kites, that was it, contraptions of tissue paper held at the end of a string, ornaments not to be taken seriously."

Muriel Rukeyser's violent verse, "M-Day," might also stand as text for a large amount of writing in prose and poetry.

> M-day's child is fair of face,
> Drill-day's child is full of grace,
> Gun-day's child is breastless and blind,
> Shell-day's child is out of its mind,
> Bomb-day's child will always be dumb,
> Cannon-day's child can never quite come,
> But the child that's born on the Battle-day
> Is blithe and bonny and rotted away.[4a]

The military system itself was the theme of one of the strongest novels of the period, Humphrey Cobb's *Paths of Glory*. It is a volley of savage machine gun fire directed at the brass hats of the army and the military mind and code. It is founded partly on actual happenings of a court martial in the French army in the first World War. The theme is the execution of a group of soldiers selected arbitrarily as a face-saving gesture of a general eager for promotion. The soldiers are executed as a punishment inflicted on a company for failure to accomplish an utterly impossible feat of capturing an impregnable position known as "The Pimple." The letters written by the men before execution are powerful in their effect. Its condemnation of war is much more effective than reiterated peace propaganda. It presents not merely the shame and horror of a single chapter in the vast volume of the war, but in doing so, conveys the impression of the obscenity of war as a whole. One of the most theatrically effective plays on war was Paul Green's *Johnny Johnson*. The hero is an idealist who overcomes a vague but strong pacifism by taking with a deadly,

[4a] *A Turning Wing* by Muriel Rukeyser. The Viking Press, 1939.

if naive, seriousness, Woodrow Wilson's eloquence in stating the aims of the war. His idealisms meet cruel and cynical rebuffs in the army itself. When he tries to end the war by an appeal to what seems at the time to Johnny, (and to the spectator and reader, looking backward sixteen years,) as common sense, the strong arm of army discipline descends upon him and he is sent to a military insane asylum. (In war, reason must be shut up in a mad house, lest it spoil the show!) The serious purpose of the play is made all the stronger by its refusal to pound steadily on the moral, and by its inclusion of elements of musical comedy and even horseplay farce. The play carries an effective satire of war. Johnny holds up an allied war council with a bomb, while he tries to persuade them to try persuasion instead of "making a pile of dead men in tomorrow's battle, higher'n that big tower in Paris." His unsophisticated enthusiasm carries the central theme of the play and a common indictment of war:

"I ask you—you know what it means? All these boys—young fellows like me—like what you used to be—going out to die—shot down—killed—murdered—to lie dead and stiff and rotten in a trench with rats and mud. We were meant for something better, I tell you. (*vehemently*) We want to live and you could let us live. We want to be let alone to do our work in peace, to have our homes, to raise our families. We want to look back some day and say our life has meant something." [5]

Undoubtedly the most original of the plays designed to strip war of its last tattered shred of glamor and stirring drum beat was Irwin Shaw's *Bury the Dead*. It is a fantasy in which grotesqueness and humor combine with emotional force in an unusual mixture. Six dead soldiers with the dirt and smell of the grave upon them decide to rise from the dead. Once grant that initial, impossible situation, and the one act play

[5] *Johnny Johnson* by Paul Green. Samuel French, Inc., 1937.

moves along almost merrily, showing the embarrassment of the army and political authorities in their efforts to get them to lie down and be good. All the official authority of the captains and generals fails. The wives of the six soldiers are appealed to over the radio to try to show them the bad form in dead men coming alive in a scandalous manner, to the upsetting of the status quo. The play rises to a powerful climax in the replies given by the risen corpses to their wives, telling why they refuse to stay in the grave. In these replies are put two deeply gripping pictures. One is the rebellion of the earth at receiving so many young bodies. The earth will not have any more of her children senselessly killed. In the replies of the soldiers to the persuasion of the women appear not only the frustration of the boys having been killed before they had a chance to live, but also, in some instances, the frustrations of their lives back home before they went to war. One soldier puts it eloquently in simple words, giving a history of his life: "They made a speech, and played a trumpet and dressed me in a uniform and then they killed me." The epitaph on ten million lives!

Robert E. Sherwood's *Idiot's Delight* carries some grim and powerful eloquence against war, in the midst of very smooth theatrical craftsmanship and comedy on the level, at times, of horseplay filled with what are known as "wise-cracks." The principal characters are a leader of a group of night club performers, stranded in a Swiss hotel near the Italian border, a munitions magnate (the villain of the play) and his mistress, cynical but clear eyed. Into her mouth the dramatist puts the most powerful speech of the play, damning the part the munitions industry plays in perpetrating war. The defense which Weber, the armament king, makes reveals his own rationalizing, and also the part gullible peoples and vicious goverments play in the whole natural history of war.

"Who are the greater criminals,—those who sell the instruments of death, or those who buy and use them? All these little people consider me an arch-villain because I furnish them with what they want, which is the illusion of power. That is what they vote for in their frightened governments—what they cheer for on their national holidays, what they glorify in their anthems and their monuments and their waving flags! Yes, they shout bravely about something they call 'national honor'. And what does it amount to? Mistrust of motives of everyone else! Dog in the manger defense of what they've got, and greed for the other fellow's possessions! Honor among thieves! I assure you, Irene—for such little people the deadliest weapons are the most merciful." [6]

Harry Vane, the vaudeville "hoofer," gives his diagnosis of the disease, "We have become a race of drug addicts, hopped up with false beliefs, false fears, false enthusiasms."

There is a challenge in the conception of God put into the mouth of the leading woman character. She ironically compliments the munitions manufacturer on his success in fomenting the war. But he answers, "Don't forget to do honor to Him up there, who put fear into men. I am but the humble instrument of His divine will." She says, "Yes, that's quite true. We don't do half enough justice to Him. Poor lonely old soul, sitting up in Heaven with nothing to do but play solitaire." [7]

The ironical ending with Vane sitting down to the piano, just as the bombs begin to crash on the hotel, playing,

> "Onward, Christian soldiers,
> Marching as to war"

was too strong for the movies to take. In the film version, the satire was removed and the innocuous "Give My Regards to Broadway" substituted.

Mr. Sherwood's play, produced in the spring of 1940, *There Shall Be No Night*, is in a very different mood from

[6] *Idiot's Delight* by Robert E. Sherwood. Charles Scribner's Sons, 1936.
[7] *Ibid.*

Idiot's Delight, reflecting the new war era, and the great change in the world situation. The action is laid in Finland before and during the attack by Soviet Russia. The play is not directly about war. It is rather a deeply moving portrayal of the values of democracy, and the threat made upon it by the totalitarian assault. There is nobility in the Finnish characters and in the writing, treating the supreme issues before the world with great emotional force.

Very few of the anti-war plays trace the roots of war to economic interests and rivalries. That would be, for one thing, a far more difficult dramatic task. Eleanor Flexner calls a war play which refuses even to glimpse at the economic causes of war an evasion. "To-day," she writes, "an anti-war play which ignores the economic basis of war lacks any impact, dwindles to a Snow White and the Seven Dwarfs in which a witch is the cause of all evil." For this reason among others, *Peace On Earth,* by George Sklar and Albert Maltz, deserves recognition as the first anti-war play in the United States which explicitly attacks war as an inescapable outcome, not of devilish Zara-hoffs, Krupps, and Bethlehem Steel, or of imperialist politics, but of an economic and social system based on private profit. It was timely in its appearance in 1934, just as the Committee of the Senate, headed by Senator Nye, began its investigations of the munitions industry. It presents the old dream, to which hope and imagination return so often, a dream which has always evaporated, of labor preventing war. A longshoremen's union refuses to handle munitions. The play presents the many ramifications of that imagined situation, including the instant hue and cry against anyone sympathizing with the strike, or standing for the "subversive" ideas of free speech and assembly. In the play, it is a liberal professor, hounded out of his job and finally joining the strike, whose experience dramatizes the forces at work. The authors make clear by the

dramatic means of conversation and incident, not by an inter-
polated soap box harangue, that if the evils of our present
acquisitive system are tolerated without opposition, the result
of war must be tolerated. That affirmation may be passed off
as partisan Marxian formula. But how much proof of it has
been furnished by the course of action and inaction by the
class and economic interests in Great Britain and France!

In *The Cradle Will Rock*, Marc Blitzstein's impressionistic
play in the form of a musical comedy without scenery, there
is the sharpest attack on the church and its clergy as baptizers
of war, marionettes lulled by not very clearly hidden economic
strings, to be found in any production of the 1930's. The play
deals with the totalitarian domination of a steel town by
Mister Mister, the owner of the steel mills, faithfully aided
by Mrs. Mister, who conveys his wishes to the pastor, the
Reverend Salvation. In satire filled with gusto and ribaldry,
the author records the shift in the message of the pulpit, from
calling for peace to screaming for war. It is a burlesque which
has sharpened relevance for the church and its ministry in
the war atmosphere of 1940. It has a bitter picture of what has
been well called an "appendage religion," a church which
does not stand on its own feet and declare a divine revelation,
but exists as a mere appendage to something else, an economic
system, or a political state. Mrs. Mister brings to the preacher
from the steel overlord the message he is to proclaim, a message always accompanied by a contribution. The first scene is
in 1915, when peace was popular.

> Please, in your sermon Sunday
> I rely on you to implore that we stay out of the War.

So the Reverend Salvation mounts the pulpit:

> Thou shalt not kill
> So saith it in the Bible. So it must be.

But in the second scene in 1916—the situation is a bit more complex. So the message from the power behind the throne is:

Please don't be so downright.
Simply answer both yes and no.
It's true you've preached so much for peace—
But now it seems that peace may be a little expensive;
Please don't think me offensive!
Just restrain your intensive ardor.
You might mention that you do deplore
The German side of the war!

The Reverend Salvation mounts the pulpit:

Thou shalt not—um.
Righteousness conquers, iniquity perishes,
Peace is a wonderful thing!
But when I say peace, I'm referring to *inner* peace,
Let there be no misconception!
The peace, you remember, which passeth beyond understanding.
We must remember our honor,
And the valor and pride which is ours to cherish and use.
Knowing well that peace without honor
NO good American should excuse!

But in 1917—a new message:

Mrs. Mister: WAR! WAR! We're entering the war
              For Mr. Mister's shown the President how things
                  are—
              England has simply been a darling!
              Eyes right! Think of the rallies!
              Eyes left! I'm going to knit socks!
              Eyes front! Steel's going to go up skyhigh!
              All you clergy must now prepare a special prayer
              And do your share! OH, yes, your share . . .
                      (Hands Rev. Salv. an envelope)

Rev. Salvation from the pulpit:

> Thou—shalt—
>> Both (and chorus)
> WAR! WAR! Kill all the dirty Huns!
> And those Austrungarians!
> WAR! WAR! We're entering the war!
> The Lusitania's an unpaid debt,
> Remember Troy! Remember Lafayette!
> Remember the Alamo! Remember our womanhood!
> Remember those innocent unborn babies!
> Make the world safe for Democracy!
> Make the world safe for Liberty!
> Make the world safe for Steel and the Mister family!

Rev. Salvation:

>> Of course, it's peace we're for—
>> This is war to end all war!
> All: Amen.
> Mrs. Mister: I can see the market rising like a beautiful bird! [7]

Two novels deal with the aftermath of war, portrayed by histories of individuals. Millen Brand's *The Heroes* does not pile horror upon horror. It shows some of the backwash of the war twenty years later in a Veterans' Home. They are literally still "prisoners of war" shut off from the world, no job to work at, no satisfying human contacts. Their souls are bottled up. Property is gone, youth is gone. Here is the real "lost generation," not the noisy expatriates wallowing in self-pity in the Paris cafés in the nineteen twenties.

Very different, but also a story of the glory of war, seen through a glass very darkly, is Dalton Trumbo's *Johnny Got His Gun*. It is an unrelieved horror tale, with too much loading of the dice to be artistically effective. It is the life of

[7] *The Cradle Will Rock* by Marc Blitzstein. Random House, 1937.

Johnny who comes out of the first world war without arms, legs, face, sight or hearing, the nearest approach to a living corpse which could be imagined. Given these insuperable handicaps, the author lands close to genius in his achievement in making anything endurable out of it. He answers with imaginative skill the question, how can a man go on living minus so much of human endowment? Memories of the dead life are interwoven to make by contrast the complete devastation of war all the more powerful.

The poetry dealing with war sounds all the possible notes, ranging the whole human keyboard, grief, sympathy, despair, bitterness, satire, appeal to struggle. Even to suggest the main features of this large body of poetry, (and verse, for some of the most arresting things are more accurately labelled verse than by the august name of poetry) would call for an anthology larger than the present volume. Four samples, selected arbitrarily, must suffice as indications of the strong and turbulent feeling which flowed through the poetry and verse of the years. One poet, Shirley Baker, gives passionate expression to a feeling deeply and widely present in the opening year of the second world war. It is the feeling that perhaps it is one's duty, as well as wisdom and compassion, in such a world as ours, not to bring any more children into it, to deny oneself one of life's highest satisfactions, that of parenthood. Miss Baker entitles her poem, "Child That I Never Had":

> Child that I never had, you owe me more
> Than any man of flesh can owe his mother:
> Armor no mob can spit upon or bore
> With lead; the knowledge no man is your brother
> And hence deserving of you. Nothingness?
> There are worse legacies of stain and blight.
> You might have paid with fifty years duress
> For sport I took at kissing in the night.

Girl that I never had, you will not know
All earth's horizons in one tall young man
As I have done, but you are better so
Than bound in service to the futile plan
Of generation. Oh unwaking son,
Infallible and unbetrayed to clay,
Not by the crumbling forts my fathers won
Shall I appoint you heir to their decay.

Women who cannot see beyond delight
Or women who believe, or those who hope,
Cling to the strong arm, claim their ancient right,
And curse with breath the children who must grope
Into an ever-darker chaos. Shrinking
Back from the baffled girl, the bleeding lad,
I shall go down my last road proudly linking
My arms with arms of heirs I never had.[8]

The most bitter despair over the human race, touched with
a savage contempt for its imbecility in failing to find a substitute for war, is in the savage lines of Edna St. Vincent Millay in her "Epitaph for The Race of Man." It recalls the bitterness of Swift:

"Detestable race, continue to expunge your-
      self, die out,
   Breed faster, crowd, encroach, sing hymns
      build bombing airplanes;
   Make speeches, unveil statues, issue
      bonds, parade;
   Convert again into explosives the bewildered
      ammonia and the distracted cellulose;
   Convert again into putrescent matter draw-
      ing flies
   The hopeful bodies of the young; exhort,
   Pray, pull long faces, be earnest, be all
      but overcome, be photographed;

[8] *The Saturday Review of Literature*, May 27, 1939.

Confer, perfect your formulae, commer-
cialize
Bacteria harmful to human tissue,
Put death on the market;
Breed, crowd, encroach, expand, expunge
yourself, die out,
HOMO called SAPIENS" [9]

Modern warfare, in its benevolent "difference" from other
wars, is memorably portrayed in lines from Archibald Mac-
Leish's radio play of truly terrifying effectiveness, *Air Raid*.
That one short half-hour play could more adequately stand as
a history of the world in 1940 than any other piece of writing
equally brief.

Strange and curious times these times
we live in:
You watch from kitchens for the bloody
signs:
You watch for breaking war above the
washing on the lines.
In the old days they watched along the
borders;
They called their warfare in the old
days wars
And fought with men and men who fought
were killed:
We call it peace and kill the women
and the children.
Our women die in peace beneath the lintels
of their doors.[10]

One of the most notable and metrically skillful of the treatments of war in verse, by irony and corrosive satire, is Phyllis

[9] *Wine From These Grapes* by Edna St. Vincent Millay. Harper &
Brothers, 1934.
[10] *Air Raid* by Archibald MacLeish. Harcourt, Brace & Co., 1938.

McGinley's widely known and much quoted "Christmas Carol, with Variations":

Oh little town of Bethlehem, how still we see thee
lie;
Your flocks are folded in to sleep, and sleep your
little ones.
Behold there is a Star again that climbs the eastern
sky.
And seven million living men are picking up their
guns.

> Hark the happy cannons roar—
> Glory to the Dictator,
> Death and fear, and peace defiled,
> And a world unreconciled!

Once more the bells of Christendom ring out a proclamation
Of joy to all the universe, and mercy, and good will;
While brother shoots his brother down, and nation
scowls at nation,
Seven million uniforms are decorated at drill.

> Hail to Dupont and to Krupp!
> Steel is strong and going up,
> Let the tidings glad be sent—
> Tis the Morn of Armament.

God rest you merry, gentlemen, whose will these armies
are.
Go proudly in your colored shirts, let nothing you
dismay.
(Oh, little town of Bethlehem, how fades your
shining star?
While seven million fighting men stand up on Christmas Day.)

> Sing hosanna, sing Noel
> Sing the gunner, and the shell
> Sing the candle, sing the lamp,
> Sing the Concentration Camp.

Sing the Season born anew,
Sing of exile for the Jew,
Wreathe the world with evergreen.
Praise the cunning submarine.
Sing the barbed and bitter wire,
Poison gas, and liquid fire,
Bullet, bomb, and hand grenade,
And the heart of man, afraid.
Christ is come, the Light hath risen,
All our foes are safe in prison,
And the Christmastide begets
Seven million bayonets.

Hear the carol once again—
Peace on earth, good will to men.[11]

The next ten years will certainly see more literature dealing with war and its measureless effects than was produced in the nineteen thirties. War is to be the unceasing preoccupation of men's minds and lives. This literature will show many various approaches and points of view. There will be many reflections of the crucial character of the struggles, both those now going on and others, of a nature undisclosed, still to come. But it is safe to predict that there will continue to be powerful expression in literature of the conviction that the chief enemy of man is not the Nazi state, or fascism, or communism, but war itself.

[11] *One More Manhattan* by Phyllis McGinley. Harcourt, Brace & Co., 1937.

INDEX

293